FROM ADAM SMITH
TO
MICHAEL PORTER

EVOLUTION OF
COMPETITIVENESS THEORY

(Extended Edition)

ASIA-PACIFIC BUSINESS SERIES (ISSN: 1793-3137)

Series Editor
Philippe Lasserre
Emeritus Professor of Strategy and Asian Business
INSEAD

Published

Asia-Pacific Business Series – Vol. 7

FROM ADAM SMITH
TO
MICHAEL PORTER

EVOLUTION OF
COMPETITIVENESS THEORY

(Extended Edition)

Dong-Sung Cho & Hwy-Chang Moon

Seoul National University, Korea

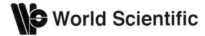 **World Scientific**

NEW JERSEY · LONDON · SINGAPORE · BEIJING · SHANGHAI · HONG KONG · TAIPEI · CHENNAI

Published by

World Scientific Publishing Co. Pte. Ltd.

5 Toh Tuck Link, Singapore 596224

USA office: 27 Warren Street, Suite 401-402, Hackensack, NJ 07601

UK office: 57 Shelton Street, Covent Garden, London WC2H 9HE

Library of Congress Cataloging-in-Publication Data
Cho, Tong-song.
    From Adam Smith to Michael Porter : evolution of competitiveness theory / Dong-Sung Cho
(Seoul National University, Korea) & Hwy-Chang Moon (Seoul National University, Korea). --
Extended edition.
        pages cm -- (Asia-Pacific Business Series : v. 7)
        Includes bibliographical references.
        ISBN 978-9814401654 (hard back : alk. paper) -- ISBN 978-9814401661 (e-book) --
        ISBN 978-9814401678 (mobile book) -- ISBN 978-9814407540 (paper back : alk. paper)
        1. Competition, International. I. Mun, Hwi-ch'ang. II. Title.
        HF1414.C456 2013
        338.6'048--dc23
                                                                2012046741

British Library Cataloguing-in-Publication Data
A catalogue record for this book is available from the British Library.

In-house Editors: Chye Shu Wen and Agnes Ng

Typeset by Stallion Press
Email: enquiries@stallionpress.com

Printed in Singapore.

To Our Colleagues Past, Current and Future

FOREWORD

Cho and Moon have long been important contributors to knowledge about competitiveness in Korea and elsewhere — a subject that only gets more important as competition among firms continues to globalize in this day and age.

This book provides an excellent overview of competitiveness thinking, and exposes the flaws in prominent ideas that continue to affect policy in many parts of the world. Cho and Moon provide an insightful overview of my thinking, but also offer their own interesting extensions. This is an invaluable book for anyone seriously interested in this vital topic.

Michael Porter
Bishop William Lawrence University Professor
Harvard Business School

PREFACE

People may view academic theories as impractical and useless, and make strategic decisions based on their personal ideas. However, these personal ideas are in fact their personal theories. These decisions may lead to disastrous consequences, if they are based on personal theories that are not fully discussed. In contrast, good academic theories have been discussed and tested by scholars. Strategies should be formulated based on the good academic theories, rather than on unproven personal theories. A good theory is a shortcut to understanding the complex real world.

This book deals with important theories of international competitiveness and their strategic implications. The theories range from classical theories such as Adam Smith's absolute advantage to more recent theories such as Michael Porter's diamond model. This book also incorporates the theoretical advances beyond Michael Porter such as the double diamond, the nine-factor model, double-diamond-based nine-factor model, and other methodologies for analyzing national competitiveness. In addition to the theoretical extensions, this second edition presents practical applications of these models at different levels of analysis.

A theory is often complex and controversial. In addition, a theory can be misused and overused. A theory, like a medicine, is most effective when it is appropriately used. Applying a theory without considering its weaknesses is like taking a medicine without knowing its side effects. To develop a critical perspective, readers first need to fully understand each theory. They should then study its strengths and weaknesses; previous research and the need for further study; and its strategic implications. Following the organization of this book, readers will be able to easily understand each theory with its historical background and practical applications.

This book is suitable for Business Strategy and International Business courses at both the graduate and upper-division undergraduate levels. This book is also suitable for policy makers and corporate managers. In this second edition, we pay special attention to how theories can be easily understood and how they can be appropriately applied to the real world. We hope that educators, students, and practitioners will find useful implications from this book's systematic integration of important competitiveness models and their applications.

CONTENTS

ACKNOWLEDGMENTS

We express our sincere appreciation to those who have influenced this work. We remain grateful to Wenyan Yin and Dongho Choi for their excellent help with editing and advice. Special thanks go to Jimmyn Parc and So Hyun Yim for their suggestions for improving this book. Additional and warm thanks go to the staff at World Scientific Publishing Co., who proposed to revise the first edition and helped in the entire process of publishing this new edition.

In addition, we would like to thank the following publishers for allowing us to reproduce their articles, which are newly included in this second edition.

Reproduced by permission of *Asian Business & Management*. Does One Size Fit All? A Dual Double Diamond Approach to Country-Specific Advantages, by Dong-Sung Cho, Hwy-Chang Moon, and Min-Young Kim, 8(1): 83–102, 2009.

Reproduced by permission of *Research in International Business and Finance*. Characterizing International Competitiveness in International Business Research: A MASI Approach to National Competitiveness, by Dong-Sung Cho, Hwy-Chang Moon, and Min-Young Kim, 22(2): 175–192, 2008.

Reproduced by permission of *Journal of International and Area Studies*. The Competitiveness of Multinational Firms: A Case Study of Samsung Electronics and Sony, by Hwy-Chang Moon and Donghun Lee, 11(1): 1–21, 2004.

Reproduced by permission of *Journal of Fashion Marketing and Management*. The Diamond Approach to the Competitiveness of Korea's Apparel Industry: Michael Porter and Beyond, by Byoungho Jin and Hwy-Chang Moon, 10(2): 195–208, 2006.

Reproduced by permission of *Journal of Korea Trade*. Northeast Asian Cluster through Business and Cultural Cooperation, by Hwy-Chang Moon and Jin-Sup Jung, 14(2): 29–53, 2010.

The acknowledgments for help and advice with the second edition of this book should go in conjunction with the thanks for the first edition. These are clearly still relevant and are reproduced below.

Acknowledgments in the First Edition

We were lucky to have a dedicated assistant, Young-Kyun Hur. Without his extraordinary effort, this book could not have been completed within a reasonable timeline. He is a man of talent and responsibility. Warm thanks go to Diana Hinds for editing the manuscripts. Additional thanks go to Yubing Zhai and Karen Quek of World Scientific Publishing Co., for their valuable help. Our most profound acknowledgment, however, is to Professor Michael E. Porter, who introduced a new paradigm of competitiveness and Professor Alan M. Rugman, who sparked the debate on competitiveness.

We would also like to thank the following publishers for allowing us to reproduce their articles.

Reproduced by permission of *Foreign Affairs*. Competitiveness: A Dangerous Obsession, by Paul Krugman, March/April: 28–44. Responses: The Fight Over Competitiveness, July/August: 186–203. Copyright (1994) by the Council on Foreign Relations, Inc.

Reproduced by permission of *Harvard Business Review*. The Competitive Advantage of Nations, by Michael E. Porter, March–April: 73–93, 1990.

Reproduced by permission from Elsevier Science from *International Business Review*. A Generalized Double Diamond Approach to the Global Competitiveness of Korea and Singapore, by Hwy-Chang Moon, Alan M. Rugman, and Alain Verbeke, 7: 135–150, 1998.

Reproduced by permission of *Journal of Far Eastern Business*. A Dynamic Approach to International Competitiveness: The Case of Korea, by Dong-Sung Cho, 1(1): 17–36, 1994.

LIST OF TABLES AND FIGURES

EPILOGUE

Why and how is Michael Porter different?

Michael E. Porter is indisputably recognized as the father of modern business. In a variety of rankings and surveys, he has been identified as the world's most influential thinker on management and competitiveness. Many people know that Porter is the foremost authority on modern competitive strategy, but few can articulate why or how he is so different from other scholars and practitioners. Let us explain Porter's uniqueness and competitiveness based on the four following factors.

First, Porter's overarching business strategy is very simple and clear: value creation. Porter's theory that business should be a positive-sum game where all players can win revolutionized prior thoughts on the need to beat the competition to be successful. This positive sum game can be achieved when focusing on value creation. To paraphrase Porter's words, the firm is the only organization that can create values, versus other organizations (e.g., government and non-profit organizations) that can only distribute values.

Second, Porter uses well-defined frameworks and models that are organized and easy to follow in order to solve problems. On the other hand, most other scholars often simply argue new perspectives or solutions without providing an analytical framework. Also, when they do provide an analytical framework, it is often missing important variables and not well organized. Porter's use of succinct yet comprehensive models has been a crucial element in making him the leader in the field of modern business.

Third, Porter's background across engineering, economics, and business administration has proved to complement his development of scientific and comprehensive solutions to issues in modern business. Porter's diverse background has allowed him to view the real world from an economist's viewpoint, analyze it scientifically, and provide useful business implications. Thus, Porter's models are not specific to a certain time period or industry, but are applicable to a variety of industries over a long period of time.

Lastly, Porter's broad research scope allows him to meet the changing demands of social needs. He began by developing business models of generic strategy with the five forces model and value chain. As businesses became more globalized, he introduced a global model of coordination and configuration. When competitiveness at the national level was at hand, Porter developed the diamond model. The progression of Porter's research shows that Porter's analysis is applicable from the corporate all the way to the national level. Lately, Porter has also extended his research scope outside of the business arena, providing new conceptual frameworks including those of creating shared value.

Although all of Porter's analytical tools are useful, the diamond model is particularly important because it provides a basic guideline to the understanding of competitiveness. The diamond model is also useful because it can be applied to various units of analysis, including national, regional, industrial, corporate, and even individual levels. As a matter of fact, the diamond model was used to explain the four factors used to analyze Porter's competitiveness above: Strategy Context (Business Context), Basic Approach (Factor Conditions), Supporting Background (Related and Supporting Sectors), and Research Scope (Demand Conditions).

This book is founded upon the diamond model. We have extended Porter's original diamond model in two directions: from domestic to international, and from physical to human factors. This book's extension of the diamond model uncovers another contribution from Porter: it provides a platform for other scholars to formulate new theories based on further development of Porter's original model. We want to thank Professor Porter for his revolutionary contributions to the field of business to date and hope that he will continue to develop new concepts and analytical tools to advance the strategic thinking in the fields of business and economics.

INTRODUCTION

The effect of *The Wealth of Nations* was revolutionary. Adam Smith's thoughts on trade gave businessmen a significant place in history. Their pursuit of profit was justified. Their social respectability as an important class was identified. Most importantly, a new concept of a nation's wealth was introduced.

Some economists argue that very little of what Smith said on the subject of trade was new, but the scope of Smith's work, the completeness of his analysis, and the timeliness of its appearance all conspired to make his book a landmark in economic thought. Since Smith published his book in 1776, many economists have made important contributions to this theory. However, many of the new trade theories are based on two important concepts — specialization and free exchange — which were introduced by Smith more than 200 years ago. This is why we respect Adam Smith as the grandfather of economics.

Although Smith and his followers provided some important bases for economic thoughts, today's global economy is too complicated to be understood with this rather simple version of trade theory. There was a breakthrough in 1990. Michael Porter introduced a new competitiveness theory, the diamond model. According to Porter, nations are most likely to succeed in industries or industry segments where the national "diamond" is the most favorable. The diamond has four interrelated components — (1) factor conditions; (2) demand conditions; (3) related and supporting industries; and (4) firm strategy, structure, and rivalry. In addition, there are two exogenous factors — chance and government.

The principle of the diamond is excellent, but its geographical constituency has to be established on different criteria. In particular, Porter's single diamond is not very relevant in small economies because their domestic variables are limited. They have to actively utilize international variables to enhance their competitiveness. In fact, Porter recognized the importance of international or global variables for a nation's competitiveness, but his diamond model did not explicitly include these variables. The debate on the diamond model in Chapter 4 has thus centered on the treatment of international variables.

Notwithstanding, the extended models by other scholars are based on the principle of the diamond model that was originally introduced by Porter. Likewise, the debate in Chapter 2 is based on the principle of Adam Smith and his followers. The debates are sometimes very harsh and acute, but we can understand the theories better through these debates. From Chapter 5 to Chapter 8, we present more sophisticated and comprehensive theoretical models that are extended from the diamond model. And from Chapter 9 to Chapter 12, we show applications of these models to the real world at different levels of analysis, including firm, industry, nation, and international cluster. To sum up, Adam Smith is the pioneer of trade theory and Michael Porter is the pioneer of competitiveness theory. Yet, no theory is perfect in a changing environment. We need to go further.

Part I

**FROM ADAM SMITH
TO MICHAEL PORTER**

1

TRADITIONAL MODEL: THEORY

SUMMARY AND KEY POINTS

Mercantilism viewed trade as a zero-sum game in which a trade surplus of one country is offset by a trade deficit of another country. In contrast, Adam Smith viewed trade as a positive-sum game in which all trading partners can benefit if countries specialize in the production of goods in which they have absolute advantages. Ricardo extended absolute advantage theory to comparative advantage theory. According to Ricardo, even if a country does not have an absolute advantage in any good, this country and other countries would still benefit from international trade. However, Ricardo did not satisfactorily explain why comparative advantages are different between countries. Heckscher and Ohlin explained that comparative advantage arises from differences in factor endowments. This theory appears to be virtually self-evident. However, Leontief found a paradoxical result.

Source:
Smith, A. (1937) (orig. pub. 1776). An inquiry into the nature and causes of the wealth of nations, in Eliot, C. W. (ed.), *The Harvard Classics*, New York: P. F. Collier & Son Corporation.

Some economists have developed alternative theories because the Heckscher–Ohlin model did not work well in the real world. These theories include product cycle, country similarity, and trade based on economies of scale. There are many other theories. However, the purpose of this chapter is not to extensively review the economic theories but to provide background knowledge for understanding the evolution of competitiveness theory. Notwithstanding, all of the theories discussed in this chapter are still useful to some extent in understanding today's industrial and trade policies. They are also helpful in evaluating the debate over competitiveness in Chapter 2, which is an initial step to the understanding of a new comprehensive approach of this book.

MERCANTILISM

In 1492 Columbus reached the New World; in 1501, Amerigo Vespucci discovered the mainland of the continent; and in 1519 Magellan reached the Philippines around the southern tip of South America and opened the Western route to India. These discoveries were possible because of scientific development in the areas such as astronomy and shipbuilding. Merchants and traders wanted to expand their business to the East because trading Eastern and Western products was profitable. International business became important in the age of discovery and exploration during the 15th century.

Ricardo, D. (1971) (orig. pub. 1817). *The Principles of Political Economy and Taxation*, Baltimore: Penguin.

Heckscher, E. F. (1949) (orig. pub. 1919). The effect of foreign trade on the distribution of income, in Howard, S. E. and Metzler, L. A. (eds.), *Readings in the Theory of International Trade*, Homewood: Irwin.

Leontief, W. (1953). Domestic production and foreign trade: The American capital position re-examined. *Proceedings of the American Philosophical Society*, **97**: 331–349. Reprinted in Caves, R. and Johnson, H. (eds.), *Readings in International Economics*, Homewood, Illinois: Richard D. Irwin, Inc.

Vernon, R. (1966). International investments and international trade in the product cycle. *Quarterly Journal of Economics*, **80**: 190–207.

Linder, S. B. (1961). *An Essay on Trade and Transformation*, New York: John Wiley.

Krugman, P. R. (1979). Increasing returns, monopolistic competition and international trade. *Journal of International Economics*, **9**: 469–479.

Lancaster, K. J. (1979). *Variety, Equity and Efficiency*, New York: Columbia University Press.

An economic theory at this time was called mercantilism. It continued to be the dominant economic thought until the 18th century. The mercantilists thought of wealth as gold and silver, or treasure, a term common at that time. The policy of accumulating precious metals was called bullionism. In the earliest period, bullionist philosophy translated into encouraging imports and forbidding exports of bullion. This policy soon shifted toward regulating international trade to achieve a favorable balance of trade. Mercantilism emphasized the necessity of a country to acquire an abundance of precious metals. To do this, the country had to export the maximum of its own manufactures and to import the minimum from other countries. The excess of exports over imports would be paid for in gold and silver.

The policy then shifted toward encouraging domestic production. The rationale was that the country, producing more goods for export, could achieve a favorable balance of trade and thus a bullion inflow. This policy was well explained by Thomas Mun (1571–1641), a director of the East India Company and a principal mercantile theorist. His main contention was that to increase the wealth of the nation, England must sell to other countries more than she bought from them. He advised his people to cultivate unused lands; reduce the consumption of foreign wares; be frugal in the use of natural resources, saving them as much as possible for export; and develop industries at home to supply necessities. These are the tenets of the thrifty businessman. However, these are not only the responsibility of individual merchants. The government should also have an obligation. It could thus be advised for the government to prohibit imports and subsidize exports.

At this time a tax policy was important. The country could achieve mercantilist goals by lowering taxes for exports and imposing high tariffs on imports. However, taxes were often superimposed on the areas which were not directly related to trade. For example, in England, there were even taxes on windows, births, burials, marriages, and bachelors. In addition, high tariffs on imported items caused the smuggling industry to thrive. Another important policy was to grant monopoly for certain important sectors such as glass manufacturing, paper manufacturing, and copper mining. However, this policy was also abused frequently and became less helpful to the industrial structure.

ABSOLUTE ADVANTAGE

The major problem with mercantilism was that it viewed trade as a zero-sum game in which a trade surplus of one country is offset by a trade deficit of another country. In contrast, Adam Smith viewed trade as a positive-sum game in which all trading partners can benefit. A large part of *The Wealth of Nations* (Smith, 1776) was devoted to an attack upon mercantilism. Smith believed in the operation of natural law, or invisible hand, and thus favored individualism and free trade. Smith said that each man is more understanding than any other as to his own needs and desires. If each man were allowed to seek his own welfare, he would in the long run contribute most to the common good. Natural law, rather than government restraint, would serve to prevent abuses of this freedom. Specifically, the advantage of this natural law in Smith's eyes came from the division of labor. Smith explained this with the example of a pin factory:

> *To take an example, . . . the pin-maker; a workman not educated to this business, not acquainted with the use of the machinery employed in it, could make one pin in a day, and certainly could not make twenty. But in the way in which this business is divided into a number of branches, . . . One man draws out the wire, another straights it, a third cuts it, a fourth points it, a fifth grinds it at the top for receiving the head; to make the head requires two or three distinct operations; to put it on, is a peculiar business, to whiten the pins is another; it is even a trade by itself to put them into the paper; and the important business of making a pin is, in this manner, divided into about eighteen distinct operations, which, in some manufactories, are all performed by distinct hands, though in others the same man will sometimes perform two or three of them. I have seen a small manufactory of this kind where ten men were employed. . . . Those ten persons could make 48,000 pins in a day. Each person, therefore, making a tenth part, might be considered as making 4,800 pins in a day. But if they had all wrought separately and independently, they certainly could not each of them have made twenty, perhaps not one pin in a day. . .* (Smith, 1776, p. 10)

Smith extended this idea of "division of labor" to that of "international division of labor." Now consider how much more production there would be if countries specialized in production just as the pin-makers did in his example. Specialization, cooperation, and exchange were responsible for the world's economic progress, and therein lay the road to future achievements. International trade was thus a positive game to Smith. In practice, however,

Smith saw various barriers set by governments that restricted the free flow of international trade. His famous passage is as follows:

> *It is the maxim of every prudent master of a family, never to attempt to make at home what it will cost him more to make than to buy. The taylor does not attempt to make his own shoes, but buys them of the shoemaker. The shoemaker does not attempt to make his own clothes, but employs a taylor. The farmer attempts to make neither the one nor the other, but employs those different artificers. . . ."*
>
> "What is prudence in the conduct of every private family, can scarce be folly in that of a great kingdom. If a foreign country can supply us with a commodity cheaper than we ourselves can make it, better buy it of them with some part of the produce of our own industry, employed in a way in which we have some advantage. . . ."
>
> "The natural advantages which one country has over another in producing particular commodities are sometimes so great, that it is acknowledged by all the world to be in vain to struggle with them. By means of glasses, hotbeds, and hotwalls, very good grapes can be raised in Scotland, and very good wine too can be made of them at about thirty times the expence for which at least equally good can be brought from foreign countries. Would it be a reasonable law to prohibit the importation of all foreign wines, merely to encourage the making of claret and burgundy in Scotland?   (Smith, 1776, p. 336–338)

In criticizing mercantilism, Smith showed how all forms of government interference, such as granting monopolies, subsidizing exports, restricting imports, and regulating wages, hampered the natural growth of economic activity. In contrast, Smith argued the advantages of specialization by regions and nations. Beginning with such reasoning, Smith showed how each nation would be far better off economically by concentrating on what it could do best rather than following the mercantilist doctrine of national self-sufficiency.[1] Following Smith's thoughts, the protection of trade as a government policy actually reduced in England.

---

[1] Very little of what Smith said on the subject of trade was new, most of it had been said before; but the scope of Smith's work, the completeness of his analysis and the timeliness of its appearance all conspired to make his book a landmark in economic thought.

Competition was important in the society that Smith proposed. Competition assured that each person and nation would do what they were best fitted to do, and it assured each one the full reward of their services and the maximum contribution to the common good. Therefore, the role of the government, or *sovereign*, should be minimum. Smith argued as follows:

> *All systems either of preference or of restraint, therefore, being thus completely taken away, the obvious and simple system of natural liberty establishes itself of its own accord. Every man, as long as he does not violate the laws of justice, is left perfectly free to pursue his own interest his own way, and to bring both his industry and capital into competition with those of any other man. . . According to the system of natural liberty, the sovereign has only three duties to attend to: three duties of great importance, indeed, but plain and intelligible to common understandings; first, the duty of protecting the society from the violence and invasion of other independent societies; secondly, the duty of protecting, as far as possible, every member of the society from the injustice or oppression of every other member of it, or the duty of establishing an exact administration of justice; and, thirdly, the duty of erecting and maintaining certain public works and certain public institutions, which it can never be for the interest of any individual, or small number of individuals, to erect and maintain; because the profit could never repay the expence to any individual or small number of individuals, though it may frequently do much more than repay it to a great society.* (Smith, 1776, p. 445–446)

The most important economic policy of government was thus to eliminate monopolies and preserve competition. However, Smith's position on the government regulation was not absolute. As shown in the third duty of the government, Smith admitted that necessary projects that were too large for private enterprise should be undertaken by public authority. He also believed The Navigation Acts, requiring the use of English vessels to transport goods to and from England, were necessary to safeguard the marine service as a matter of national defense. Smith said, "The act of navigation is perhaps the wisest of all the commercial regulations of England." (Smith, 1776, p. 344)

It has often been said that it was more than a coincidence that both the Declaration of Independence and *The Wealth of Nations* were given to the world in 1776. One was a declaration of political freedom. The other was a declaration of commercial independence. The effect of *The Wealth of Nations* was revolutionary. Smith's thoughts on trade gave businessmen a significant place in history. Their pursuit of profit was justified. Their social respectability as an important class was identified. In the same year of 1776, individuals attained political freedom in the U.S. and economic freedom in England.

COMPARATIVE ADVANTAGE

Since Adam Smith published his book in 1776, many economists have made important contributions to this theory. Among them, David Ricardo's contribution to international trade theory was so important that this classical theory is sometimes referred to as Ricardian theory.[2] There was a problem with the theory of absolute advantage. What if one country had an absolute advantage in both goods? According to Smith, such a superior country might have no benefits from international trade. In contrast, according to Ricardo, the superior country should specialize where it has the greatest absolute advantage and the inferior country should specialize where it has the least absolute disadvantage. This rule is known as the theory of comparative advantage. One important implication of this theory is that even if a country did not have an absolute advantage in any good, this country and other countries would still benefit from international trade.

To explain this, Ricardo used an illustration as shown in Table 1-1 (see "On Foreign Trade" in Ricardo, 1817). In trade between England and Portugal, if Portugal could produce cloth with the labor of 90 men and wine with the labor of 80 men, and England could produce the same quantity of cloth with 100 men and the wine with 120, it would be advantageous for these nations to exchange English cloth for Portuguese wine. By concentrating upon what each nation could do with the least effort, each had a greater comparative advantage. Thus each nation had more wine and more cloth than it could have had by producing each commodity independently without the benefit of exchange.

In this example, Portugal can benefit from trading with the less efficient England because Portugal's cost advantage is relatively greater in wine than in cloth. Portugal's production cost of wine is only two-thirds the cost in England, but its cost of cloth is nine-tenths the cost in England. Portugal has thus greater

---

[2]Although Ricardo is known as the author of the theory of comparative advantage, some economists say there is substantial evidence that Robert Torrens developed the notion of comparative advantage years earlier, in 1808.

efficiency in wine than in cloth, while England has less inefficiency in cloth than in wine.

Ricardo used another illustration which resulted in the same point. Two men could both make shoes and hats, and one was superior to the other in both employments; but in making hats, he could only exceed his competitor by one-fifth or 20 percent, and in making shoes he can exceed him by one-third or 33 percent. Would it not be for the interest of both, that the superior man should employ himself exclusively in making shoes, and the inferior man in making hats? Ricardo contended that imports could be profitable to a nation even though that nation could produce the imported article at a lower cost. Therefore, it was not true, as Adam Smith believed, that under free trade each commodity would be produced by that country which produced it at the lowest real cost.

It is the principle of comparative advantage that underlies the advantages of the division of labor, whether between individuals, regions, or nations. The Ricardian model of international trade is thus a very useful tool for explaining the reasons why trade may happen and how trade increases the welfare of the trading partners. However, this model is incomplete. In particular, there are two major problems. First, the simple Ricardian model predicts an extreme degree of specialization, but in practice, countries produce not one but many products, including import-competing products. Second, it explains trade based on differences in productivity levels between countries, but it does not explain why these differences exist.

The first problem can be solved when we assume diminishing returns to scale (i.e., a convex production possibility frontier), implying that as resources are shifted from one sector to another sector, the opportunity cost of each additional unit of another sector increases. Such increasing costs may arise because factors of production vary in quality and in suitability for producing different commodities. Under these circumstances, the theory can predict

Table 1-1   Ricardo's Comparative Advantage

Country	Production Cost	
	Cloth	Wine
Portugal	90	80
England	100	120

that a country will specialize up to the point where gains from specialization become equal to increasing costs of specialization. The theory can then explain the reason why a country does not specialize its production completely. The second problem is solved by the theory of factor endowments.

FACTOR ENDOWMENTS

Ricardo explained that comparative advantage arises from differences in labor productivity, but did not satisfactorily explain why labor productivity is different between countries. In the early twentieth century an important new theory of international trade, the Heckscher–Ohlin (HO) model, was developed by two Swedish economists.[3] Heckscher and Ohlin argued that comparative advantage arises from differences in factor endowments. According to the HO model, there are two basic characteristics of countries and products. Countries differ from each other depending on the factors of production they possess. Goods differ from each other depending on the factors that are required in their production. The HO model says that a country will have comparative advantage in, and therefore will export, that good whose production is relatively intensive in the factor with which that country is relatively well endowed. The logic is that the more abundant a factor is, the lower its cost. Therefore, differences in the factor endowments of various countries explain differences in factor costs, which result in different comparative advantages.

There are two factors of production, capital and labor, in the HO model, while labor is the only factor of production in the Ricardian model. The HO model assumes that technology is identical but production methods are different between countries. Different production methods indicate different combinations of capital and labor. That is, different countries may choose different production methods depending upon factor prices in those countries. Therefore, patterns of production and trade are explained by different factor endowments or factor prices.

The HO model has been expanded by three important theorems: the factor price equalization theorem, the Stolpe–Samuelson theorem, and the Rybczynski theorem.

---

[3] Eli Heckscher's original work, published in 1919 in Swedish, received little attention until it was translated into English in 1949. Bertil Ohlin, Heckscher's student, elaborated on Heckscher's ideas in his doctoral dissertation in 1924, which was also written in Swedish, and did not receive attention until it was published in English in 1933.

The Factor Price Equalization Theorem

This theorem states that free trade will equalize factors of production between countries.[4] Suppose there is a free trade between the U.S. and Mexico. With free trade, output of the comparative advantage good increases, thereby demand for the abundant factor and consequently its price increase. At the same time, output of the comparative disadvantage good decreases, thereby demand for the scarce factor and consequently its price decrease. Therefore, rental rates increase and wages decrease in the capital-abundant country (the U.S.), while the opposite happens in the labor-abundant country (Mexico). Prior to free trade, rental rates were relatively low and wages were relatively high in the U.S. With free trade, these prices move in the direction of equalization.

However, we need strong conditions for factor price equalization to occur. These conditions include no transportation costs, no trade barriers, and identical technology. One interesting implication of factor price equalization is that foreign investment may not be necessary if there is free trade. We can understand foreign investment as an international transfer of production factors such as technology, capital, and labor. This is a viable strategy only when the prices of these factors are not equal between countries. With factor price equalization, there is no need to invest abroad. In the real world, however, there are many obstacles or market imperfections (for example, see Hymer, 1960) that stand in the way of complete equalization of factor prices.

The factor price equalization theorem is still useful and we can derive some important implications from it. For example, how trade liberalization affects income gaps between countries. The theorem predicts that income gaps will reduce by lowering trade barriers. Two important conclusions can be derived. First, with the formation of a trading bloc, the country of low income will benefit more than the country of high income. Second, a less developed country should actively pursue an open door policy to increase its income level.

---

[4]This theorem was first suggested by Heckscher and Ohlin, and later proved by Samuelson (1948). Interestingly, shortly after Samuelson's article appeared, he learned that Abba Lerner, while a student in England in 1933, had written a term paper that also proved the theorem.

The Stolper–Samuelson Theorem

The Stolper and Samuelson (1941) theorem links international trade to the domestic distribution of income. As we have seen in the case of factor price equalization, free trade will increase the price, or income, of the relatively abundant factor and reduce that of the relatively scarce factor. Therefore, according to this theorem, free trade benefits the abundant factor and harms the scarce factor. Why should the scarce factor lose? Precisely because the income of the scarce factor has been too high. With free trade, the scarce factor, say, U.S. labor, has to compete with its foreign competitor, say, Mexican labor. Although labor is immobile between countries, its price can change through international trade because labor is embodied in the goods.

Everyone is a winner in the classical one-factor model. In the two-factor HO model, one factor is a loser. We can now understand why the abundant factor (e.g., U.S. capitalists) is for and the scarce factor (e.g., U.S. workers) is against trade liberalization (e.g., North American Free Trade Agreement). The scarce factor may want to lobby to restrict free trade, but may have to accept a reduction of income in the end. However, it is important to note that although the scarce factor loses, the country as a whole gains from trade liberalization. A policy of income redistribution such as taxation may then be important. Otherwise, a group of people will lose permanently.

The Rybczynski Theorem

This theorem says that at constant prices, an increase in one factor endowment will increase by a greater proportion the output of the good intensive in that factor and reduce the output of the other. Suppose a country's capital stock increases by 10 percent and its labor force is unchanged. As the capital stock increases, the output of the capital-intensive good expands to utilize the extra supply of capital. In contrast, the output of the labor-intensive good decreases because labor is moving out of this sector. As the capital stock increases, the production possibility frontier bulges out in the direction of the capital-intensive good so that the country's production should be larger than before. Since the output of the labor-intensive good decreases absolutely, the output of the capital-intensive good should increase more than 10 percent.

This theorem is useful in explaining the pattern of economic development of Japan and Korea. These countries have had high savings and investment and produced more capital-intensive goods. Labor-intensive sectors have actually shrunk in these countries because labor force has been released to the booming capital-intensive sectors. Therefore, an important implication of this theorem is that a country can change its relative factor endowments by changing its investment patterns, while factor endowments are fixed in the world of the classical theories of Smith and Ricardo.

The HO model is referred to as the neoclassical theory of international trade because it builds upon and complements the classical theory of comparative advantage. The HO model contains several appealing elements. It is simple, logical, makes common sense, and appears to be virtually self-evident. However, an empirical test produced a paradoxical result.

LEONTIEF PARADOX

The famous empirical study of the HO model was conducted by Leontief (1953), who was awarded the Nobel prize in 1973. Leontief expected that the U.S., the most capital-abundant country in the world, should export capital-intensive goods and import labor-intensive goods, but found that U.S. import-competing goods required 30 percent more capital per worker than U.S. export goods. According to his calculations, the capital-labor ratio was about $14,000 per worker-year in export goods and about $18,100 per worker-year in import-competing goods. This finding was the opposite of what the HO model predicted. It has become known as the Leontief Paradox.

How can we reconcile the Leontief's findings with the HO model? Many economists, including Leontief, have attempted to explain this.

Labor Skills

The first attempt was made by Leontief himself. He argued that U.S. workers are much more productive than foreign workers. Specifically, he suggested that one man-year of U.S. labor is equivalent to three man-years of foreign labor. Thus, the number of U.S. workers must be multiplied by three. However, his estimate about the superiority of U.S. labor was overstated. Other studies (e.g., Kreinin, 1965) showed that the superiority was not 300 percent, as Leontief claimed, but about 20 to 25 percent, which was not sufficient to convert the paradox.

Natural Resources

Leontief tested only capital and labor, but omitted other important factors such as resources. Vanek (1963) argued that the U.S. is relatively scarce in natural resources but abundant in both capital and labor. The production of certain natural resources requires large quantities of capital. Importing natural resources then means importing capital which is embodied in natural resources. Since the HO model includes basically capital and labor, many economists recalculated the factor content of U.S. trade after excluding the natural resource sectors. Studies generally show that the capital intensity of U.S. import-competing sectors drops substantially, but not enough to reverse the paradox.

Factor Intensity Reversals

Because foreign data on trade were not available, Leontief calculated the factor content of U.S. import-competing goods rather than analyzing actual imports. For example, Leontief calculated the factor content of the U.S. textile industry that competed with imports, instead rather than calculating the factor content of the foreign textile industry. However, textiles may be labor-intensive in Mexico, for example, but relatively capital-intensive in the U.S. For another example, agriculture is labor-intensive in many foreign countries, but capital-intensive in the U.S. Yet, many economists believe that factor intensity reversals are not significant in the real world.

Several other explanations have been attempted, but failed to satisfactorily reconcile the Leontief paradox. The paradox continues. Some economists have developed alternative theories of international trade because the HO model does not work well in the real world. Recognizing the increasing diversity of international trade, the new theories are useful in explaining some special cases of international trade. These theories include product cycle, country similarity, and trade based on economies of scale.

PRODUCT CYCLE

Raymond Vernon (1966) argued that many manufactured goods go through a product cycle of introduction, growth, maturity, and decline. Thus, comparative advantages of these goods shift over time from one country to another. The product cycle hypothesis begins with the assumption that the stimulus to innovation is typically provided by some threat or promise in the market. In other words, firms tend to be stimulated by the needs and opportunities of the market closest at hand, the home market, which plays a dual role in this hypothesis. Not only is it the source of stimulus for the innovation firm; it is also the preferred location for production.

In the introduction stage, the U.S. has been a pioneer in inventing and producing new products such as televisions and computers. Two reasons account for this dominant position. First, the wealth and size of the U.S. market gave U.S. firms a strong incentive to develop new consumer products. Second, the high cost of U.S. labor gave U.S. firms an incentive to develop cost-saving innovations.[5] If innovating firms scan their home markets with special intensity, the chances are greatly increased that their first production facilities will also be located in the home market. The propensity to cluster in the home market is fortified by the fact that there are some well-recognized economies to be captured by an innovating team that is brought together in a common location.

In this introduction stage, the demand for new products tends to be based on non-price factors. Firms can charge relatively high prices for new products, which obviates the need to look for low-cost production sites in other countries. As the market in the U.S. and other developed countries matures, the product becomes more standardized, and price becomes the main competitive weapon. Thus the locus of production shifts to other developed countries, and then to less developed countries.

The product cycle model is useful in reconciling the Leontief paradox. Suppose the U.S. has comparative advantage in new manufactured products. The production method of these new products may be quite labor-intensive because investment in fixed capital is not likely to occur at this stage. Producers still need to know how to manufacture products most efficiently and how the market reacts to these new products. Thus, U.S. exports tend to be labor-intensive. When the product becomes standardized, producers are familiar with the efficient engineering and market feedback. A large amount of fixed capital can now be invested. The production method may thus be quite capital-intensive. The Leontief paradox can be reconciled because the U.S. exports in the introducing stage where the production is labor-intensive and imports in the maturing stage where the production is capital-intensive.

In his later work, Vernon (1979) suggested that the power of the product cycle hypothesis has been changing. Two reasons account for that change: one, an increase in the geographical reach of many of the enterprises that are involved in the introduction of new products, a consequence of their establishment of many overseas subsidiaries; and two, a change in the national markets of the advanced industrialized countries, which has reduced some of the differences that had previously existed between such markets.

---

[5] European technology is material-saving and Japanese technology is space-saving.

In industries such as electronics and chemicals, innovating firms that are limited to their own home markets are no longer very common. Instead, firms with highly developed multinational networks introduce the new products simultaneously in the Triad — the U.S., Europe, and Japan — and in some less developed countries. With a multinational network, U.S. firms also feel at ease in foreign production. The interval of time between the introduction of any new product in the U.S. and its first production in a foreign location has thus been rapidly shrinking.

The U.S. income was higher than that of other developed countries. Recently, however, the income gap has narrowed. This shrinkage weakened a critical assumption of the product cycle hypotheses, namely, that the entrepreneurs of large enterprises confronted different conditions in their respective home markets. As European and Japanese incomes approached those of the U.S., these differences were reduced.

The product cycle hypothesis had strong predictive power in the first two or three decades after World War II, especially in explaining the composition of U.S. trade and in projecting the likely patterns of foreign direct investment by U.S. firms. However, Vernon said that certain conditions of that period no longer exist. For one thing, the leading multinational firms have developed global networks of subsidiaries; on the other, the U.S. market is no longer unique among national markets. Thus, the predictive power of the hypothesis is weakened. However, the hypothesis is still useful for a multinational firm that has not yet acquired a capacity for global scanning, but tries to move from home-based innovation to the possibility of exports and ultimately of overseas investment. The hypothesis may also provide useful guidelines for many less developed countries that try to absorb a developed country's innovations as introduced earlier.

COUNTRY SIMILARITY

Staffan Linder's (1961) country similarity theory is different from other trade theories because it deals with the demand side rather than the supply side. This theory explains international trade among countries that have similar characteristics. The theory has two assumptions. First, a country exports those manufactured products for which there is a significant home market. According to Linder, manufacturers introduce new products in order to serve the domestic market because they are familiar with the domestic market. Production for the domestic market must be large enough for firms to achieve economies of scale and thus to reduce costs. Second, the country exports the product to other countries with similar tastes and income levels. Linder believed that countries with similar income levels would have similar tastes. Each country will produce primarily for its home market, but part of the output will be exported to other similar countries.

The first assumption, the home-oriented myopic view of the managers, is similar to the product cycle hypothesis in explaining the early stage of product life. In today's global economy, however, this view is less appealing because firms often target the global market rather than domestic markets. For example, artificial Christmas trees are exported by non-Christian countries such as China, where the market for this product is small, to countries such as the U.S., where there is a high demand for this product. For another example, Japan exported typewriters to the U.S. when the market for this product was not yet developed in Japan. Other counter-examples include OEM manufacturing and international subcontracting, which are popular in many less developed countries. These are not for the domestic market, but for exports.

There is also a problem with the second assumption. Suppose there are two countries with similar tastes and income levels. Why can one country originate a particular product? The U.S. exports Cadillac cars to Japan while importing Lexus cars from them. The origins of these products may not be explained in Linder's thesis. To explain this, we need to know different factor endowments and different characteristics of technology of the two countries, which can be explained by the HO model. Despite these problems, the Linder model is useful in explaining some trade patterns. Much of the international trade in manufactured goods takes place among the countries with high income: the U.S., Europe, and Japan. Much of this trade is in fact the exchange of similar products.

There are two important differences between the HO model and the Linder model. First, in the HO model, there will be more trade between countries that have more dissimilarities in factor endowments because more dissimilarities will give larger differences in relative factor prices. In contrast, in the Linder model, there will be more trade between countries that have more similarity in incomes and tastes. Second, in the HO model, a country's exports and imports are different products with different factor proportions. In contrast, in the Linder model, a country's exports and imports are similar products. These differences are due to the different perspectives of the two theories: the HO model on a production side and the Linder model on a demand side.

The theoretical contribution of the Linder model is its identification of two important variables, domestic demand and economies of scale, in explaining different types of international trade. These two variables are revitalized in two more recent theories. The first variable, domestic demand, is one of the four determinants of Porter's (1990) diamond model, which will be discussed in Chapter 3. The second variable, economies of scale, is a major explanatory variable in the theory of intraindustry trade, which will be discussed in the next section.

ECONOMIES OF SCALE

The basic HO model assumes constant returns to scale. Thus, if inputs were doubled, output would be doubled. In many industries, however, there exist economies of scale (or increasing returns). Thus, if inputs were doubled, output would be more than doubled. The existence of economies of scale can explain some trade patterns which are not explained by the HO model. If there are economies of scale, countries (or firms) would benefit if they specialize in the production of a limited range of goods. The problem of specifying a market structure consistent with economies of scale internal to firms delayed for many years the formal modeling of trade based on increasing returns to scale. The breakthrough came in the late 1970s, when Krugman (1979) and Lancaster (1979) independently developed models of trade in differentiated products.[6]

Suppose there are two countries (the U.S. and Japan) and two types of cars (large cars and small cars). Also suppose there is a demand for both cars in each of the two countries. If there are economies of scale, it would be advantageous for each country to specialize in the production of only one type of car rather than both types. If there is free trade between the two countries, consumers in each country can buy both cars. Economies of scale and international trade make it possible for each country to produce goods more efficiently without sacrificing of variety of goods.

There are basically two types of trade: interindustry trade and intraindustry trade. Interindustry trade reflects comparative advantage. Countries that are relatively similar and so have few comparative differences may not engage in interindustry trade. For an extreme example, suppose that two countries have identical factor endowments. The HO model would then predict no trade. If there are economies of scale, however, there would be benefits of trade from specialization by each country. Therefore, we can conclude that trade between

---

[6]Krugman emphasized individuals' desire for variety in consumption. In contrast, Lancaster introduced consumer heterogeneity. For more information, see Grossman (1992).

countries with dissimilar factor endowments is largely interindustry, but trade between countries with similar factor endowments is largely intraindustry.

The intraindustry trade model, based on economies of scale, is useful in explaining the trade of manufactured goods among developed countries. For example, cars made by General Motors are exported to other countries at the same time that the U.S. imports foreign-made cars. This is similar to the prediction of the country similarity theorem. However, the intraindustry trade model focuses on the production side, while the country similarity theory emphasizes the demand side.

There are two problems with this model. First, the empirical measures of intraindustry trade are overstated because aggregation is too broad. Much of the apparent intraindustry trade would disappear if goods were further disaggregated. Second, the model does not explain which country produces which goods, so the pattern of intraindustry trade is unpredictable. However, the trade pattern may not be just arbitrary, as we have seen in the case of the country similarity theory. In fact, it is not difficult to explain why, for example, the U.S. exports large cars and Japan exports small cars. This pattern may be based on different factor endowments between the two countries.

CONCLUSION

We have discussed traditional trade theories. None of these theories has died. They remain useful in understanding many of today's industrial and trade policies. For example, the theory of comparative advantage is a basic guideline for many countries when they consider industrial and trade policies. Even mercantilism, a popular theory before Adam Smith, is important for some countries. However, no single theory is satisfactory in explaining today's international trade because today's world is much more complicated than before. The primary goal of model building is to recognize the most important variable or variables to simplify the phenomena and to easily understand the world. For example, the theory of comparative advantage treats only one variable, i.e., factor endowments, but not other important variables such as demand conditions. It was effective at the time this theory was introduced because the world was not so complicated. Today's global economy is different. Several important variables have to be considered simultaneously in the trade or competitiveness formula. One recent, important development that addresses this issue is Michael Porter's (1990) "diamond model," which will be introduced in Chapter 3. In the next chapter, we will discuss the relationship between international trade and competitiveness.

REFERENCES

Grossman, G. M. (ed.) (1992). *Imperfect Competition and International Trade*, Cambridge: MIT Press.

Heckscher, E. F. (1949) (orig. pub. 1919). The effect of foreign trade on the distribution of income, in Howard, S. E. and Metzler, L. A. (eds.), *Readings in the Theory of International Trade*, Homewood: Irwin.

Hymer, S. H. (1976) (orig. pub. 1960). *The International Operations of National Firms: A Study of Direct Foreign Investment*, Cambridge: MIT Press.

Krugman, P. R. (1979). Increasing returns, monopolistic competition and international trade. *Journal of International Economics*, **9**: 469–479.

Kreinin, M. (1965). Comparative labor effectiveness and the Leontief scarce factor paradox. *American Economic Review*, **64**: 143–155.

Lancaster, K. J. (1979). *Variety, Equity and Efficiency*, New York: Columbia University Press.

Leontief, W. (1953). Domestic production and foreign trade: The American capital position re-examined. *Proceedings of the American Philosophical Society*, **97**: 331–349. Reprinted in Caves, R. and Johnson, H. (eds.), *Readings in International Economics*, Homewood, Illinois: Richard D. Irwin, Inc.

Linder, S. B. (1961). *An Essay on Trade and Transformation*, New York: John Wiley.

Porter, M. E. (1990). *The Competitive Advantage of Nations*, New York: Free Press.

Ricardo, D. (1971) (orig. pub. 1817). *The Principles of Political Economy and Taxation*, Baltimore: Penguin.

Samuelson, P. (1948). International trade and the equalization of factor prices. *Economic Journal*, **58**: 165–184.

Smith, A. (1937) (orig. pub. 1776). An inquiry into the nature and causes of the wealth of nations, in Eliot, C. W. (ed.), *The Harvard Classics*, New York: P. F. Collier & Son Corporation.

Stolper, W. and Samuelson, P. (1941). Protection and real wages. *Review of Economic Studies*, **9**: 58–73.

Vanek, J. (1963). *The Natural Resource Content of United States Foreign Trade, 1870–1955*, Cambridge: MIT Press.

Vernon, R. (1966). International investments and international trade in the product cycle. *Quarterly Journal of Economics*, **80**: 190–207.

Vernon, R. (1979). The product cycle hypothesis in a new international environment. *Oxford Bulletin of Economics and Statistics*, **41**(4): 255–267. Reprinted in Wortzel, H. and Wortzel, L. (eds.) (1985), *Strategic Management of Multinational Corporations: The Essentials*, New York: John Wiley & Sons.

2

TRADITIONAL MODEL: DEBATE

SUMMARY AND KEY POINTS

The rhetoric of competitiveness — the view that, in the words of President Clinton, each nation is "like a big corporation competing in the global marketplace" — has become pervasive. According to Krugman, competitiveness poses three dangers. First, it could result in the waste of money to enhance U.S. competitiveness. Second, it could lead protectionism and trade wars. Finally, it could result in bad public policy. This chapter introduces his key points and responses by others.

Since this debate in 1994, Krugman has continuously claimed that talking about "competitiveness" as a goal is fundamentally misleading. In 2011, in the wake of President Obama's State of the Union address and his appointment of Jeff Immelt of GE to chair his new Council on Jobs and Competitiveness, there was a heated debate in the U.S. about the role of government in improving the competitiveness of American businesses. Again, on this issue,

Source:
March/April 1994 and July/August 1994 issues of *Foreign Affairs*.
Krugman, P. (2011). The competition myth. *New York Times*, 23 January.

Krugman criticized that it was a misdiagnosis of the problems and it could lead to policies based on the false idea that what's good for corporations is good for America.

This kind of debate is highly intellectual and practical, but sometimes confusing. The knowledge of trade models discussed in Chapter 1 is useful in evaluating this debate. For example, Krugman argues that many policy makers and economists are mercantilists because they view trade as a zero-sum game. However, Krugman can also be criticized for not clearly distinguishing between competitive advantage and comparative advantage as a basis of a nation's competitiveness. There are two important issues in this debate. First, it is difficult to define competitiveness. Second, trade balance may not be a good measure for competitiveness. We need a new, comprehensive model that can effectively deal with these two issues. For this purpose, Michael Porter has provided the diamond model, which will be discussed in Chapter 3.

COMPETITIVENESS: A DANGEROUS OBSESSION

Paul Krugman

THE HYPOTHESIS IS WRONG

In June 1993, Jacques Delors made a special presentation to the leaders of the nations of the European Community, meeting in Copenhagen, on the growing problem of European unemployment. Economists who study the European situation were curious to see what Delors, president of the EC Commission, would say. Most of them share more or less the same diagnosis of the European problem: the taxes and regulations imposed by Europe's elaborate welfare states have made employers reluctant to create new jobs, while the relatively generous level of unemployment benefits has made workers unwilling to accept the kinds of low-wage jobs that help keep unemployment comparatively low in the U.S. The monetary difficulties associated with preserving the European Monetary System (EMS) in the face of the costs of German reunification have reinforced this structural problem.

It is a persuasive diagnosis, but a politically explosive one, and everyone wanted to see how Delors would handle it. Would he dare tell European leaders that their efforts to pursue economic justice have produced unemployment as an unintended by-product? Would he admit that the EMS could be sustained only at the cost of a recession and face the implications of that admission for European monetary union?

Guess what? Delors didn't confront the problems of either the welfare state or the EMS. He explained that the root cause of European unemployment was

25

a lack of competitiveness with the U.S. and Japan and that the solution was a program of investment in infrastructure and high technology.

It was a disappointing evasion, but not a surprising one. After all, the rhetoric of competitiveness — the view that, in the words of President Clinton, each nation is "like a big corporation competing in the global marketplace" — has become pervasive among opinion leaders throughout the world. People who believe themselves to be sophisticated about the subject take it for granted that the economic problem facing any modern nation is essentially one of competing on world markets — that the U.S. and Japan are competitors in the same sense that Coca Cola competes with Pepsi — and are unaware that anyone might seriously question that proposition. Every few months a new bestseller warns the American public of the dire consequences of losing the "race" for the 21st century.[1] A whole industry of councils on competitiveness, "geo-economists" and managed trade theorists has sprung up in Washington. Many of these people, having diagnosed America's economic problems in much the same terms as Delors did Europe's, are now in the highest reaches of the Clinton administration formulating economic and trade policy for the U.S. So Delors was using a language that was not only convenient but comfortable for him and a wide audience on both sides of the Atlantic.

Unfortunately, his diagnosis was deeply misleading as a guide to what ails Europe, and similar diagnoses in the U.S. are equally misleading. The idea that a country's economic fortunes are largely determined by its success on world markets is a hypothesis, not a necessary truth; and as a practical,

---

[1] See, for just a few examples, Laura D'Andrea Tyson, *Who's Bashing Whom: Trade Conflict in High-Technology Industries*, Washington: Institute for International Economics, 1992; Lester C. Thurow, *Head to Head: The Coming Economic Battle among Japan, Europe, and America*, New York: Morrow, 1992; Ira C. Magaziner and Robert B. Reich, *Minding America's Business. The Decline and Rise of the American Economy*, New York: Vintage Books, 1983; Ira C. Magaziner and Mark Patinkin, *The Silent War: Inside the Global Business Battles Shaping Americas Future*, New York: Vintage Books, 1990; Edward N. Luttwak, *The Endangered American Dream: How to Stop the United States from Becoming a Third World Country and How to Win the Geo-economic Struggle for Industrial Supremacy*, New York: Simon and Schuster, 1993; Kevin P. Phillips, *Staying on Top: The Business Case for a National Industrial Strategy*, New York: Random House, 1984; Clyde V. Prestowitz, Jr., *Trading Places: How We Allowed Japan to Take the Lead*, New York: Basic Books, 1988; William S. Dietrich, *In the Shadow of the Rising Sun: The Political Roots of American Economic Decline*, University Park: Pennsylvania State University Press, 1991; Jeffrey E. Garten, *A Cold Peace: America, Japan, Germany, and the Struggle for Supremacy*, New York: Times Books, 1992; and Wayne Sandholtz *et al.*, *The Highest Stakes: The Economic Foundations of the Next Security System*, Berkeley Roundtable on the International Economy (BRIE), Oxford University Press, 1992.

empirical matter, that hypothesis is flatly wrong. That is, it is simply not the case that the world's leading nations are to any important degree in economic competition with each other, or that any of their major economic problems can be attributed to failures to compete on world markets. The growing obsession in most advanced nations with international competitiveness should be seen, not as a well-founded concern, but as a view held in the face of overwhelming contrary evidence. And yet it is clearly a view that people very much want to hold — a desire to believe that is reflected in a remarkable tendency of those who preach the doctrine of competitiveness to support their case with careless, flawed arithmetic.

This article makes three points. First, it argues that concerns about competitiveness are, as an empirical matter, almost completely unfounded. Second, it tries to explain why defining the economic problem as one of international competition is nonetheless so attractive to so many people. Finally, it argues that the obsession with competitiveness is not only wrong but dangerous, skewing domestic policies and threatening the international economic system. This last issue is, of course, the most consequential from the standpoint of public policy. Thinking in terms of competitiveness leads, directly and indirectly, to bad economic policies on a wide range of issues, domestic and foreign, whether it be in health care or trade.

MINDLESS COMPETITION

Most people who use the term "competitiveness" do so without a second thought. It seems obvious to them that the analogy between a country and a corporation is reasonable and that to ask whether the U.S. is competitive in the world market is no different in principle from asking whether General Motors is competitive in the North American minivan market.

In fact, however, trying to define the competitiveness of a nation is much more problematic than defining that of a corporation. The bottom line for a corporation is literally its bottom line: if a corporation cannot afford to pay its workers, suppliers, and bondholders, it will go out of business. So when we say that a corporation is uncompetitive, we mean that its market position is unsustainable — that unless it improves its performance, it will cease to exist. Countries, on the other hand, do not go out of business. They may be happy or unhappy with their economic performance, but they have no well-defined bottom line. As a result, the concept of national competitiveness is elusive.

One might suppose, naively, that the bottom line of a national economy is simply its trade balance, that competitiveness can be measured by the ability of a country to sell more abroad than it buys. But in both theory and practice, a trade surplus may be a sign of national weakness, a deficit a sign of strength. For example, Mexico was forced to run huge trade surpluses in the 1980s in order to pay the interest on its foreign debt since international investors refused to lend it any more money; it began to run large trade deficits after 1990 as foreign investors recovered confidence and began to pour in new funds. Would anyone want to describe Mexico as a highly competitive nation during the debt crisis era or describe what has happened since 1990 as a loss in competitiveness?

Most writers who worry about the issue at all have therefore tried to define competitiveness as the combination of favorable trade performance and something else. In particular, the most popular definition of competitiveness nowadays runs along the lines of the one given in Council of Economic Advisors Chairman Laura D'Andrea Tyson's *Who's Bashing Whom?*: competitiveness is "our ability to produce goods and services that meet the test of international competition while our citizens enjoy a standard of living that is both rising and sustainable." This sounds reasonable at first. If you think about it, however, and test your thoughts against the facts, you will find out that there is much less to this definition than meets the eye.

Consider, for a moment, what the definition would mean for an economy that conducted very little international trade, like the U.S. in the 1950s. For such an economy, the ability to balance its trade is mostly a matter of getting the exchange rate right. But because trade is such a small factor in the economy, the level of the exchange rate is a minor influence on the standard of living. So in an economy with very little international trade, the growth in living standards — and thus "competitiveness" according to Tyson's definition — would be determined almost entirely by domestic factors, primarily the rate of productivity growth. That's domestic productivity growth, period — not productivity growth relative to other countries. In other words, for an economy with very little international trade, "competitiveness" would turn out to be a funny way of saying "productivity" and would have nothing to do with international competition.

But surely this changes when trade becomes more important, as indeed it has for all major economies? It certainly could change. Suppose that a country finds that although its productivity is steadily rising, it can succeed in exporting only if it repeatedly devalues its currency, selling its exports ever more cheaply on world markets. Then its standard of living, which depends on its purchasing power over imports as well as domestically produced goods, might actually decline. In the jargon of economists, domestic growth might be outweighed by deteriorating terms of trade.[2] So "competitiveness" could turn out really to be about international competition after all.

There is no reason, however, to leave this as a pure speculation; it can easily be checked against the data. Have deteriorating terms of trade in fact been a major drag on the U.S. standard of living? Or has the rate of growth of U.S. real income continued essentially to equal the rate of domestic productivity growth, even though trade is a larger share of income than it used to be?

To answer this question, one need only look at the national income accounts data the Commerce Department publishes regularly in the Survey of Current Business. The standard measure of economic growth in the U.S. is, of course, real GNP — a measure that divides the value of goods and services produced in the U.S. by appropriate price indexes to come up with an estimate of real national output. The Commerce Department also, however, publishes something called "command GNP." This is similar to real GNP except that it divides U.S. exports not by the export price index, but by the price index for U.S. imports. That is, exports are valued by what Americans can buy with the money exports bring. Command GNP therefore measures the volume of goods and services the U.S. economy can "command" — the nation's purchasing power — rather than the volume it produces.[3] And as we have just seen, "competitiveness" means something different from "productivity" if and only if purchasing power grows significantly more slowly than output.

Well, here are the numbers. Over the period 1959–1973, a period of vigorous growth in U.S., living standards and few concerns about international

---

[2]An example may be helpful here. Suppose that a country spends 20 percent of its income on imports, and that the prices of its imports are set not in domestic but in foreign currency. Then if the country is forced to devalue its currency — reduce its value in foreign currency — by 10 percent, this will raise the price of 20 percent of the country's spending basket by 10 percent, thus raising the overall price index by 2 percent. Even if domestic *output* has not changed, the country's real *income* will therefore have fallen by 2 percent. If the country must repeatedly devalue in the face of competitive pressure, growth in real income will persistently lag behind growth in real output. [It is] important to notice, however, that the size of this lag depends not only on the amount of devaluation but on the share of imports in spending. A 10 percent devaluation of the dollar against the yen does not reduce U.S. real income by 10 percent — in fact, it reduces U.S. real income by only about 0.2 percent because only about 2 percent of U.S. income is spent on goods produced in Japan.

[3]In the example in the previous footnote, the devaluation would have no effect on real GNP, but command GNP would have fallen by 2 percent. The finding that in practice command GNP has grown almost as fast as real GNP therefore amounts to saying that events like the hypothetical case in footnote one are unimportant in practice.

competition, real GNP per worker-hour grew 1.85 percent annually, while command GNP per hour grew a bit faster, 1.87 percent. From 1973 to 1990, a period of stagnating living standards, command GNP growth per worker-hour slowed to 0.65 percent. Almost all (91 percent) of that slowdown, however, was explained by a decline in domestic productivity growth: real GNP per hour grew only 0.73 percent.

Similar calculations for the European Community and Japan yield similar results. In each case, the growth rate of living standards essentially equals the growth rate of domestic productivity — not productivity relative to competitors, but simply domestic productivity. Even though world trade is larger than ever before, national living standards are overwhelmingly determined by domestic factors rather than by some competition for world markets.

How can this be in our interdependent world? Part of the answer is that the world is not as interdependent as you might think: countries are nothing at all like corporations. Even today, U.S. exports are only 10 percent of the value-added in the economy (which is equal to GNP). That is, the U.S. is still almost 90 percent an economy that produces goods and services for its own use. By contrast, even the largest corporation sells hardly any of its output to its own workers; the "exports" of General Motors — its sales to people who do not work there — are virtually all of its sales, which are more than 2.5 times the corporation's value-added.

Moreover, countries do not compete with each other the way corporations do. Coke and Pepsi are almost purely rivals: only a negligible fraction of Coca Cola's sales go to Pepsi workers, only a negligible fraction of the goods Coca Cola workers buy are Pepsi products. So if Pepsi is successful, it tends to be at Coke's expense. But the major industrial countries, while they sell products that compete with each other, are also each other's main export markets and each other's main suppliers of useful imports. If the European economy does well, it need not be at U.S. expense; indeed, if anything a successful European economy is likely to help the U.S. economy by providing it with larger markets and selling it goods of superior quality at lower prices.

International trade, then, is not a zero-sum game. When productivity rises in Japan, the main result is a rise in Japanese real wages; American or European wages are in principle at least as likely to rise as to fall, and in practice seem to be virtually unaffected.

It would be possible to belabor the point, but the moral is clear: while competitive problems could arise in principle, as a practical, empirical matter, the major nations of the world are not, to any significant degree, in economic competition with each other. Of course, there is always a rivalry for status and power — countries that grow faster will see their political rank rise. So it is always interesting to compare countries. But asserting that Japanese growth diminishes U.S. status is very different from saying that it reduces the U.S. standard of living and it is the latter that the rhetoric of competitiveness asserts.

One can, of course, take the position that words mean what we want them to mean, that all are free, if they wish, to use the term "competitiveness" as a poetic way of saying productivity, without actually implying that international competition has anything to do with it. But few writers on competitiveness would accept this view. They believe that the facts tell a very different story, that we live, as Lester Thurow put it in his best-selling book, *Head to Head*, in a world of "win-lose" competition between the leading economies. How is this belief possible?

CARELESS ARITHMETIC

One of the remarkable, startling features of the vast literature on competitiveness is the repeated tendency of highly intelligent authors to engage in what may perhaps most tactfully be described as "careless arithmetic." Assertions are made that sound like quantifiable pronouncements about measurable magnitudes, but the writers do not actually present any data on these magnitudes and thus fail to notice that the actual numbers contradict their assertions. Or data are presented that are supposed to support an assertion, but the writer fails to notice that his own numbers imply that what he is saying cannot be true. Over and over again one finds books and articles on competitiveness that seem to the unwary reader to be full of convincing evidence but that strike anyone familiar with the data as strangely, almost eerily inept in their handling of the numbers. Some examples can best illustrate this point. Here are three cases of careless arithmetic, each of some interest in its own right.

Trade Deficits and the Loss of Good Jobs. In a recent article published in Japan, Lester Thurow explained to his audience the importance of reducing the Japanese trade surplus with the U.S. He pointed out that U.S. real wages had fallen 6 percent during the Reagan and Bush years, and the reason was that trade deficits in manufactured goods had forced workers out of high-paying manufacturing jobs into much lower-paying service jobs.

This is not an original view; it is very widely held. But Thurow was more concrete than most people, giving actual numbers for the job and wage loss. A million manufacturing jobs have been lost because of the deficit, he asserted, and manufacturing jobs pay 30 percent more than service jobs.

Both numbers are dubious. The million job number is too high, and the 30 percent wage differential between manufacturing and services is primarily due to a difference in the length of the workweek, not a difference in the hourly wage rate. But let's grant Thurow his numbers. Do they tell the story he suggests?

The key point is that total U.S. employment is well over 100 million workers. Suppose that a million workers were forced from manufacturing into services and as a result lost the 30 percent manufacturing wage premium. Since these workers are less than 1 percent of the U.S. labor force, this would reduce the average U.S. wage rate by less than 1/100 of 30 percent — that is, by less than 0.3 percent.

This is too small to explain the 6 percent real wage decline *by a factor of 20*. Or to look at it another way, the annual wage loss from deficit induced deindustrialization, which Thurow clearly implies is at the heart of U.S. economic difficulties, is on the basis of his own numbers roughly equal to what the U.S. spends on health care every week.

Something puzzling is going on here. How could someone as intelligent as Thurow, in writing an article that purports to offer hard quantitative evidence of the importance of international competition to the U.S. economy, fail to realize that the evidence he offers clearly shows that the channel of harm that he identifies was not the culprit?

High Value-added Sectors. Ira Magaziner and Robert Reich, both now influential figures in the Clinton Administration, first reached a broad audience with their 1982 book, *Minding America's Business*. The book advocated a U.S. industrial policy, and in the introduction the authors offered a seemingly concrete quantitative basis for such a policy: "Our standard of living can only rise if (I) capital and labor increasingly flow to industries with high value-added per worker and (II) we maintain a position in those industries that is superior to that of our competitors."

Economists were skeptical of this idea on principle. If targeting the right industries was simply a matter of moving into sectors with high value-added, why weren't private markets already doing the job?[4] But one might dismiss this as simply the usual boundless faith of economists in the market; didn't Magaziner and Reich back their case with a great deal of real world evidence?

---

[4] "Value-added" has a precise, standard meaning in national income accounting: the value added of a firm is the dollar value of its sales, minus the dollar value of the inputs it purchases from other firms, and as such it is easily measured. Some people who use the term, however, may be unaware of this definition and simply use "high value-added" as a synonym for "desirable."

Well, *Minding America's Business* contains a lot of facts. One thing it never does, however, is actually justify the criteria set out in the introduction. The choice of industries to cover clearly implied a belief among the authors that high value-added is more or less synonymous with high technology, but nowhere in the book do any numbers compare actual value-added per worker in different industries.

Such numbers are not hard to find. Indeed, every public library in America has a copy of the *Statistical Abstract of the United States*, which each year contains a table presenting value-added and employment by industry in U.S. manufacturing. All one needs to do, then, is to spend a few minutes in the library with a calculator to come up with a table that ranks U.S. industries by value-added per worker.

Table 2-1 shows selected entries from pages 740–744 of the 1991 *Statistical Abstract*. It turns out that the U.S. industries with really high value-added per worker are in sectors with very high ratios of capital to labor, like cigarettes and petroleum refining. (This was predictable: because capital-intensive industries must earn a normal return on large investments, they must charge prices that are a larger markup over labor costs than labor-intensive industries, which means that they have high value-added per worker.) Among large industries, value-added per worker tends to be high in traditional heavy manufacturing sectors like steel and autos. High-technology sectors like aerospace and electronics turn out to be only roughly average.

This result does not surprise conventional economists. High value-added per worker occurs in sectors that are highly capital-intensive, that is, sectors in which an additional dollar of capital buys little extra value-added. In other words, there is no free lunch.

Table 2-1 Value Added Per Worker, 1988 (in thousands of dollars)

Cigarettes	488
Petroleum Refining	283
Autos	99
Steel	97
Aircraft	68
Electronics	64
All Manufacturing	66

But let's leave on one side what the table says about the way the economy works, and simply note the strangeness of the lapse by Magaziner and Reich. Surely they were not calling for an industrial policy that would funnel capital and labor into the steel and auto industries in preference to high-tech. How, then, could they write a whole book dedicated to the proposition that we should target high value-added industries without ever checking to see which industries they meant?

Labor Costs. In his own presentation at the Copenhagen summit, British Prime Minister John Major showed a chart indicating that European unit labor costs have risen more rapidly than those in the U.S. and Japan. Thus he argued that European workers have been pricing themselves out of world markets.

But a few weeks later Sam Brittan of the *Financial Times* pointed out a strange thing about Major's calculations: the labor costs were not adjusted for exchange rates. In international competition, of course, what matters for a U.S. firm are the costs of its overseas rivals measured in dollars, not marks or yen. So international comparisons of labor costs, like the tables the Bank of England routinely publishes, always convert them into a common currency. The numbers presented by Major, however, did not make this standard adjustment. And it was a good thing for his presentation that they didn't. As Brittan pointed out, European labor costs have not risen in relative terms when the exchange rate adjustment is made.

If anything, this lapse is even odder than those of Thurow or Magaziner and Reich. How could John Major, with the sophisticated statistical resources of the U.K. Treasury behind him, present an analysis that failed to make the most standard of adjustments?

These examples of strangely careless arithmetic, chosen from among dozens of similar cases, by people who surely had both the cleverness and the resources to get it right, cry out for an explanation. The best working hypothesis is that in each case the author or speaker wanted to believe in the competitive hypothesis so much that he felt no urge to question it; if data were used at all, it was only to lend credibility to a predetermined belief, not to test it. But why are people apparently so anxious to define economic problems as issues of international competition?

THE THRILL OF COMPETITION

The competitive metaphor — the image of countries competing with each other in world markets in the same way that corporations do — derives much of its attractiveness from its seeming comprehensibility. Tell a group of businessmen that a country is like a corporation writ large, and you give them the comfort of feeling that they already understand the basics. Try to tell them about economic concepts like comparative advantage, and you are asking them to learn something new. It should not be surprising if many prefer a doctrine that offers the gain of apparent sophistication without the pain of hard thinking. The rhetoric of competitiveness has become so widespread, however, for three deeper reasons.

First, competitive images are exciting, and thrills sell tickets. The subtitle of Lester Thurow's huge best-seller, *Head to Head*, is "The Coming Economic Battle among Japan, Europe, and America"; the jacket proclaims that "the decisive war of the century has begun . . . and America may already have decided to lose." Suppose that the subtitle had described the real situation: "The coming struggle in which each big economy will succeed or fail based on its own efforts, pretty much independently of how well the others do." Would Thurow have sold a tenth as many books?

Second, the idea that U.S. economic difficulties hinge crucially on our failures in international competition somewhat paradoxically makes those difficulties seem easier to solve. The productivity of the average American worker is determined by a complex array of factors, most of them unreachable by any likely government policy. So if you accept the reality that our "competitive" problem is really a domestic productivity problem pure and simple, you are unlikely to be optimistic about any dramatic turnaround. But if you can convince yourself that the problem is really one of failures in international competition — that imports are pushing workers out of high-wage jobs, or subsidized foreign competition is driving the U.S. out of the high value-added sectors — then the answers to economic malaise may seem to you to involve simple things like subsidizing high technology and being tough on Japan.

Finally, many of the world's leaders have found the competitive metaphor extremely useful as a political device. The rhetoric of competitiveness turns out to provide a good way either to justify hard choices or to avoid them. The example of Delors in Copenhagen shows the usefulness of competitive metaphors as an evasion. Delors had to say something at the EC summit; yet to say anything that addressed the real roots of European unemployment would have involved huge political risks. By turning the discussion to essentially irrelevant but plausible sounding questions of competitiveness, he bought himself some time to come up with a better answer (which to some extent he provided in December's white paper on the European economy — a paper that still, however, retained "competitiveness" in its title).

By contrast, the well-received presentation of Bill Clinton's initial economic program in February 1993 showed the usefulness of competitive rhetoric as a motivation for tough policies. Clinton proposed a set of painful spending cuts and tax increases to reduce the Federal deficit. Why? The real reasons for cutting the deficit are disappointingly undramatic: the deficit siphons off funds that might otherwise have been productively invested, and thereby exerts a steady if small drag on U.S. economic growth. But Clinton was able instead to offer a stirring patriotic appeal, calling on the nation to act now in order to make the economy competitive in the global market — with the implication that dire economic consequences would follow if the U.S. does not.

Many people who know that "competitiveness" is a largely meaningless concept have been willing to indulge competitive rhetoric precisely because they believe they can harness it in the service of good policies. An overblown fear of the Soviet Union was used in the 1950s to justify the building of the interstate highway system and the expansion of math and science education. Cannot the unjustified fears about foreign competition similarly be turned to good, used to justify serious efforts to reduce the budget deficit, rebuild infrastructure, and so on?

A few years ago this was a reasonable hope. At this point, however, the obsession with competitiveness has reached the point where it has already begun dangerously to distort economic policies.

THE DANGERS OF OBSESSION

Thinking and speaking in terms of competitiveness poses three real dangers. First, it could result in the wasteful spending of government money supposedly to enhance U.S. competitiveness. Second, it could lead to protectionism and trade wars. Finally, and most important, it could result in bad public policy on a spectrum of important issues.

During the 1950s, fear of the Soviet Union induced the U.S. government to spend money on useful things like highways and science education. It also, however, led to considerable spending on more doubtful items like bomb shelters. The most obvious if least worrisome danger of the growing obsession with competitiveness is that it might lead to a similar misallocation of resources. To take an example, recent guidelines for government research funding have stressed the importance of supporting research that can improve U.S. international competitiveness. This exerts at least some bias toward inventions that can help manufacturing firms, which generally compete on international markets, rather than service producers, which generally do not. Yet most of our employment and value-added is now in services, and lagging productivity in services rather than manufactures has been the single most important factor in the stagnation of U.S. living standards.

A much more serious risk is that the obsession with competitiveness will lead to trade conflict, perhaps even to a world trade war. Most of those who have preached the doctrine of competitiveness have not been old-fashioned protectionists. They want their countries to win the global trade game, not drop out. But what if, despite its best efforts, a country does not seem to be winning, or lacks confidence that it can? Then the competitive diagnosis inevitably suggests that to close the borders is better than to risk having foreigners take away high-wage jobs and high-value sectors. At the very least, the focus on the supposedly competitive nature of international economic relations greases the rails for those who want confrontational if not frankly protectionist policies.

We can already see this process at work, in both the U.S. and Europe. In the U.S., it was remarkable how quickly the sophisticated interventionist arguments advanced by Laura Tyson in her published work gave way to the simple-minded claim by U.S. Trade Representative Mickey Kantor that Japan's bilateral trade surplus was costing the U.S. millions of jobs. And the trade rhetoric of President Clinton, who stresses the supposed creation of high-wage jobs rather than the gains from specialization, left his administration in a weak position when it tried to argue with the claims of NAFTA foes that competition from cheap Mexican labor will destroy the U.S. manufacturing base.

Perhaps the most serious risk from the obsession with competitiveness, however, is its subtle indirect effect on the quality of economic discussion and policy-making. If top government officials are strongly committed to a particular economic doctrine, their commitment inevitably sets the tone for policy-making on all issues, even those which may seem to have nothing to do with that doctrine. And if an economic doctrine is flatly, completely, and demonstrably wrong, the insistence that discussion adhere to that doctrine inevitably blurs the focus and diminishes the quality of policy discussion across a broad range of issues, including some that are very far from trade policy per se.

Consider, for example, the issue of health care reform, undoubtedly the most important economic initiative of the Clinton administration, almost surely an order of magnitude more important to U.S. living standards than anything that might be done about trade policy (unless the U.S. provokes a full-blown trade war). Since health care is an issue with few direct international linkages, one might have expected it to be largely insulated from any distortions of policy resulting from misguided concerns about competitiveness.

But the administration placed the development of the health care plan in the hands of Ira Magaziner, the same Magaziner who so conspicuously failed to do his homework in arguing for government promotion of high value-added industries. Magaziner's prior writings and consulting on economic policy focused almost entirely on the issue of international competition, his views on which may be summarized by the title of his 1990 book, *The Silent War*. His appointment reflected many factors, of course, not least his long personal friendship with the first couple. Still, it was not irrelevant that in an administration committed to the ideology of competitiveness Magaziner, who has consistently recommended that national industrial policies be based on the corporate strategy concepts he learned during his years at the Boston Consulting Group, was regarded as an economic policy expert.

We might also note the unusual process by which the health care reform was developed. In spite of the huge size of the task force, recognized experts in the health care field were almost completely absent, notably though not exclusively economists specializing in health care, including economists with impeccable liberal credentials like Henry Aaron of the Brookings Institution. Again, this may have reflected a number of factors, but it is probably not irrelevant that anyone who, like Magaziner, is strongly committed to the ideology of competitiveness is bound to have found professional economists notably unsympathetic in the past — and to be unwilling to deal with them on any other issue.

To make a harsh but not entirely unjustified analogy, a government wedded to the ideology of competitiveness is as unlikely to make good economic policy as a government committed to creationism is to make good science policy, even in areas that have no direct relationship to the theory of evolution.

ADVISERS WITH NO CLOTHES

If the obsession with competitiveness is as misguided and damaging as this article claims, why aren't more voices saying so? The answer is, a mixture of hope and fear.

On the side of hope, many sensible people have imagined that they can appropriate the rhetoric of competitiveness on behalf of desirable economic policies. Suppose that you believe that the U.S. needs to raise its savings rate and improve its educational system in order to raise its productivity. Even if you know that the benefits of higher productivity have nothing to do with international competition, why not describe this as a policy to enhance competitiveness if you think that it can widen your audience? It's tempting to pander to popular prejudices on behalf of a good cause, and I have myself succumbed to that temptation.

As for fear, it takes either a very courageous or very reckless economist to say publicly that a doctrine that many, perhaps most, of the world's opinion leaders have embraced is flatly wrong. The insult is all the greater when many of those men and women think that by using the rhetoric of competitiveness they are demonstrating their sophistication about economics. This article may influence people, but it will not make many friends.

Unfortunately, those economists who have hoped to appropriate the rhetoric of competitiveness for good economic policies have instead had their own credibility appropriated on behalf of bad ideas. And somebody has to point out when the emperor's intellectual wardrobe isn't all he thinks it is.

So let's start telling the truth: competitiveness is a meaningless word when applied to national economies. And the obsession with competitiveness is both wrong and dangerous.

RESPONSE 1: PLAYING TO WIN

Clyde V. Prestowitz, Jr.

Paul Krugman first achieved a measure of public recognition with a study of competition in the aircraft industry, which proved mathematically the potential efficacy of strategic — that is to say managed — trade. That this analysis was considered important might seem odd in view of the fact that the German-American scholar Friedrich List had done more or less the same work nearly 150 years ago and in view of the experience of the Japanese, who had been practicing strategic trade for more than 40 years at the time of Krugman's study. But given the narrow scope of the research considered permissible by the conventional wisdom of U.S. economists, as well as their ignorance of history and other disciplines, Krugman's analysis was a notable, iconoclastic achievement.

Indeed, it may have been too daring because ever since its publication Krugman has been running away from the implications of his own findings. His diatribe in *Foreign Affairs* (March/April) against the concept of competitiveness and those who espouse it is only the most recent example.

Krugman not only claims that concern with competitiveness is misplaced. He attacks all those who think otherwise — including leading members of the Clinton administration such as Robert B. Reich, Ira C. Magaziner, Laura D'Andrea Tyson and the president himself — as protectionists whose work is careless if not dishonest and whose motives run from simple greed to chauvinism and demagoguery.

Krugman contends that concern about competitiveness is silly because as a practical matter the major countries of the world are not in economic competition with each other. He attempts to prove this by making three points. First he argues that trade is not a zero-sum game. Trade between the U.S. and Japan is not like competition between Coca-Cola and Pepsi because whereas Pepsi's gain is almost always Coke's loss, the U.S. and its trading partners can both be winners through the dynamics of comparative advantage.

Although true to some extent, this rationale ignores that different kinds of trade take place. Surely Krugman is correct in the case of trade between the U.S. and Costa Rica, where America imports bananas it does not grow and exports airplanes and machinery that Costa Rica does not make. Both countries come out winners by devoting their resources to what each does best. But what about the kind of trade typified by the recent Saudi Arabian order for $6 billion of new airplanes? Why were the Europeans so upset and Clinton so happy when the Saudis announced that U.S. producers would win all the orders? Both the Europeans and the Americans make airplanes, and this order means that the U.S. will gain jobs and income that Europe might have had but lost. This was largely a zero-sum trade situation, and ironically it was precisely the case that first brought Krugman to prominence. Maybe he was right the first time.

IT'S LIVING STANDARDS, STUPID

In fact, Krugman later concedes the point by allowing that "in principle" competitiveness problems could arise between countries. But he insists that they do not in practice because trade is a relatively small part of GNP in the major countries. Consequently, living standards are determined almost wholly by how well the economy works domestically rather than by international performance. In this vein, he observes that exports constitute only 10 percent of U.S. output, apparently leaving 90 percent of the economy to purely domestic factors. Moreover, he attributes 91 percent of the 1973 to 1990 stagnation in U.S. living standards to declining domestic productivity growth and only 9 percent to deteriorating terms of trade.

But competitiveness proponents have never denied the importance of domestic economic performance. Indeed, virtually all competitiveness prescriptions emphasize domestic savings and investment rates, education, cost of capital and research and development. Trade is typically treated as a secondary issue — more a symptom than a cause of subpar competitiveness.

Second, Krugman ignores America's imports — which equal 11 percent of GNP and nearly half of U.S. manufacturing output. Thus, overall trade is equivalent to about 21 percent of GNP, and by some estimates the impact of trade is felt directly by at least half the U.S. economy. Take the U.S. auto industry. It is not a big exporter, and imports account for only about 15 percent of the U.S. market. But the prices and quality of those imports help determine the retail prices U.S. automakers can charge, wages of U.S. auto workers, and incomes of those who service the U.S. auto industry.

Krugman does not explain the slowdown in U.S. productivity growth, but he implies that domestic factors are the sole culprits. Yet the slowdown came just when U.S. imports were soaring and entire industries such as consumer electronics were being wiped out by foreign competitors pursuing mercantilist tactics. Surely these dislocations had some impact on U.S. productivity growth.

Krugman's third and final argument is that although countries may be rivals for status and power, such rivalry is something apart from economics and has no impact on living standards. A high relative growth rate may enhance Japan's status, for example, but it does not reduce the living standard of other countries. Although this notion may be true in the short-term, absolute sense, it is not necessarily true in the long-term, potential sense. Since the end of World War II, the U.S. has grown faster than Great Britain. The U.S. has done so in part by taking British inventions such as jet planes and radar and commercializing them faster than the British, thereby closing off those industries as potential avenues of British growth. Of course, if Britain could enter other high-growth, high-wage industries, the U.S. position would make no difference. But at any one time, the number of those industries is limited; missing the boat on one can mean losing potential gains in living standards. In the extreme, loss of economic competitiveness can weaken national security and cause greater vulnerability to political regimes and international cartels that may severely constrain a country's economic potential. This competition is, after all, what imperialism and its opposition has been all about.

SPLITTING HAIRS

To buttress his arguments, Krugman attacks his critics' arithmetic as careless. Yet Krugman's own arithmetic is careless and selective. His analysis of how manufacturing job loss affects real average wages ignores the relationship between service and manufacturing wages. American barbers are not notably more productive than Bangladeshi barbers. But their wages are much higher because their customers work with much higher productivity than the customers of their Bangladeshi counterparts. Loss of high-wage U.S. manufacturing jobs also depresses not only manufacturing wages but also service industry wages. Krugman, however, fails to mention this drag.

Krugman's discussion of value added is even more questionable. He may have a point in that "high value added" has become a kind of shorthand for technology-intensive and high-wage industries when that is not always the case. But Krugman uses very broad industry categories to make his point, although the data he draws on clearly show that a huge industry like electronics consists of many sectors, some with high value added and others with low. Overall, Krugman notes a figure of value added per worker in the electronics industry of only $64,000. But why did he ignore the tables showing the figures of $443,000 for computers and $234,000 for semiconductors?

Krugman concludes by expressing fear of the possible distortion of the U.S. economy through the application of flawed competitiveness policies. He could, of course, be right. But can the U.S. be confident that an analyst who has such obvious gaps of his own and who has now argued both sides of the competitiveness issue can be relied on as the guide? Perhaps he is wrong, and competitiveness, far from being a dangerous obsession, is an essential concern.

RESPONSE 2: MICROCHIPS, NOT POTATO CHIPS

Lester C. Thurow

The Gang of Eight (Bill Clinton, John Major, Jacques Delors, Robert Reich, Laura D'Andrea Tyson, Mickey Kantor, Ira Magaziner, Lester Thurow) pleads not guilty to Paul Krugman's charges that it is grossly exaggerating the importance of international competitiveness.

Krugman asserts that, economically, nations have "no well-defined bottom line." Wrong! Nations seek to raise the living standards of each citizen. Higher living standards depend on rising productivity, and in any economy the rate of productivity growth is principally determined by the size of domestic investments in plant and equipment, research and development, skills and public infrastructure, and the quality of private management and public administration.

I have written articles referring to strategic trade policies as the "seven percent solution." 93 percent of economic success or failure is determined at home with only 7 percent depending on competitive and cooperative arrangements with the rest of the world. My book, *The Zero-Sum Solution: Building a World-Class American Economy*, contains 23 pages on competitiveness issues, 45 pages on the importance of international cooperation and 333 pages on getting things right at home. The centrality of domestic invention and innovation is precisely why I agreed to lead the Lemelson-MIT program in invention and innovation, one part of which is a $500,000 prize for the American inventor and innovator of the year. The corpus of writings, speeches, and actions of the rest of the Gang of Eight contains similar quotations, proportions, and actions.

But remembering this sense of proportion, what is the role for competitiveness? Clearly something is wrong with Krugman's arithmetic that shows international trade cannot make much difference to American productivity. If his arithmetic were correct, then it follows that a lot of American protection might be quite a good thing.

Today 6 million Americans are working part-time who would like to work full-time, and almost 9 million are unemployed. In the last 20 years the bottom two-thirds of the male work force has taken a 20 percent reduction in real wages. The American work force could use a few million extra high-wage jobs. Suppose the U.S. were to impose quotas on manufactured imports so as to bring American imports (now 14 percent of gross domestic product) down to the 10 percent of GDP currently exported — that is, increase the domestically produced GDP by $250 billion. According to the U.S. Department of Commerce, if one divides manufacturing output by manufacturing employment, every $45 billion in extra output represents one million jobs. Production of current imports would absorb more than 5 million of those 15 million underemployed and unemployed people.

Since more Americans would be working in a sector with above-average productivity, national output and earnings would rise. The losses to the American consumer in the form of higher prices would be smaller than the gains to American producers in the form of higher earnings unless American producers were less than half as efficient as those abroad (an unlikely event). But even if that were the case, the economic burden of their inefficiency would be trivial relative to American GDP of $6.5 trillion. The gains to workers would be well worth the loss in output. But certainly none of the Gang of Eight advocates such policies, although they would seem to be called for by Krugman's simple arithmetic. Why?

WELCOME TO THE REAL WORLD

The simple arithmetic of what economists call "comparative statics" is technically right but economically wrong. If the domestic economy is to succeed in moving to higher levels of productivity and income, it must first compete successfully in the global economy. Foreign competition simultaneously forces a faster pace of economic change at home and produces opportunities to learn new technologies and new management practices that can be used to improve domestic productivity. Put bluntly, those who don't compete abroad won't be productive at home.

Although he denies saying it, Michael J. Boskin, chairman of President Bush's Council of Economic Advisers, will go down in history as the man who said, "It doesn't make any difference whether a country makes potato chips or computer chips!" The statement is wrong because wages and rates of return to capital are not everywhere equal.

The real world is in a perpetual state of dynamic disequilibrium where differentials in wages and rate of return to capital by industry are both large and persistent (these above-average wages or returns to capital are technically called disequilibrium quasi-rents). Within manufacturing in 1992 there was an almost four-to-one wage gap between those working in the highest- and lowest-paid industries. The industries at the top and bottom have changed little since World War II. Rates of return to capital similarly ranged from plus 27 percent in pharmaceuticals to minus 26 percent in building materials.

Pharmaceuticals top the rate of return charts every year. The market is always eliminating the high rates of return on existing drugs, but disequilibrium quasi-rents are always being created on new drugs. Because every successful pharmaceutical firm requires huge amounts of time and capital to build physical and human infrastructure, those already in the industry find it relatively easy to stay ahead of those who might seek to enter.

PUTTING PEOPLE FIRST

Those who lost jobs in autos and machine tools as American firms lost market share at home and abroad typically took a 30 to 50 percent wage reduction, if they were young. If they were older than 50 years, they were usually permanently exiled to the periphery of the low-wage, part-time labor market. Their losses might not be a large faction of GDP, but those losses are important to the millions of affected workers and their families. The correct redressal for their problems, however, is not to keep Japanese autos or machine tools out of the American market but to organize ventures such as the government–industry auto battery consortium that seeks to expand the American auto industry's market share by taking the lead in producing tomorrow's electric cars.

Since aircraft manufacturing generates technologies that later spread to the rest of the economy and above-average wages, the U.S. cannot simply ignore the government–financed European Airbus Industry challenge in an industry America currently dominates.

The fastest-growing and technologically most exciting industry over the next decade is expected to be the industry that lies at the intersection of telecommunications, computers, television, and the media arts. Given this prospect, the U.S. cannot afford to let itself be locked out of the Japanese wireless telecommunications market or permit the Europeans to limit American movies and television programs to 40 percent of their markets. To do so is to make the entire American economy less dynamic and less technologically sophisticated and to generate lower American incomes than would otherwise be the case.

In the traditional theory of comparative advantage, Boskin and Krugman are correct. Natural resource endowments and factor proportions (capital–labor ratios) determine what countries should produce. Governments can and should do little when it comes to international competitiveness. With a world capital market, however, all now essentially borrow in London, New York, or Tokyo, regardless of where they live. There is no such thing as a capital-rich or capital-poor country. Modern technology has also pushed natural resources out of the competitive equation. Japan, with no coal or iron ore deposits, can have the best steel industry in the world.

This is now a much more dynamic world of brainpower industries and synthesized comparative advantage. Industries such as microelectronics, biotechnology, the new materials industries, telecommunications, civilian aircraft production, machine tools, and computer hardware and software have no natural geographic home. They will be located wherever someone organizes the brainpower to capture them. With man-made comparative advantage, one seeks not to find disequilibrium quasi-rents (the gold mine of yore) but to create the new products and processes that generate above-average wages and rates of return.

In their funding of education, skills, and research and development, governments have an important role to play in organizing the brainpower necessary to create economic leadership. Just as military intelligence estimates about U.S.S.R. intentions partly guided yesterday's strategic military research and development, so the actions of U.S. economic competitors will partly guide tomorrow's civilian research and development. If the Japanese have an insurmountable lead in flat-screen video technology, it does not make sense to invest government or private resources or talent in a hopeless attempt to catch up.

The smart private firm benchmarks itself *vis-à-vis* its best domestic and international competition. Where it is not the world's best, it seeks to adopt the better practices found elsewhere. A smart country will do the same. Is America's investment in plant and equipment, research and development, skills and infrastructure world class? Do American managers, private and public, have something to learn from practices in the rest of the world? The purpose of such benchmarking is not to declare economic warfare on foreign competitors but to emulate them and elevate U.S. standards of performance.

Obsessions are not always wrong or dangerous. A passion for building a world-class economy that is second to none in generating a high living standard for every citizen is exactly what the U.S. and every other country should seek to achieve. Achieving that goal in any one country in no way stops any other country from doing likewise.

RESPONSE 3:
SPEAKING FREELY

Stephen S. Cohen

Paul Krugman contends that those who speak of competitiveness fail to understand three important points. First, nations are not like companies. No single number indicates their bottom line and the analogy does not apply. Second, he says that competitiveness is at best a meaningless concept. If it has any meaning whatever, it is "a poetic way of saying productivity." Productivity is the robust and unique measure of the performance of a national economy. Third, international trade is not a zero-sum game.

These are not stinging revelations but merely oft-repeated truisms. All his assertions are set out mundanely in The Report of the President's Commission on Competitiveness, written for the Reagan administration in 1984. The report provides what even Krugman acknowledges has become the standard definition:

> *Competitiveness has different meanings for the firm and for the national economy. . . . A nation's competitiveness is the degree to which it can, under free and fair market conditions, produce goods and services that meet the test of international markets while simultaneously expanding the real incomes of its citizens. Competitiveness at the national level is based on superior productivity performance.*

So all of Krugman's revelations are on page one of the basic text: no simple analogy equates a nation and a business, productivity lies at the center of competitiveness, and trade is not a zero-sum game; it can and should be free and fair.

What then, if anything, is Krugman flailing at? Nobody with whom Krugman should deign to take difference has ever said the silly things he pokes with his jousting spear. Lots of people vulgarize competitiveness, but that is true of just about every other idea in economics.

Krugman objects to President Clinton's likening of the U.S. economy to "a big corporation competing in the global marketplace." Presidential metaphors, which try to encapsulate complicated matters for purposes of political mobilization, have their own logic and history. Perhaps Clinton's simile is akin to Franklin D. Roosevelt's famous likening of the Lend-Lease Act to lending a neighbor a fire hose. Clinton was neither mendacious nor wrong. To remind Americans that in many ways they are all in this together is important, and in a sense the national economy can be likened to a huge corporation — not big in the rude, trivializing example Krugman uses, Pepsi versus Coke, but big in the Mitsubishi, Mitsui, or Sumitomo sense. The six main *keiretsu* — massive structures of grouped companies — which for many purposes come very close to being the Japanese economy, produce about half the Japanese total output of transportation equipment, banking, insurance, oil, glass, cement, and shipping. Over one-half of all intermediate products are produced and bought within the cozy network of the six main groups, not to mention the lesser vertical *keiretsu*.

Lots of people, not just politicians, use "competitiveness" as a metaphor and do so a bit freely. Scientists talk of national competitiveness in biology; educators, in math. Part of the problem is the need for a single substantive term for "competitive position." Part is a heightened awareness, all to the good, that the U.S. is no longer supreme, benchmarking is a first step toward serious improvement, and comparative measures — even of economic welfare — have important and legitimate meanings.

Krugman criticizes those who write about competitiveness for their tendency to "engage in what may perhaps most tactfully be described as 'careless arithmetic.'" Yet Krugman's own arithmetic is, to say the least, careless. He provides a table that purports to demonstrate arithmetically that value-added production correlates not with technology but with capital intensity. But relating capital intensity to value added by sector contains a concealed correlation because the same table also ranks sectors by degree of monopoly power. And nothing generates more value added than monopoly. Furthermore,

Krugman omitted at least one sector: pharmaceuticals. This sector should be number three on his list, with value added almost twice as high as autos. But value added in pharmaceuticals is not explained by lots of capital per worker; instead the pharmaceutical industry has lots of research per worker along with lots of sales effort and monopoly concentration. And for a more sophisticated understanding, one should look beyond production to sales figures in the U.S., which include competition from imports. In cigarettes, the number-one industry in value added and number-one in monopoly concentration, competition from imports is trivial. That is a major reason for the high value added in cigarette production. But that raises big questions, such as what determines productivity? What operationally can and cannot be done with simple productivity numbers?

Krugman warns that an obsession with competitiveness is dangerous and advises cathecting onto productivity. A near-exclusive focus on productivity, however, has some particular dangers and problems. Competitiveness puts productivity at the center of its concerns but not as an explanation. Instead competitiveness points out that overall productivity rates, which are very complex syntheses, are the things to explain, and that economics does not know how to do that.

BEGGAR-THY-QUESTION

Krugman unwittingly illustrates the problem of relying on a single number for overall production rates when he provides an alternative to a competitiveness approach. To say that 91 percent of the slowdown in the growth of per capita GNP "was explained by a decline in domestic productivity growth" does not explain the decline but rephrases it. To say that GNP grew slowly because the growth in output per hour grew slowly is simply to push aside the real question: What caused the decline? Krugman's numerical exercise does not even adequately fulfill the smaller role he assigns to it — to show that foreign competition played a trivial part in lowering the rate of growth of national welfare. This failure occurs because Krugman counts only the prices and quantities of imports, not their impact on profits, investment, jobs, and wages. The typical case outlining the advantages of trade to the U.S. economy always focuses on these elements because they are much bigger than the simple, first-round effects of the prices and quantities of imports, which, with a modicum of craftsmanship, can be manipulated to demonstrate whatever one wishes. Similar problems of logic and data flaw the calculations that yield Krugman's most sweeping single-number assertion — that the U.S.

trade deficit in manufactured goods has only a very small impact on wages, a reduction at most of only 0.3 percent. The problem, again, is not just with the single number but with the static approach Krugman adopts. Only a dynamic understanding and methodology can appreciate those impacts because that is how they proceed, iteratively, with real and consequential feedback. Finally, national productivity data have several smaller, technical difficulties that radically reduce the reliability of the numbers. It is impossible to get reliable productivity numbers for the core sectors of the service economy, for example well over a third of GNP. And operationally, market and institutional structures lead economists to assign low productivity growth rates to industries such as semiconductors although engineers know that productivity has grown at fabulous rates.

The clean simplicity and apparent analytic power of the simple, one-number approach, though it fits snugly with the models and methods of traditional American economics, has given rise to efforts to define a different organizing concept — competitiveness — in order to open a broader, more open-minded and modest approach. The competitiveness approach poses a sensible question: How are we doing as an economy? No single number sums it all up, especially given the follow-up: How are we doing compared to the other guys? And why? Competitiveness is a reconsideration of a broad set of indicators, none of which tells the whole story but that together provide a highly legitimate focus.

COUNTER-RESPONSE: PROVING MY POINT

Paul Krugman

My article in the March/April issue of *Foreign Affairs* has obviously upset many people. Some of my critics claim that I misrepresented their position, that despite their insistent use of the word "competitiveness" they have never believed that the major industrial nations are engaged in a competitive economic struggle. Others claim that I have gotten the economics wrong: that countries are engaged in a competitive struggle. Indeed, some of them make both claims in the same response.

MOVING TARGET

Lester C. Thurow vigorously denies ever asserting that international competition is a central issue for the U.S. economy. In particular, he cites page counts from his 1985 book, *The Zero-Sum Solution*, to demonstrate that domestic factors are his principal concern. But Thurow's most recent book is *Head to Head*, which follows its provocative title with the subtitle, *The Coming Battle Among Japan, Europe and America*. The book jacket asserts that the "decisive war of the century has begun." The text asserts over and over that the major economic powers are now engaged in "win-lose" competition for world markets, a competition that has taken the place of the military competition between East and West. Thurow now says that international strategic competition is no more than 7 percent of the problem; did the typical reader of *Head to Head* get this message?

Similarly, Stephen S. Cohen denies that he, or indeed anyone else with whom I should "deign to take difference," has ever said the things I claim competitiveness advocates believe. But in 1987 Cohen, together with John Zysman, published *Manufacturing Matters*, a book that seemed to say two (untrue) things: the long-term downward trend in the share of manufacturing in U.S. employment is largely due to foreign competition, and this declining share is a major economic problem.

After their initial denial, both Cohen and Thurow proceed to argue that international competition is of crucial importance after all. In this they are joined by Clyde V. Prestowitz, Jr., who at least makes no bones about believing that trade and trade policy are the central issues for the U.S. economy. Does Cohen believe that Prestowitz — or James Fallows, who expressed similar views in his new book, *Looking at the Sun* — is one of those people with whom I should not deign to argue?

SLOPPY MATH: PART II

Of all the elements in my article, the section on careless arithmetic — the strange pattern of errors in reporting or using data in articles and books on competitiveness — has enraged the most people. Both Thurow and Prestowitz have taken care to fill their responses with a blizzard of numbers and calculations. However, some of the numbers are puzzling.

For example, Thurow says that imports are 14 percent of U.S. GDP, while exports are only 10 percent, and that reducing imports to equal exports would add $250 billion to the sales of U.S. manufacturers. But according to Economic Indicators, the monthly statistical publication of the Joint Economic Committee, U.S. imports in 1993 were only 11.4 percent of GDP, while exports were 10.4 percent. Even the current account deficit, a broader measure that includes some additional debit items, was only $109 billion. If the U.S. were to cut imports by $250 billion, far from merely balancing its trade as Thurow asserts, the U.S. would run a current account surplus of $140 billion — that is, more than the 2 percent maximum of GDP U.S. negotiators have demanded Japan set as a target!

Or consider Prestowitz, who derides my claim that high-technology industries, commonly described as "high value" sectors, actually have much lower value added per worker than traditional "high volume," heavy industrial sectors. I have aggregated too much by looking at broad sectors like electronics, he says; I should look at the highest-tech lines of business, like semiconductors, where value added per worker is $234,000. Prestowitz should report the results of his research to the Department of Commerce, whose staff has obviously incorrectly calculated (in the *Annual Survey of Manufactures*) that in 1989 value added per worker in Standard Industrial Classification 3674 (semiconductors and related devices) was $96,487 — closer to the $76,709 per worker in SIC 2096 (potato chips and related snacks) than to the $187,569 in SIC 3711 (motor vehicles and car bodies).[5]

Everyone makes mistakes, although it is surprising when men who are supposed to be experts on international competition do not have even a rough idea of the size of the U.S. trade deficit or know how to look up a standard industrial statistic. The interesting point, however, is that the mistakes made by Thurow, Prestowitz, and other competitiveness advocates are not random errors; they are always biased in the same direction. That is, the advocates always err in a direction that makes international competition seem more important than it really is.

Beyond these petty, if revealing, errors of fact are a series of conceptual misunderstandings. For example, Prestowitz argues that productivity in sectors that compete on world markets is much more important than productivity in non-traded service sectors because the former determine wage rates throughout the economy. For example, because U.S. manufacturing workers are much more productive than their Third World counterparts, U.S. barbers, who do not have a comparable productivity advantage, also get high wages. But Prestowitz fails to notice that the converse is also true: service productivity affects the real wages of manufacturing workers. Because the high relative productivity of U.S. manufacturing is not matched in the haircut sector, haircuts by those well-paid barbers are much more expensive than haircuts in the Third World; as a result real wages of U.S. manufacturing workers (that is, wages in terms of what they can buy, including haircuts) are not as high as they would be if U.S. barbers were more productive. With careful thought, one realizes that real wages depend on the overall productivity of the economy, with no special presumption that productivity in manufacturing — or in internationally traded sectors in general — deserves any more attention or active promotion than productivity elsewhere.

---

[5] I don't know why Thurow thinks the U.S. trade deficit is four times as big as it actually is. I have, however, tracked down Prestowitz's number. It is not value added per employee; it is shipments (which are always larger than value added) divided by the number of production workers (who are only a fraction of total employment, especially in high-technology industries).

Cohen makes essentially the same mistake when he complains that I underestimated the effects of competitive pressure because I focused only on import and export prices and did not consider the further impacts of that pressure on profits and wages. He somehow fails to realize that a change in wages or profits that is not reflected in import or export prices cannot change overall U.S. real income — it can only redistribute profits to one group within the United States at the expense of another. That is why the effect of international price competition on U.S. real income can be measured by the change in the ratio of export to import prices — full stop. And the effects of changes in this ratio on the U.S. economy have, as I showed in my article, been small.

Or consider Thurow's analysis of the benefits that would accrue to the U.S. if it could roll back imports (leaving aside the inaccuracy of his numbers). He asserts that the U.S. could create five million new jobs in import-competing sectors, and he assumes that all five million jobs represent a net addition to employment. But this assumption is unrealistic. As this reply was being written, the Federal Reserve was raising interest rates in an effort to rein in a recovery that it feared would proceed too far, that is, lead to excessive employment, producing a renewed surge in inflation. Some people think that the Fed is tightening too soon, but the essential point is that the growth of employment is not determined by the ability of the U.S. to sell goods on world markets or to compete with imports, but by the Fed's judgement of what will not set off inflation. So suppose that the U.S. were to impose import quotas, adding millions of jobs in import-competing sectors. The Fed would respond by raising interest rates to prevent an overheated economy, and most if not all of the job gains would be matched by job losses elsewhere.

THINGS ADD UP

In each of these cases, my critics seem to have forgotten the most basic principle of economics: things add up. Higher employment in import-competing industries must come either through a reduction in unemployment, in which case one must ask whether the implied unemployment rate (about 3 percent in Thurow's example) is feasible, or at the expense of jobs elsewhere in the economy, in which case no overall job gain takes place. If higher manufacturing wages lead to a higher wage rate for barbers without higher tonsorial productivity, the gain must come at someone else's expense. Since it is hard to see how foreigners pay for more expensive American haircuts, that wage gain can only redistribute the benefits of manufacturing productivity from one set of American workers to another, not increase the total gains. In their haste to assign great importance to international competition, my critics, like the inventors of perpetual motion machines, have failed to realize that there are conservation principles that any story about the economy must honor.

But perhaps Cohen, Thurow, and Prestowitz stumble on economic basics because they are so eager to get to their main point, which is that advanced economic theory, and in particular the theory of strategic trade policy, supports their obsession with competitiveness.

Prestowitz's central assertion is that the theory of strategic trade policy, which he for some reason thinks I invented in a paper about aircraft competition (the actual inventors were James Brander and Barbara Spencer, who never mentioned aircraft), justifies aggressively interventionist trade policies. He further asserts that economists in general, and I in particular, have run away from that implication for ideological reasons.

Well, that's not quite the real story. It is true that in the early 1980s professional economists became aware that one of the implications of new theories of international trade was a possible role for strategic policies to promote exports in certain industries. Confronted with a new idea that was exciting, potentially important but untested, these economists began a sustained process of research, probing the weak points, confronting the new idea with the data. After all, lots of things could be true in principle. For example in certain theoretical situations a tax cut could definitely stimulate the economy so much that government revenues would actually rise, and it would be very nice if that were the actual situation; but unfortunately it isn't. Similarly, it is definitely possible to imagine a situation in which, because of all of the market imperfections Thurow dwells on, a clever strategic trade policy would sharply raise U.S. real income. And it would be very nice if the U.S. could devise such a policy. But is that possibility really there? To answer that question requires looking hard at the facts.

And so over the course of the last ten years a massive international research program has explored the prospects for strategic trade policy.[6] Two

---

[6]The original paper on strategic trade policy was James Brander and Barbara Spencer, "Export Subsidies and International Market Share Rivalry," *Journal of International Economics*, February 1985, pp. 83–100. See also Paul Krugman, ed., *Strategic Trade Policy and the New International Economics*, Cambridge: MIT Press, 1986; Robert Feenstra, ed., *Empirical Methods for International Trade*, Chicago: University of Chicago Press, 1988; Robert Baldwin, ed., *Trade Policy Issues and Empirical Analysis*, Chicago: University of Chicago Press, 1988; and

broad conclusions emerge. First, to identify which industries should receive strategic promotion or the appropriate form and level of promotion is very difficult. Second, the payoffs of even a successful strategic trade policy are likely to be very modest — certainly far less even than Thurow's "seven percent solution," which is closer to the entire share of international trade in the U.S. economy.

Research results are always open to challenge, especially in an inexact field like economics. If Prestowitz wants to point out specific failings in the dozens of painstaking empirical studies of strategic trade that have been carried out over the past decade, by all means let him do so. His remarks about the subject, however, strongly suggest that while he is happy to mention strategic trade theory in support of his policy writing, Prestowitz has not read any of the economic literature.

I do, however, agree with Prestowitz on one point. More people should read the works of Friedrich List. If they do, they may wonder why this turgid, confused writer — whose theory led him to predict that Holland and Denmark would be condemned to permanent economic backwardness unless they sought political union with Germany — has suddenly become a favorite of Fallows, Prestowitz, and others. The new cult of List bears an uncanny resemblance to the right-wing supply-siders' canonization of the classical French economist Jean-Baptiste Say, who claimed that the economy as a whole could never suffer from the falls in aggregate demand that produce recessions.[7] The motive of the supply-siders was, of course, to cover simplistic ideas with a veneer of faux scholarship.

In contrast to Prestowitz and Thurow, who offer coherent if flawed reasons to worry about international competition, Cohen offers a more difficult target. Basically, he asks us to accept "competitiveness" as a kind of ineffable essence that cannot be either defined or measured. Data that seem to suggest the importance of this essence are cited as "indicators," whatever that means, while those that do not are dismissed as unreliable. Both in his article and other writings he has persistently used a rhetoric that seems to portray international

---

Paul Krugman and Alasdair Smith, eds., *Empirical Studies of Strategic Trade Policy*, Chicago: University of Chicago Press, 1994.

[7] Fallows officially elevated List to guru status in his article "How the World Works," *The Atlantic Monthly*, December 1993, pp. 60–87. Readers may wish to compare the elevation of Say by Jude Wanniski in his influential supply-side tract, *The Way the World Works*, New York: Basic Books, 1978.

trade as a game with winners and losers, but when challenged on any particular point he denies having said it. I guess I don't understand how a concept so elusive can be a useful guide to policy.

My original article in *Foreign Affairs* argued that a doctrine that views world trade as a competitive struggle has become widely accepted, that this view is wrong but that there is nonetheless an intense desire to believe in that doctrine. The article enraged many, especially when it asserted that the desire to believe in competitive struggle repeatedly leads highly intelligent authors into surprising lapses in their handling of concepts and data. I could not, however, have asked for a better demonstration of my point than the responses published in this issue.

REFERENCES

Baldwin, R. (ed.) (1988). *Trade Policy Issues and Empirical Analysis*, Chicago: University of Chicago Press.

Brander, J. and Spencer, S. (1985). Export subsidies and international market share rivalry. *Journal of International Economics*, **February**: 83–100.

Dietrich, W. S. (1991). *In the Shadow of the Rising Sun: The Political Roots of American Economic Decline*, University Park: Pennsylvania State University Press.

Fallows, J. (1993). How the world works. *The Atlantic Monthly*, **December**: 60–87.

Feenstra, R. (ed.) (1988). *Empirical Methods for International Trade*, Chicago: University of Chicago Press.

Garten, J. E. (1992). *A Cold Peace: America, Japan, Germany, and the Struggle for Supremacy*, New York: Times Books.

Krugman, P. (ed.) (1986). *Strategic Trade Policy and the New International Economics*, Cambridge: MIT Press.

Krugman, P. and Smith, A. (eds.) (1994). *Empirical Studies of Strategic Trade Policy*, Chicago: University of Chicago Press.

Luttwak, E. N. (1993). *The Endangered American Dream: How to Stop the United States from Becoming a Third World Country and How to Win the Geo-economic Struggle for Industrial Supremacy*, New York: Simon and Schuster.

Magaziner, I. C. and Reich, R. B. (1983). *Minding America's Business. The Decline and Rise of the American Economy*, New York: Vintage Books.

Magaziner, I. C. and Patinkin, M. (1990). *The Silent War: Inside the Global Business Battles Shaping Americas Future*, New York: Vintage Books.

Phillips, K. P. (1984). *Staying on Top: The Business Case for a National Industrial Strategy*, New York: Random House.

Prestowitz, Jr., C. V. (1988). *Trading Places: How We Allowed Japan to Take the Lead*, New York: Basic Books.

Sandholtz, W., Borrus, M., Zysman, J., Conca, K., Stowsky, J., Vogel, S. and Weber, S. (1992). *The Highest Stakes: The Economic Foundations of the Next Security System*, Berkeley Roundtable on the International Economy (BRIE), Oxford University Press.

Thurow, L. C. (1992). *Head to Head: The Coming Economic Battle among Japan, Europe, and America*, New York: Morrow.

Tyson, L. D. (1992). *Who's Bashing Whom: Trade Conflict in High-Technology Industries*, Washington: Institute for International Economics.

Wanniski, J. (1978). *The Way the World Works*, New York: Basic Books.

3

NEW MODEL: THEORY

SUMMARY AND KEY POINTS

To investigate why nations gain competitive advantage in particular industries and the implications for company strategy and national economies, Porter (1990) conducted a four-year study of ten important trading nations. Porter defined a nation's industry as internationally successful if it possessed competitive advantage relative to the best worldwide competitors. As the best indicators he chose the presence of substantial and sustained exports and/or significant outbound foreign investment based on skills and assets created in the home country. Porter concluded that nations succeed in particular industries because their home environment is the most forward-looking, dynamic, and challenging. Specifically, the determinants are factor conditions; demand conditions; related and supporting industries; and firm strategy, structure, and rivalry. In addition, there are two outside variables: government and chance.

Source:
Porter, M. E. (1990). The competitive advantage of nations. *Harvard Business Review*, **March–April**: 73–93.
Institute for Strategy and Competitiveness. *Harvard Business School*. Available at: www.isc.hbs.edu.

Porter criticized the traditional doctrine, whose origins date back to Adam Smith and David Ricardo, that it is at best incomplete and at worst incorrect. According to Porter, national prosperity is created, not inherited. Porter's model is thus dynamic. Porter's model is also comprehensive because it includes not just factor conditions, as most traditional models do, but also other important variables. With this framework, Porter has analyzed the competitiveness of several countries, including Canada, Saudi Arabia, Rwanda, Malaysia, Nigeria, as well as the U.S. Porter also helped the World Economic Forum's Global Competitiveness Report on the comparative strengths and weaknesses of leading economies of the world.

However, the Porter model is not without criticism. In particular, Porter's treatment of multinational activities and government is not convincing. We will discuss this in Chapter 4.

THE COMPETITIVE
ADVANTAGE OF NATIONS

National prosperity is created, not inherited. It does not grow out of a country's natural endowments, its labor pool, its interest rates, or its currency's value, as classical economics insists.

A nation's competitiveness depends on the capacity its industry to innovate and upgrade. Companies gain advantage over the world's best competitors, because of pressure and challenge. They benefit from having strong domestic rivals, aggressive home-based suppliers, and demanding local customers.

In a world of increasingly global competition, nations have become more, not less, important. As the basis of competition has shifted more and more to the creation and assimilation of knowledge, the role of the nation has grown. Competitive advantage is created and sustained through a highly localized process. Differences in national values, culture, economic structures, institutions, and histories all contribute to competitive success. There are striking differences in the patterns of competitiveness in every country; no nation can or will be competitive in every or even most industries. Ultimately, nations succeed in particular industries because their home environment is the most forward-looking, dynamic, and challenging.

These conclusions, the product of a four-year study of the patterns of competitive success in ten leading trading nations, contradict the conventional wisdom that guides the thinking of many companies and national governments — and that is pervasive today in the U.S. (For more about the study, see Appendix A "Patterns of National Competitive Success.") According to prevailing thinking, labor costs, interest rates, exchange rates, and economies of scale are the most potent determinants of competitiveness. In companies, the words of the day are merger, alliance, strategic partnerships, collaboration, and supranational globalization. Managers are pressing for more government support for particular industries. Among governments, there is a growing tendency to experiment with various policies intended to promote national competitiveness — from efforts to manage exchange rates to new measures to manage trade to policies to relax antitrust — which usually end up only undermining it. (See Appendix B)

These approaches, now much in favor in both companies and governments, are flawed. They fundamentally misperceive the true sources of competitive advantage. Pursuing them, with all their short-term appeal, will virtually guarantee that the U.S. — or any other advanced nation — never achieves real and sustainable competitive advantage.

We need a new perspective and new tools — an approach to competitiveness that grows directly out of an analysis of internationally successful industries, without regard for traditional ideology or current intellectual fashion. We need to know, very simply, what works and why. Then we need to apply it.

HOW COMPANIES SUCCEED IN INTERNATIONAL MARKETS

Around the world, companies that have achieved international leadership employ strategies that differ from each other in every respect. But while every successful company will employ its own particular strategy, the underlying mode of operation — the character and trajectory of all successful companies — is fundamentally the same.

Companies achieve competitive advantage through acts of innovation. They approach innovation in its broadest sense, including both new technologies and new ways of doing things. They perceive a new basis for competing or find better means for competing in old ways. Innovation can be manifested in a new product design, a new production process, a new marketing approach, or a new way of conducting training. Much innovation is mundane and incremental, depending more on accumulation of small insights and advances than on a single, major technological breakthrough. It often involves ideas that are not even "new" — ideas that have been around, but never vigorously pursued. It always involves investments in skill and knowledge, as well as in physical assets and brand reputation.

Some innovations create competitive advantage by perceiving an entirely new market opportunity or by serving a market segment that others have ignored. When competitors are slow to respond, such innovation yields competitive advantage. For instance, in industries such as autos and home electronics, Japanese companies gained their initial advantage by emphasizing smaller, more compact, lower capacity models that foreign competitors disdained as less profitable, less important, and less attractive.

In international markets, innovations that yield competitive advantage anticipate both domestic and foreign needs. For example, as international concern for product safety has grown, Swedish companies like Volvo, Atlas Copco, and AGA have succeeded by anticipating the market opportunity in this area. On the other hand, innovations that respond to concerns or circumstances that are peculiar to the home market can actually retard international competitive success. The lure of the huge U.S. defense market, for instance, has diverted the attention of U.S. materials and machine-tool companies from attractive, global commercial markets.

Information plays a large role in the process of innovation and improvement — Information that either is not available to competitors or that they do not seek. Sometimes it comes from simple investment in research and development or market research; more often, it comes from effort and from openness and from looking in the right place unencumbered by blinding assumptions or conventional wisdom.

This is why innovators are often outsiders from a different industry or a different country. Innovation may come from a new company, whose founder has a non-traditional background or was simply not appreciated in an older, established company. Or the capacity for innovation may come into an existing company through senior managers who are new to the particular industry and thus more able to perceive opportunities and more likely to pursue them. Or innovation may occur as a company diversifies, bringing new resources, skills, or perspectives to another industry. Or innovations may come from another nation with different circumstances or different ways of competing.

With few exceptions, innovation is the result of unusual effort. The company that successfully implements a new or better way of competing pursues its approach with dogged determination, often in the face of harsh criticism and tough obstacles. In fact, to succeed, innovation usually requires pressure, necessity, and even adversity: the fear of loss often proves more powerful than the hope of gain.

Once a company achieves competitive advantage through an innovation, it can sustain it only through relentless improvement. Almost any advantage can be imitated. Korean companies have already matched the ability of their Japanese rivals to mass-produce standard color televisions and VCRs; Brazilian companies have assembled technology and designs comparable to Italian competitors in casual leather footwear.

Competitors will eventually and inevitably overtake any company that stops improving and innovating. Sometimes early-mover advantages such as customer relationships, scale economies in existing technologies, or the loyalty of distribution channels are enough to permit a stagnant company to retain its entrenched position for years or even decades. But sooner or later, more dynamic rivals will find a way to innovate around these advantages or create a better or cheaper way of doing things. Italian appliance producers, which competed successfully on the basis of cost in selling midsize and compact appliances through large retail chains, rested too long on this initial advantage. By developing more differentiated products and creating strong brand franchises, German competitors have begun to gain ground.

Ultimately, the only way to sustain a competitive advantage is to *upgrade it* — to move to more sophisticated types. This is precisely what Japanese automakers have done. They initially penetrated foreign markets with small, inexpensive compact cars of adequate quality and competed on the basis of lower labor costs. Even while their labor-cost advantage persisted, however, the Japanese companies were continuously upgrading. They invested aggressively to build large modern plants to reap economies of scale. Then they became innovators in process technology, pioneering just-in-time production and a host of other quality and productivity practices. These process improvements led to better product quality, better repair records, and better customer-satisfaction ratings than that of foreign competitors. Most recently, Japanese automakers have advanced to the vanguard of product technology and are introducing new, premium brand names to compete with the world's most prestigious passenger cars.

The example of the Japanese automakers also illustrates two additional prerequisites for sustaining competitive advantage. First, a company must adopt a global approach to strategy. It must sell its product worldwide, under its own brand name, through international marketing channels that it controls. A truly global approach may even require the company to locate production or R&D facilities in other nations to take advantage of lower wage rates, to gain or improve market access, or to take advantage of foreign technology. Second, creating more sustainable advantages often means that a company must make its existing advantage obsolete — even while it is still an advantage. Japanese auto companies recognized this; either they would make their advantage obsolete, or a competitor would do it for them.

As this example suggests, innovation and change are inextricably tied together. But change is an unnatural act, particularly in successful companies; powerful forces are at work to avoid and defeat it. Past approaches become institutionalized in standard operating procedures and management controls. Training emphasizes the one correct way to do anything; the construction of specialized, dedicated facilities solidifies past practice into expensive brick and mortar; the existing strategy takes on an aura of invincibility and becomes rooted in the company culture.

Successful companies tend to develop a bias for predictability and stability; they work on defending what they have. Change is tempered by the fear that there is much to lose. The organization at all levels filters out information that would suggest new approaches, modifications, or departures from the norm. The internal environment operates like an immune system to isolate or expel "hostile" individuals who challenge current directions or established thinking. Innovation ceases; the company becomes stagnant; it is only a matter of time before aggressive competitors overtake it.

THE DIAMOND OF NATIONAL ADVANTAGE

Why are certain companies based in certain nations capable of consistent innovation? Why do they ruthlessly pursue improvements, seeking an ever-more sophisticated source of competitive advantage? Why are they able to overcome the substantial barriers to change and innovation that so often accompany success?

The answer lies in four broad attributes of a nation, attributes that individually and as a system constitute the diamond of national advantage, the playing field that each nation establishes and operates for its industries. These attributes are:

1. *Factor Conditions.* The nation's position in factors of production, such as skilled labor or infrastructure, necessary to compete in a given industry
2. *Demand Conditions.* The nature of home-market demand for the industry's product or service

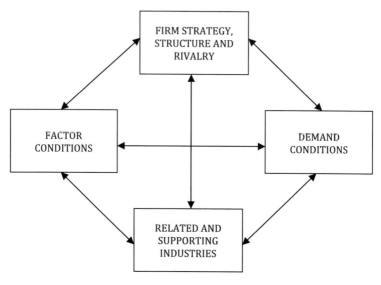

Fig. 3-1 Determinants of National Competitiveness

3. ***Related and Supporting Industries.*** The presence or absence in the nation of supplier industries and other related industries that are internationally competitive
4. ***Firm Strategy, Structure, and Rivalry.*** The conditions in the nation governing how companies are created, organized, and managed, as well as the nature of domestic rivalry

These determinants create the national environment in which companies are born and learn how to compete (see Figure 3-1) Each point on the diamond — and the diamond as a system — affects essential ingredients for achieving international competitive success: the availability of resources and skills necessary for competitive advantage in an industry; the information that shapes the opportunities that companies perceive and the directions in which they deploy their resources and skills; the goals of the owners, managers, and individuals in companies; and most important, the pressures on companies to invest and innovate (see Appendix C).

When a national environment permits and supports the most rapid accumulation of specialized assets and skills — sometimes simply because of greater effort and commitment — companies gain a competitive advantage. When a national environment affords better ongoing information and insight into product and process needs, companies gain a competitive advantage. Finally, when the national environment pressures companies to innovate and invest, companies both gain a competitive advantage and upgrade those advantages over time.

Factor Conditions. According to standard economic theory, factors of production — labor, land, natural resources, capital, infrastructure — will determine the flow of trade. A nation will export those goods that make most use of the factors with which it is relatively well endowed. This doctrine, whose origins date back to Adam Smith and David Ricardo and that is embedded in classical economics, is at best incomplete and at worst incorrect.

In the sophisticated industries that form the backbone of any advanced economy, a nation does not inherit but instead creates the most important factors of production — such as skilled human resources or a scientific base. Moreover, the stock of factors that a nation enjoys at a particular time is less important than the rate and efficiency with which it creates, upgrades, and deploys them in particular industries.

The most important factors of production are those that involve sustained and heavy investment and are specialized. Basic factors, such as a pool of labor or a local raw-material source, do not constitute an advantage in knowledge-intensive industries. Companies can access them easily through a global strategy or circumvent them through technology. Contrary to conventional wisdom, simply having a general work force that is high school or even college educated represents no competitive advantage in modern international competition. To support competitive advantage, a factor must be highly specialized to an industry's particular needs — a scientific institute specialized in optics, a pool of venture capital to fund software companies. These factors are more scarce, more difficult for foreign competitors to imitate — and they require sustained investment to create.

Nations succeed in industries where they are particularly good at factor creation. Competitive advantage results from the presence of world-class institutions that first create specialized factors and then continually work to upgrade them. Denmark has two hospitals that concentrate in studying and treating diabetes — and a world-leading export position in insulin. Holland has premier research institutes in the cultivation, packaging, and shipping of flowers, where it is the world's export leader.

What is not so obvious, however, is that selective disadvantages in the more basic factors can prod a company to innovate and upgrade — a disadvantage in a static model of competition can become an advantage in a dynamic one. When there is an ample supply of cheap raw materials or abundant labor, companies can simply rest on these advantages and often deploy them inefficiently. But when companies face a selective disadvantage, like high land costs, labor shortages, or the lack of local raw materials, they must innovate and upgrade to compete.

Implicit in the oft-repeated Japanese statement, "We are an island nation with no natural resources," is the understanding that these deficiencies have only served to spur Japan's competitive innovation. Just-in-time production, for example, economized on prohibitively expensive space. Italian steel producers in the Brescia area faced a similar set of disadvantages: high capital costs, high energy costs, and no local raw materials. Located in Northern Lombardy, these privately owned companies faced staggering logistics costs due to their distance from southern ports and the inefficiencies of the state-owned Italian transportation system. The result: they pioneered technologically advanced minimills that require only modest capital investment, use less energy, employ scrap metal as the feedstock, are efficient at small scale, and permit producers to locate close to sources of scrap and end-use customers. In other words, they converted factor disadvantages into competitive advantage.

Disadvantages can become advantages only under certain conditions. First, they must send companies proper signals about circumstances that will spread to other nations, thereby equipping them to innovate in advance of foreign rivals. Switzerland, the nation that experienced the first labor shortages after World War II, is a case in point. Swiss companies responded to the disadvantage by upgrading labor productivity and seeking higher value, more sustainable market segments. Companies in most other parts of the world, where there were still ample workers, focused their attention on other issues, which resulted in slower upgrading.

The second condition for transforming disadvantages into advantages is favorable circumstances elsewhere in the diamond — a consideration that applies to almost all determinants. To innovate, companies must have access to people with appropriate skills and have home-demand conditions that send the right signals. They must also have active domestic rivals who create pressure to innovate. Another precondition is company goals that lead to sustained commitment to the industry. Without such a commitment and the presence of active rivalry, a company may take an easy way around a disadvantage rather than using it as a spur to innovation.

For example, U.S. consumer-electronics companies, faced with high relative labor costs, chose to leave the product and production process largely unchanged and move labor-intensive activities to Taiwan and other Asian countries. Instead of upgrading their sources of advantage, they settled for labor-cost parity. On the other hand, Japanese rivals, confronted with intense domestic competition and a mature home market, chose to eliminate labor through automation. This led to lower assembly costs, to products with fewer components and to improved quality and reliability. Soon Japanese companies were building assembly plants in the U.S. — the place U.S. companies had fled.

Demand Conditions. It might seem that the globalization of competition would diminish the importance of home demand. In practice, however, this is simply not the case. In fact, the composition and character of the home market usually has a disproportionate effect on how companies perceive, interpret, and respond to buyer needs. Nations gain competitive advantage in industries where the home demand gives their companies a clearer or earlier picture of emerging buyer needs, and where demanding buyers pressure companies to innovate faster and achieve more sophisticated competitive advantages than their foreign rivals. The size of home demand proves far less significant than the character of home demand.

Home-demand conditions help build competitive advantage when a particular industry segment is larger or more visible in the domestic market than in foreign markets. The larger market segments in a nation receive the most attention from the nation's companies; companies accord smaller or less desirable segments a lower priority. A good example is hydraulic excavators, which represent the most widely used type of construction equipment in the Japanese domestic market — but which comprise a far smaller proportion of the market in other advanced nations. This segment is one of the few where there are vigorous Japanese international competitors and where Caterpillar does not hold a substantial share of the world market.

More important than the mix of segments per se is the nature of domestic buyers. A nation's companies gain competitive advantage if domestic buyers are the world's most sophisticated and demanding buyers for the product or service. Sophisticated, demanding buyers provide a window into advanced customer needs; they pressure companies to meet high standards; they prod them to improve, to innovate, and to upgrade into more advanced segments. As with factor conditions, demand conditions provide advantages by forcing companies to respond to tough challenges.

Especially stringent needs arise because of local values and circumstances. For example, Japanese consumers, who live in small, tightly packed homes, must contend with hot, humid summers and high-cost electrical energy — a daunting combination of circumstances. In response, Japanese companies have pioneered compact, quiet air-conditioning units powered by energy-saving rotary compressors. In industry after industry, the tightly constrained requirements of the Japanese market have forced companies to innovate, yielding products that are *kei-haku-tan-sho* — light, thin, short, small — and that are internationally accepted.

Local buyers can help a nation's companies gain advantage if their needs anticipate or even shape those of other nations — if their needs provide ongoing "early-warning indicators" of global market trends. Sometimes anticipatory needs emerge because a nation's political values foreshadow needs that will grow elsewhere. Sweden's long-standing concern for handicapped people has spawned an increasingly competitive industry focused on special needs. Denmark's environmentalism has led to success for companies in water-pollution control equipment and windmills.

More generally, a nation's companies can anticipate global trends if the nation's values are spreading — that is, if the country is exporting its values and tastes as well as its products. The international success of U.S. companies in fast food and credit cards, for example, reflects not only the American desire for convenience but also the spread of these tastes to the rest of the world. Nations export their values and tastes through media, through training foreigners, through political influence, and through the foreign activities of their citizens and companies.

Related and Supporting Industries. The third broad determinant of national advantage is the presence in the nation of related and supporting industries that are internationally competitive. Internationally competitive home-based suppliers create advantages in downstream industries in several ways. First, they deliver the most cost-effective inputs in an efficient, early, rapid, and sometimes preferential way. Italian gold and silver jewelry companies lead the world in that industry in part because other Italian companies supply two-thirds of the world's jewelry-making and precious-metal recycling machinery.

Far more significant than mere access to components and machinery, however, is the advantage that home-based related and supporting industries provide in innovation and upgrading — an advantage based on close working relationships. Suppliers and end-users located near each other can take advantage of short lines of communication, quick and constant flow of information, and an ongoing exchange of ideas and innovations. Companies have the opportunity to influence their suppliers' technical efforts and can serve as test sites for R&D work, accelerating the pace of innovation.

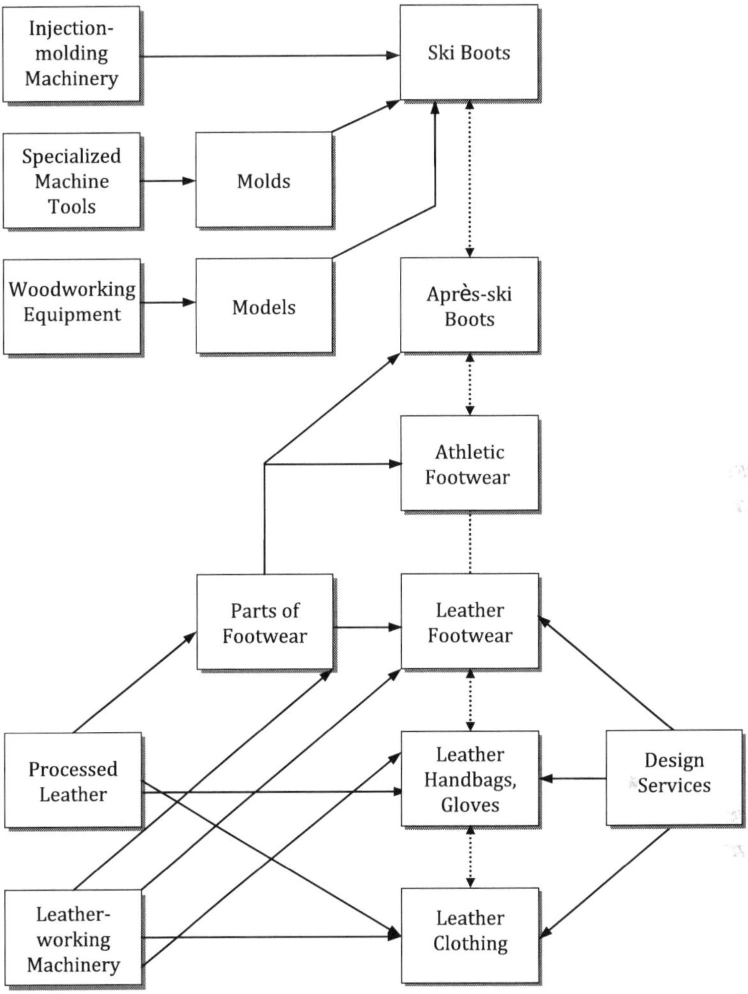

Fig. 3-2 The Italian Footwear Cluster

Figure 3-2 offers a graphic example of how a group of close-by, supporting industries creates competitive advantage in a range of interconnected industries that are all internationally competitive. Shoe producers, for instance, interact regularly with leather manufacturers on new styles and manufacturing techniques and learn about new textures and colors of leather when they are still on the drawing boards. Leather manufacturers gain early insights into fashion trends, helping them to plan new products. The interaction is mutually advantageous and self-reinforcing, but it does not happen automatically: it is helped by proximity, but occurs only because companies and suppliers work at it.

The nation's companies benefit most when the suppliers are, themselves, global competitors. It is ultimately self-defeating for a company or country to create "captive" suppliers who are totally dependent on the domestic industry and prevented from serving foreign competitors. By the same token, a nation need not be competitive in all supplier industries for its companies to gain competitive advantage. Companies can readily source from abroad materials, components, or technologies without a major effect on innovation or performance of the industry's products. The same is true of other generalized technologies — like electronics or software — where the industry represents a narrow application area.

Home-based competitiveness in related industries provides similar benefits: information flow and technical interchange speed the rate of innovation and upgrading. A home-based related industry also increases the likelihood that companies will embrace new skills, and it also provides a source of entrants who will bring a novel approach to competing. The Swiss success in pharmaceuticals emerged out of previous international success in the dye industry, for example; Japanese dominance in electronic musical keyboards grows out of success in acoustic instruments combined with a strong position in consumer electronics.

Firm Strategy, Structure, and Rivalry. National circumstances and context create strong tendencies in how companies are created, organized, and managed, as well as what the nature of domestic rivalry will be. In Italy, for example, successful international competitors are often small or medium-sized companies that are privately owned and operated like extended families; in Germany, in contrast, companies tend to be strictly hierarchical in organization and management practices, and top managers usually have technical backgrounds.

No one managerial system is universally appropriate — notwithstanding the current fascination with Japanese management. Competitiveness in a specific industry results from convergence of the management practices and organizational modes favored in the country and the sources of competitive advantage in the industry. In industries where Italian companies are world leaders — such as lighting, furniture, footwear, woolen fabrics, and packaging machines — a company strategy that emphasizes focus, customized products, niche marketing, rapid change, and breathtaking flexibility fits both the dynamics of the industry and the character of the Italian management system. The German management system, in contrast, works well in technical or engineering-oriented industries — optics, chemicals, and complicated machinery — where complex products demand precision manufacturing, a careful development process, after-sale service, and thus a highly disciplined management structure. German success is much rarer in consumer goods and services where image marketing and rapid new-feature and model turnover are important to competition.

Countries also differ markedly in the goals that companies and individuals seek to achieve. Company goals reflect the characteristics of national capital markets and the compensation practices for managers. For example, in Germany and Switzerland, where banks comprise a substantial part of the nation's shareholders, most shares are held for long-term appreciation and are rarely traded. Companies do well in mature industries, where ongoing investment in R&D and new facilities is essential but returns may be only moderate. The U.S. is at the opposite extreme, with a large pool of risk capital but widespread trading of public companies and a strong emphasis by investors on quarterly and annual share-price appreciation. Management compensation is heavily based on annual bonuses tied to individual results. America does well in relatively new industries, like software and biotechnology, or ones where equity funding of new companies feeds active domestic rivalry, like specialty electronics, and services. Strong pressures leading to underinvestment, however, plague more mature industries.

Individual motivation to work and expand skills is also important to competitive advantage. Outstanding talent is a scarce resource in any nation. A nation's success largely depends on the types of education its talented people choose, where they choose to work, and their commitment and effort. The goals a nation's institutions and values set for individuals and companies, and the prestige it attaches to certain industries, guide the flow of capital and human resources — which, in turn, directly affects the competitive performance of certain industries. Nations tend to be competitive in activities that people admire or depend on — the activities from which the nation's heroes emerge. In Switzerland, it is banking and pharmaceuticals. In Israel, the highest callings have been agriculture and defense-related fields. Sometimes it is hard to distinguish between cause and effect. Attaining international success can make an industry prestigious, reinforcing its advantage.

The presence of strong local rivals is a final, and powerful, stimulus to the creation and persistence of competitive advantage. This is true of small countries, like Switzerland, where the rivalry among its pharmaceutical companies, Hoffmann-La Roche, Ciba-Geigy, and Sandoz, contributes to

Table 3-1 Estimated Number of Japanese Rivals in Selected Industries

Air Conditioners	13	Motorcycles	4
Auto Equipment	25	Musical Instruments	4
Automobiles	9	Personal Computers	16
Cameras	15	Semiconductors	34
Car Audio	12	Sewing Machines	20
Carbon Fibers	7	Shipbuilding[a]	33
Construction Equipment[b]	15	Steel[c]	5
Copiers	14	Synthetic Fibers	8
Facsimile Machines	10	Television Sets	15
Large-scale Computers	6	Truck and Bus Tires	5
Lift Trucks	8	Trucks	11
Machine Tools	112	Typewriters	14
Microwave Equipment	5	Videocassette Recorders	10

Note: [a] Six companies had annual production exports in excess of 10,000 tons.
[b] The number of companies varied by product area. The smallest number, 10, produced bulldozers. Fifteen companies produced shovel trucks, truck cranes, and asphalt-paving equipment. There were 20 companies in hydraulic excavators, a product area where Japan was particularly strong.
[c] Integrated companies.
Sources:
Field interviews; *Nippon Kogyo Shinbun, Nippon Kogyo Nenkan*, 1987; Yano Research, *Market Share Jitan*, 1987; researchers' estimates.

a leading worldwide position. It is true in the U.S. in the computer and software industries. Nowhere is the role of fierce rivalry more apparent than in Japan, where there are 112 companies competing in machine tools, 34 in semiconductors, 25 in audio equipment, 15 in cameras — in fact, there are usually double figures in the industries in which Japan boasts global dominance (Table 3-1). Among all the points on the diamond, domestic rivalry is arguably the most important because of the powerfully stimulating effect it has on all the others.

Conventional wisdom argues that domestic competition is wasteful: it leads to duplication of effort and prevents companies from achieving economies of scale. The "right solution" is to embrace one or two national champions, companies with the scale and strength to tackle foreign competitors, and to guarantee them the necessary resources, with the government's blessing. In fact, however, most national champions are uncompetitive, although heavily subsidized and protected by their government. In many of the prominent industries in which there is only one national rival, such as aerospace and telecommunications, government has played a large role in distorting competition.

Static efficiency is much less important than dynamic improvement, which domestic rivalry uniquely spurs. Domestic rivalry, like any rivalry, creates pressure on companies to innovate and improve. Local rivals push each other to lower costs, improve quality and service, and create new products and processes. But unlike rivalries with foreign competitors, which tend to be analytical and distant, local rivalries often go beyond pure economic or business competition and become intensely personal. Domestic rivals engage in active feuds; they compete not only for market share but also for people, for technical excellence, and perhaps most important, for "bragging rights." One domestic rival's success proves to others that advancement is possible and often attracts new rivals to the industry. Companies often attribute the success of foreign rivals to "unfair" advantages. With domestic rivals, there are no excuses.

Geographic concentration magnifies the power of domestic rivalry. This pattern is strikingly common around the world: Italian jewelry companies are located around two towns, Arezzo and Valenza Po; cutlery companies in Solingen, West Germany and Seki, Japan; pharmaceutical companies in Basel, Switzerland; motorcycles and musical instruments in Hamamatsu, Japan. The more localized the rivalry, the more intense. And, the more intense, the better.

Another benefit of domestic rivalry is the pressure it creates for constant upgrading of the sources of competitive advantage. The presence of domestic competitors automatically cancels the types of advantage that come from simply being in a particular nation — factor costs, access to or preference in the home market, or costs to foreign competitors who import into the market. Companies are forced to move beyond them, and as a result, gain more sustainable advantages. Moreover, competing domestic rivals will keep each other honest in obtaining government support. Companies are less likely to get hooked on the narcotic of government contracts or creeping industry protectionism. Instead, the industry will seek — and benefit from — more constructive forms of government support, such as assistance in opening foreign markets, as well as investments in focused educational institutions or other specialized factors.

Ironically, it is also vigorous domestic competition that ultimately pressures domestic companies to look at global markets and toughens them to succeed in them. Particularly when there are economies of scale, local competitors force each other to look outward to foreign markets to capture greater efficiency and higher profitability. And having been tested by fierce domestic competition, the stronger companies are well equipped to win abroad. If Digital Equipment can hold its own against IBM, Data General, Prime, and Hewlett-Packard, going up against Siemens or Machines Bull does not seem so daunting a prospect.

THE DIAMOND AS A SYSTEM

Each of these four attributes defines a point on the diamond of national advantage; the effect of one point often depends on the state of others. Sophisticated buyers will not translate into advanced products, for example, unless the quality of human resources permits companies to meet buyer needs. Selective disadvantages in factors of production will not motivate innovation unless rivalry is vigorous and company goals support sustained investment. At the broadest level, weaknesses in any one determinant will constrain an industry's potential for advancement and upgrading.

But the points of the diamond are also self-reinforcing: they constitute a system. Two elements, domestic rivalry and geographic concentration, have especially great power to transform the diamond into a system — domestic rivalry because it promotes improvement in all the other determinants and geographic concentration because it elevates and magnifies the interaction of the four separate influences.

The role of domestic rivalry illustrates how the diamond operates as a self-reinforcing system. Vigorous domestic rivalry stimulates the development of unique pools of specialized factors, particularly if the rivals are all located in one city or region: the University of California at Davis has become the world's leading center of wine-making research, working closely with the California wine industry. Active local rivals also upgrade domestic demand in an industry. In furniture and shoes, for example, Italian consumers have learned to expect more and better products because of the rapid pace of new product development that is driven by intense domestic rivalry among hundreds of Italian companies. Domestic rivalry also promotes the formation of related and supporting industries. Japan's world-leading group of semiconductor producers, for instance, has spawned world-leading Japanese semiconductor-equipment manufacturers.

The effects can work in all directions: sometimes world-class suppliers become new entrants in the industry they have been supplying. Or highly sophisticated buyers may themselves enter a supplier industry, particularly when they have relevant skills and view the new industry as strategic. In the case of the Japanese robotics industry, for example, Matsushita and Kawasaki originally designed robots for internal use before beginning to sell robots to others. Today they are strong competitors in the robotics industry. In Sweden, Sandvik moved from specialty steel into rock drills, and SKF moved from specialty steel into ball bearings.

Another effect of the diamond's systemic nature is that nations are rarely home to just one competitive industry; rather, the diamond creates an environment that promotes *clusters* of competitive industries. Competitive industries are not haphazardly scattered throughout the economy but are usually linked together through vertical (buyer-seller) or horizontal (common customers, technology, channels) relationships. Nor are clusters usually scattered physically; they tend to be concentrated geographically. One competitive industry helps to create another in a mutually reinforcing process. Japan's strength in consumer electronics, for example, drove its success in semiconductors toward the memory chips and integrated circuits these products use. Japanese strength in laptop computers, which contrasts to limited success in other segments, reflects the base of strength in other compact, portable products and leading expertise in liquid-crystal display gained in the calculator and watch industries.

Once a cluster forms, the whole group of industries becomes mutually supporting. Benefits flow forward, backward, and horizontally. Aggressive rivalry in one industry spreads to others in the cluster, through spin-offs, through the exercise of bargaining power, and through diversification by established companies. Entry from other industries within the cluster spurs upgrading by stimulating diversity in R&D approaches and facilitate the introduction of new strategies and skills. Through the conduits of suppliers or customers who have contact with multiple competitors, information flows freely and innovations diffuse rapidly. Interconnections within the cluster, often unanticipated, lead to perceptions of new ways of competing and new opportunities. The cluster becomes a vehicle for maintaining diversity and overcoming the inward focus, inertia, inflexibility, and accommodation among rivals that slows or blocks competitive upgrading and new entry.

THE ROLE OF GOVERNMENT

In the continuing debate over the competitiveness of nations, no topic engenders more argument or creates less understanding than the role of the government. Many see government as an essential helper or supporter of industry, employing a host of policies to contribute directly to the competitive performance of strategic or target industries. Others accept the "free market" view that the operation of the economy should be left to the workings of the invisible hand.

Both views are incorrect. Either, followed to its logical outcome, would lead to the permanent erosion of a country's competitive capabilities. On one hand, advocates of government help for industry frequently propose policies that would actually hurt companies in the long run and only create the demand for more helping. On the other hand, advocates of a diminished government presence ignore the legitimate role that government plays in shaping the context and institutional structure surrounding companies and in creating an environment that stimulates companies to gain competitive advantage.

Government's proper role is as a catalyst and challenger; it is to encourage — or even push — companies to raise their aspirations and move to higher levels of competitive performance, even though this process may be inherently unpleasant and difficult. Government cannot create competitive industries; only companies can do that. Government plays a role that is inherently partial, that succeeds only when working in tandem with favorable underlying conditions in the diamond. Still, government's role of transmitting and amplifying the forces of the diamond is a powerful one. Government policies that succeed are those that create an environment in which companies can gain competitive advantage rather than those that involve government directly in the process, except in nations early in the development process. It is an indirect, rather than a direct, role.

Japan's government, at its best, understands this role better than anyone-including the point that nations pass through stages of competitive development and that government's appropriate role shifts as the economy progresses. By stimulating early demand for advanced products, confronting industries with the need to pioneer frontier technology through symbolic cooperative projects, establishing prizes that reward quality, and pursuing other policies that magnify the forces of the diamond, the Japanese government accelerates the pace of innovation. But like government officials anywhere, at their worst Japanese bureaucrats can make the same mistakes: attempting to manage industry structure, protecting the market too long, and yielding to political pressure to insulate inefficient retailers, farmers, distributors, and industrial companies from competition.

It is not hard to understand why so many governments make the same mistakes so often in pursuit of national competitiveness: competitive time for companies and political time for governments are fundamentally at odds.

It often takes more than a decade for an industry to create competitive advantage; the process entails the long upgrading of human skills, investing in products and processes, building clusters, and penetrating foreign markets. In the case of the Japanese auto industry, for instance, companies made their first faltering steps toward exporting in the 1950s — yet did not achieve strong international positions until the 1970s.

But in politics, a decade is an eternity. Consequently, most governments favor policies that offer easily perceived short-term benefits, such as subsidies, protection, and arranged mergers — the very policies that retard innovation. Most of the policies that would make a real difference either are too slow and require too much patience for politicians or, even worse, carry with them the sting of short-term pain. Deregulating a protected industry, for example, will lead to bankruptcies sooner and to stronger, more competitive companies only later.

Policies that convey static, short-term cost advantages but that unconsciously undermine innovation and dynamism represent the most common and most profound error in government industrial policy. In a desire to help, it is all too easy for governments to adopt policies such as joint projects to avoid "wasteful" R&D that undermine dynamism and competition. Yet even a 10 percent cost saving through economies of scale is easily nullified through rapid product and process improvement and the pursuit of volume in global markets — something that such policies undermine.

There are some simple, basic principles that governments should embrace to play the proper supportive role for national competitiveness: encourage change, promote domestic rivalry, and stimulate innovation. Some of the specific policy approaches to guide nations seeking to gain competitive advantage include the following:

Focus on specialized factor creation. Government has critical responsibilities for fundamentals like the primary and secondary education systems, basic national infrastructure, and research in areas of broad national concern such as health care. Yet these kinds of generalized efforts at factor creation rarely produce competitive advantage. Rather, the factors that translate into competitive advantage are advanced, specialized, and tied to specific industries or industry groups. Mechanisms such as specialized apprenticeship programs, research efforts in universities connected with an industry, trade association activities, and, most important, the private investments of companies ultimately create the factors that will yield competitive advantage.

Avoid intervening in factor and currency markets. By intervening in factor and currency markets, governments hope to create lower factor costs or a favorable exchange rate that will help companies compete more effectively in international markets. Evidence from around the world indicates that these policies — such as the Reagan administration's dollar devaluation — are often counterproductive. They work against the upgrading of industry and the search for more sustainable competitive advantage.

The contrasting case of Japan is particularly instructive, although both Germany and Switzerland have had similar experiences. Over the past 20 years, the Japanese have been rocked by the sudden Nixon currency devaluation shock, two oil shocks, and, most recently, the yen shock — all of which forced Japanese companies to upgrade their competitive advantages. The point is not that government should pursue policies that intentionally drive up factor costs or the exchange rate. Rather, when market forces create rising factor costs or a higher exchange rate, government should resist the temptation to push them back down.

Enforce strict product, safety, and environmental standards. Strict government regulations can promote competitive advantage by stimulating and upgrading domestic demand. Stringent standards for product performance, product safety, and environmental impact pressure companies to improve quality, upgrade technology, and provide features that I respond to consumer and social demands. Easing standards, however tempting, is counterproductive.

When tough regulations anticipate standards that will spread internationally, they give a nation's companies a head start in developing products and services that will be valuable elsewhere. Sweden's strict standards for environmental protection have promoted competitive advantage in many industries. Atlas Copco, for example, produces quiet compressors that can be used in dense urban areas with minimal disruption to residents. Strict standards, however, must be combined with a rapid and streamlined regulatory process that does not absorb resources and cause delays.

Sharply limit direct cooperation among industry rivals. The most pervasive global policy fad in the competitiveness arena today is the call for more cooperative research and industry consortia. Operating on the belief that independent research by rivals is wasteful and duplicative, that collaborative efforts achieve economies of scale, and that individual companies are likely to underinvest in R&D because they cannot reap all the benefits, governments have embraced the idea of more direct cooperation. In the U.S., antitrust laws have been modified to allow more cooperative R&D; in Europe, mega-projects such as ESPRIT, an information-technology project, bring together companies from several countries. Lurking behind much of this thinking is the fascination of Western governments with — and fundamental misunderstanding of — the countless cooperative research projects sponsored by the Ministry of International Trade and Industry (MITI), projects that appear to have contributed to Japan's competitive rise.

But a closer look at Japanese cooperative projects suggests a different story. Japanese companies participate in MITI projects to maintain good relations with MITI, to preserve their corporate images, and to hedge the risk that competitors will gain from the project — largely defensive reasons. Companies rarely contribute their best scientists and engineers to cooperative projects and usually spend much more on their own private research in the same field. Typically, the government makes only a modest financial contribution to the project.

The real value of Japanese cooperative research is to signal the importance of emerging technical areas and to stimulate proprietary company research. Cooperative projects prompt companies to explore new fields and boost internal R&D spending because companies know that their domestic rivals are investigating them.

Under certain limited conditions, cooperative research can prove beneficial. Projects should be in areas of basic product and process research, not in subjects closely connected to a company's proprietary sources of advantage. They should constitute only a modest portion of a company's overall research program in any given field. Cooperative research should be only indirect, channeled through independent organizations to which most industry participants have access. Organizational structures, like university labs and centers of excellence, reduce management problems and minimize the risk to rivalry. Finally, the most useful cooperative projects often involve fields that touch a number of industries and that require substantial R&D investments.

Promote goals that lead to sustained investment. Government has a vital role in shaping the goals of investors, managers, and employees through policies in various areas. The manner in which capital markets are regulated, for example, shapes the incentives of investors and, in turn, the behavior of companies. Government should aim to encourage sustained investment in human skills, in innovation, and in physical assets. Perhaps the single most powerful tool for raising the rate of sustained investment in industry is a tax incentive for long-term (five years or more) capital gains restricted to new investment in corporate equity. Long-term capital gains incentives should also be applied to pension funds and other currently untaxed investors, who now have few reasons not to engage in rapid trading.

Deregulate competition. Regulation of competition through such policies as maintaining a state monopoly, controlling entry into an industry, or fixing prices has two strong negative consequences: it stifles rivalry and innovation as companies become preoccupied with dealing with regulators and protecting what they already have; and it makes the industry a less dynamic and less desirable buyer or supplier. Deregulation and privatization on their own, however, will not succeed without vigorous domestic rivalry — and that requires, as a corollary, a strong and consistent antitrust policy.

Enforce strong domestic antitrust policies. A strong antitrust policy — especially for horizontal mergers, alliances, and collusive behavior — is fundamental to innovation. While it is fashionable today to call for mergers and alliances in the name of globalization and the creation of national champions, these often undermine the creation of competitive advantage. Real national competitiveness requires governments to disallow mergers, acquisitions, and alliances that involve industry leaders. Furthermore, the same standards for mergers and alliances should apply to both domestic and foreign companies. Finally, government policy should favor internal entry, both domestic and international, over acquisition. Companies should, however, be allowed to acquire small companies in related industries when the move promotes the transfer of skills that could ultimately create competitive advantage.

Reject managed trade. Managed trade represents a growing and dangerous tendency for dealing with the fallout of national competitiveness. Orderly marketing agreements, voluntary restraint agreements, or other devices that set quantitative targets to divide up markets are dangerous, ineffective, and often enormously costly to consumers. Rather than promoting innovation in a nation's industries, managed trade guarantees a market for inefficient companies.

Government trade policy should pursue open market access in every foreign nation. To be effective, trade policy should not be a passive instrument; it cannot respond only to complaints or work only for those industries that can muster enough political clout; it should not require a long history of injury or serve only distressed industries. Trade policy should seek to open markets wherever a nation has competitive advantage and should actively address emerging industries and incipient problems.

Where government finds a trade barrier in another nation, it should concentrate its remedies on dismantling barriers, not on regulating imports or exports. In the case of Japan, for example, pressure to accelerate the already rapid growth of manufactured imports is a more effective approach than a shift to managed trade. Compensatory tariffs that punish companies for unfair trade practices are better than market quotas. Other increasingly important tools to open markets are restrictions that prevent companies in offending nations from investing in acquisitions or production facilities in the host country — thereby blocking the unfair country's companies from using their advantage to establish a new beachhead that is immune from sanctions.

Any of these remedies, however, can backfire. It is virtually impossible to craft remedies to unfair trade practices that avoid both reducing incentives for domestic companies to innovate and export and harming domestic buyers. The aim of remedies should be adjustments that allow the remedy to disappear.

THE COMPANY AGENDA

Ultimately, only companies themselves can achieve and sustain competitive advantage. To do so, they must act on the fundamentals described above. In particular, they must recognize the central role of innovation — and the uncomfortable truth that innovation grows out of pressure and challenge. It takes leadership to create a dynamic, challenging environment. And it takes leadership to recognize the all-too-easy escape routes that appear to offer a path to competitive advantage, but are actually short-cuts to failure. For example, it is tempting to rely on cooperative research and development projects to lower the cost and risk of research. But they can divert company attention and resources from proprietary research efforts and will all but eliminate the prospects for real innovation.

Competitive advantage arises from leadership that harnesses and amplifies the forces in the diamond to promote innovation and upgrading. Here are just a few of the kinds of company policies that will support that effort:

Create pressures for innovation. A company should seek out pressure and challenge, not avoid them. Part of strategy is to take advantage of the home nation to create the impetus for innovation. To do that, companies can sell to the most sophisticated and demanding buyers and channels; seek out those buyers with the most difficult needs; establish norms that exceed the toughest regulatory hurdles or product standards; source from the most advanced suppliers; treat employees as permanent in order to stimulate upgrading of skills and productivity.

Seek out the most capable competitors as motivators. To motivate organizational change, capable competitors and respected rivals can be a common enemy. The best managers always run a little scared; they respect and study competitors. To stay dynamic, companies must make meeting challenge a part of the organization's norms. For example, lobbying against strict product standards signals the organization that company leadership has diminished aspirations. Companies that value stability, obedient customers, dependent suppliers, and sleepy competitors are inviting inertia and, ultimately, failure.

Establish early-warning systems. Early-warning signals translate into early-mover advantages. Companies can take actions that help them see the signals of change and act on them, thereby getting a jump on the competition. For example, they can find and serve those buyers with the most anticipatory needs; investigate all emerging new buyers or channels; find places whose regulations foreshadow emerging regulations elsewhere; bring some outsiders into the management team; maintain ongoing relationships with research centers and sources of talented people.

Improve the national diamond. Companies have a vital stake in making their home environment a better platform for international success. Part of a company's responsibility is to play an active role in forming clusters and to work with its home-nation buyers, suppliers, and channels to help them upgrade and extend their own competitive advantages. To upgrade home demand, for example, Japanese musical instrument manufacturers, led by Yamaha, Kawai, and Suzuki, have established music schools. Similarly, companies can stimulate and support local suppliers of important specialized inputs — including encouraging them to compete globally. The health and strength of the national cluster will only enhance the company's own rate of innovation and upgrading.

In nearly every successful competitive industry, leading companies also take explicit steps to create specialized factors like human resources, scientific knowledge, or infrastructure. In industries like wool cloth, ceramic tiles, and lighting equipment, Italian industry associations invest in market information, process technology, and common infrastructure. Companies can also speed innovation by putting their headquarters and other key operations where there are concentrations of sophisticated buyers, important suppliers, or specialized factor-creating mechanisms, such as universities or laboratories.

Welcome domestic rivalry. To compete globally, a company needs capable domestic rivals and vigorous domestic rivalry. Especially in the U.S. and Europe today, managers are wont to complain about excessive competition and to argue for mergers and acquisitions that will produce hoped-for economies of scale and critical mass. The complaint is only natural — but the argument is plain wrong. Vigorous domestic rivalry creates sustainable competitive advantage. Moreover, it is better to grow internationally than to dominate the domestic market. If a company wants an acquisition, a foreign one that can speed globalization and supplement home-based advantages or offset home-based disadvantages is usually far better than merging with leading domestic competitors.

Globalize to tap selective advantages in other nations. In search of "global" strategies, many companies today abandon their home diamond. To be sure, adopting a global perspective is important to creating competitive advantage. But relying on foreign activities that supplant domestic capabilities is always a second-best solution. Innovating to offset local factor disadvantages is better than outsourcing; developing domestic suppliers and buyers is better than relying solely on foreign ones. Unless the critical underpinnings of competitiveness are present at home, companies will not sustain competitive advantage in the long run. The aim should be to upgrade home-base capabilities so that foreign activities are selective and supplemental only to over-all competitive advantage.

The correct approach to globalization is to tap selectively into sources of advantage in other nations' diamonds. For example, identifying sophisticated buyers in other countries helps companies understand different needs and creates pressures that will stimulate a faster rate of innovation. No matter how favorable the home diamond, moreover, important research is going on in other nations. To take advantage of foreign research, companies must station high-quality people in overseas bases and mount a credible level of scientific effort. To get anything back from foreign research ventures, companies must also allow access to their own ideas — recognizing that competitive advantage comes from continuous improvement, not from protecting today's secrets.

Use alliances only selectively. Alliances with foreign companies have become another managerial fad and cure-all: they represent a tempting solution to the problem of a company wanting the advantages of foreign enterprises or hedging against risk, without giving up independence. In reality, however, while alliances can achieve selective benefits, they always exact significant costs: they involve coordinating two separate operations, reconciling goals with an independent entity, creating a competitor, and giving up profits. These costs ultimately make most alliances short-term transitional devices, rather than stable, long-term relationships.

Most important, alliances as a broad-based strategy will only ensure a company's mediocrity, not its international leadership. No company can rely on another outside, independent company for skills and assets that are central to its competitive advantage. Alliances are best used as a selective tool, employed on a temporary basis or involving non-core activities.

Locate the home base to support competitive advantage. Among the most important decisions for multinational companies is the nation in which to locate the home base for each distinct business. A company can have different home bases for distinct businesses or segments. Ultimately, competitive advantage is created at home: it is where strategy is set, the core product and process technology is created, and a critical mass of production takes place. The circumstances in the home nation must support innovation; otherwise the company has no choice but to move its home base to a country that stimulates innovation and that provides the best environment for global competitiveness. There are no half-measures: the management team must move as well.

THE ROLE OF LEADERSHIP

Too many companies and top managers misperceive the nature of competition and the task before them by focusing on improving financial performance, soliciting government assistance, seeking stability, and reducing risk through alliances and mergers.

Today's competitive realities demand leadership. Leaders believe in change; they energize their organizations to innovate continuously; they recognize the importance of their home country as integral to their competitive success and work to upgrade it. Most important, leaders recognize the need for pressure and challenge. Because they are willing to encourage appropriate — and painful — government policies and regulations, they often earn the title "statesmen," although few see themselves that way. They are prepared to sacrifice the easy life for difficulty and, ultimately, sustained competitive advantage. That must be the goal, for both nations and companies: not just surviving, but achieving international competitiveness. And not just once, but continuously.

APPENDIX A: PATTERNS OF NATIONAL COMPETITIVE SUCCESS

To investigate why nations gain competitive advantage in particular industries and the implications for company strategy and national economies, I conducted a four-year study of ten important trading nations: Denmark, Germany, Italy, Japan, Korea, Singapore, Sweden, Switzerland, the United Kingdom, and the U.S. I was assisted by a team of more than 30 researchers, most of whom were natives of and based in the nation they studied. The researchers all used the same methodology.

Three nations — the U.S., Japan, and Germany — are the world's leading industrial powers. The other nations represent a variety of population sizes, government policies toward industry, social philosophies, geographical sizes, and locations. Together, the 10 nations accounted for fully 50 percent of total world exports in 1985, the base year for statistical analysis.

Most previous analyses of national competitiveness have focused on single nation or bilateral comparisons. By studying nations with widely varying characteristics and circumstances, this study sought to separate the fundamental forces underlying national competitive advantage from the idiosyncratic ones.

In each nation, the study consisted of two parts. The first identified all industries in which the nation's companies were internationally successful, using available statistical data, supplementary published sources, and field interviews. We defined a nation's industry as internationally successful if it *possessed competitive advantage relative to the best worldwide competitors.* Many measures of competitive advantage, such as reported profitability, can be misleading. We chose as the best indicators the presence of substantial and sustained exports to a wide array of other nations and/or significant outbound foreign investment based on skills and assets created in the home country. A nation was considered the home base for a company if it was either a locally owned, indigenous enterprise or managed autonomously although owned by a foreign company or investors. We then created a profile of all the industries in which each nation was internationally successful at three points in time: 1971, 1978, and 1985. The pattern of competitive industries in each economy was far from random: the task was to explain it and how it had changed over time. Of particular interest were the connections or relationships among the nation's competitive industries.

In the second part of the study, we examined the history of competition in particular industries to understand how competitive advantage was created.

On the basis of national profiles, we selected over 100 industries or industry groups for detailed study; we examined many more in less detail. We went back as far as necessary to understand how and why the industry began in the nation, how it grew, when and why companies from the nation developed international competitive advantage, and the process by which competitive advantage had been either sustained or lost. The resulting case histories fall short of the work of a good historian in their level of detail, but they do provide insight into the development of both the industry and the nation's economy.

We chose a sample of industries for each nation that represented the most important groups of competitive industries in the economy. The industries studied accounted for a large share of total exports in each nation: more than 20 percent of total exports in Japan, Germany, and Switzerland, for example, and more than 40 percent in South Korea. We studied some of the most famous and important international success stories — German high-performance autos and chemicals, Japanese semiconductors and VCRs, Swiss banking and pharmaceuticals, Italian footwear and textiles, U.S. commercial aircraft and motion pictures — and some relatively obscure but highly competitive industries — South Korean pianos, Italian ski boots, and British biscuits. We also added a few industries because they appeared to be paradoxes: Japanese home demand for Western-character typewriters is nearly nonexistent, for example, but Japan holds a strong export and foreign investment position in the industry. We avoided industries that were highly dependent on natural resources: such industries do not form the backbone of advanced economies, and the capacity to compete in them is more explicable using classical theory. We did, however, include a number of more technologically intensive, natural-resource-related industries such as newsprint and agricultural chemicals.

The sample of nations and industries offers a rich empirical foundation for developing and testing the new theory of how countries gain competitive advantage. The accompanying article concentrates on the determinants of competitive advantage in individual industries and also sketches out some of the study's overall implications for government policy and company strategy. A fuller treatment in my book, *The Competitive Advantage of Nations*, develops the theory and its implications in greater depth and provides many additional examples. It also contains detailed descriptions of the nations we studied and the future prospects for their economies.

APPENDIX B: WHAT IS NATIONAL COMPETITIVENESS?

National competitiveness has become one of the central preoccupation of government and industry in every nation. Yet for all the discussion, debate, and writing on the topic, there is still not persuasive theory to explain national competitiveness. What is more, there is not even an accepted definition of the term "competitiveness" as applied to a nation. While the notion of a competitive company is clear, the notion of competitive nation is not.

Some see national competitiveness as a macro-economic phenomenon, driven by variables such as exchange rates, interest rates, and government deficits. But Japan, Italy, and South Korea have all enjoyed rapidly rising living standards despite budget deficits; Germany and Switzerland despite appreciating currencies; and Italy and Korea despite high interest rates.

Others argue that competitiveness is a function of cheap and abundant labor. But Germany, Switzerland, and Sweden have all prospered even with high wages and labor shortages. Besides, shouldn't a nation seek higher wages for its workers as a goal of competitiveness?

Another view connects competitiveness with bountiful natural resources. But how, then, can one explain the success of Germany, Japan, Switzerland, Italy, and South Korea — countries with limited natural resources?

More recently, the argument has gained favor that competitiveness is driven by government policy: targeting, protection, import promotion, and subsidies have propelled Japanese and South Korean auto, steel, shipbuilding, and semiconductor industries into global preeminence. But a closer look reveals a spotty record. In Italy, government intervention has been ineffectual — but Italy has experienced a boom in world export share second only to Japan. In Germany, direct government intervention in exporting industries is rare. And even in Japan and South Korea, government's role in such important industries as facsimile machines, copiers, robotics, and advanced materials has been modest; some of the most frequently cited examples, such as sewing machines, steel, and shipbuilding, are now quite dated.

A final popular explanation for national competitiveness is differences in management practices, including management–labor relations. The problem here, however, is that different industries require different approaches to management. The successful management practices governing small, private, and loosely organized Italian family companies in footwear/textiles, and jewelry, for example, would produce a management disaster if applied to German chemical or auto companies, Swiss pharmaceutical makers, or American aircraft producers. Nor is it possible to generalize about management–labor relations. Despite the commonly held view that powerful unions undermine competitive advantage, unions are strong in Germany and Sweden-and both countries boast internationally preeminent companies.

Clearly, none of these explanations is fully satisfactory; none is sufficient by itself to rationalize the competitive position of industries within a national border. Each contains some truth; but a broader, more complex set of forces seems to be at work.

The lack of a clear explanation signals an even more fundamental question. What is a "competitive" nation in the first place? Is a "competitive" nation one where every company or industry is competitive? No nation meets this test. Even Japan has large sectors of its economy that fall far behind the world's best competitors.

Is a "competitive" nation one whose exchange rate makes its goods price competitive in international markets? Both Germany and Japan have enjoyed remarkable gains in their standards of living — and experienced sustained periods of strong currency and rising prices. Is a "competitive" nation one with a large positive balance of trade? Switzerland has roughly balanced trade; Italy has a chronic trade deficit — both nations enjoy strongly rising national income. Is a "competitive" nation one with low labor costs? India and Mexico both have low wages and low labor costs — but neither seems an attractive industrial model.

The only meaningful concept of competitiveness at the national level is *productivity*. The principal goal of a nation is to produce a high and rising standard of living for its citizens. The ability to do so depends on the productivity with which a nation's labor and capital are employed. Productivity is the value of the output produced by a unit of labor or capital. Productivity depends on both the quality and features of products (which determine the prices that they can command) and the efficiency with which they are produced. Productivity is the prime determinant of a nation's long-run standard of living; it is the root cause of national per capita income. The productivity of human resources determines employee wages; the productivity with which capital is employed determines the return it earns for its holders.

A nation's standard of living depends on the capacity of its companies to achieve high levels of productivity-and to increase productivity over time. Sustained productivity growth requires that an economy continually *upgrade itself*. A nation's companies must relentlessly improve productivity in existing industries by raising product quality, adding desirable features, improving product technology, or boosting production efficiency. They must develop the necessary capabilities to compete in more and more sophisticated industry segments, where productivity is generally high. They must finally develop the capability to compete in entirely new, sophisticated industries.

International trade and foreign investment can both improve a nation's productivity as well as threaten it. They support rising national productivity by allowing a nation to specialize in those industries and segments of industries where its companies are more productive and to import where its companies are less productive. No nation can be competitive in everything. The ideal is to deploy the nation's limited pool of human and other resources into the most productive uses. Even those nations with the highest standards of living have many industries in which local companies are uncompetitive.

Yet international trade and foreign investment also can threaten productivity growth. They expose a nation's industries to the test of international standards of productivity. An industry will lose out if its productivity is not sufficiently higher than foreign rivals' to offset any advantages in local wage rates. if a nation loses the ability to compete in a range of high-productivity/high-wage industries, its standard of living is threatened.

Defining national competitiveness as achieving a trade surplus or balanced trade per se is inappropriate. The expansion of exports because of low wages and a weak currency, at the same time that the nation imports sophisticated goods that its companies cannot produce competitively, may bring trade into balance or surplus but lowers the nation's standard of living. Competitiveness also does not mean jobs. It's the *type* of jobs, not just the ability to employ citizens at low wages, that is decisive for economic prosperity.

Seeking to explain "competitiveness" at the national level, then, is to answer the wrong question. What we must understand instead is the determinants of productivity and the rate of productivity growth. To find answers, we must focus not on the economy as a whole but on *specific industries and industry segments*. We must understand how and why commercially viable skills and technology are created, which can only be fully understood at the level of particular industries. It is the outcome of the thousands of struggles for competitive advantage against foreign rivals in particular segments and industries, in which products and processes are created and improved, that underpins the process of upgrading national productivity.

When one looks closely at any national economy, there are striking differences among a nation's industries in competitive success. International advantage is often concentrated in particular industry segments. German exports of cars are heavily skewed toward high-performance cars, while Korean exports are all compacts and subcompacts. In many industries and segments of industries, the competitors with true international competitive advantage are *based in only a few nations.*

Our search, then, is for the decisive characteristic of a nation that allows its companies to create and sustain competitive advantage in particular fields — the search is for the competitive advantage of nations. We are particularly concerned with the determinants of international success in technology — and skill-intensive segments and industries, which underpin high and rising productivity.

Classical theory explains the success of nations in particular industries based on so-called factors of production such as land, labor, and natural resources. Nations gain factor-based comparative advantage in industries that make intensive use of the factors they possess in abundance. Classical theory, however, has been overshadowed in advanced industries and economies by the globalization of competition and the power of technology.

A new theory must recognize that in modern international competition, companies compete with global strategies involving not only trade but also foreign investment. What a new theory must explain is why a nation provides a favorable *home base* for companies that compete internationally. The home base is the nation in which the essential competitive advantages of the enterprise are created and sustained. It is where a company's strategy is set, where the core product and process technology is created and maintained, and where the most productive jobs and most advanced skills are located. The presence of the home base in a nation has the greatest positive influence on other linked domestic industries and leads to other benefits in the nation's economy. While the ownership of the company is often concentrated at the home base, the nationality of shareholders is secondary.

A new theory must move beyond comparative advantage to the competitive advantage of a nation. It must reflect a rich conception of competition that includes segmented markets, differentiated products, technology differences, and economies of scale. A new theory must go beyond cost and explain why companies from some nations are better than others at creating advantages based on quality, features, and new product innovation. A new theory must begin from the premise that competition is dynamic and evolving; it must answer the questions: Why do some companies based in some nations innovate more than others? Why do some nations provide an environment that enables companies to improve and innovate faster than foreign rivals?

APPENDIX C: HOW THE DIAMOND WORKS: THE ITALIAN CERAMIC TILE INDUSTRY*

In 1987, Italian companies were world leaders in the production and export of ceramic tiles, a $10 billion industry. Italian producers, concentrated in and around the small town of Sassuolo in the Emilia-Romagna region, accounted for about 30 percent of world production and almost 60 percent of world exports. The Italian trade surplus that year in ceramic tiles was about $1.4 billion.

The development of the Italian ceramic tile industry's competitive advantage illustrates how the diamond of national advantage works. Sassuolo's sustainable competitive advantage in ceramic tiles grew not from any static or historical advantage but from dynamism and change. Sophisticated and demanding local buyers, strong and unique distribution channels, and intense rivalry among local companies created constant pressure for innovation. Knowledge grew quickly from continuous experimentation and cumulative production experience. Private ownership of the companies and loyalty to the community spawned intense commitment to invest in the industry.

Tile producers benefited as well from a highly developed set of local machinery suppliers and other supporting industries, producing materials, services, and infrastructure. The presence of world-class, Italian-related industries also reinforced Italian strength in tiles. Finally, the geographic concentration of the entire cluster supercharged the whole process. Today foreign companies compete against an entire subculture. The organic nature of this system represents the most sustainable advantage of Sassuolo's ceramic tile companies.

The Origins of the Italian Industry

Tile production in Sassuolo grew out of the earthenware and crockery industry, whose history traces back to the thirteenth century. Immediately after World War II, there were only a handful of ceramic tile manufacturers in and around Sassuolo, all serving the local market exclusively.

---

*By Michael J. Enright and Paolo Tenti. Michael J. Enright, a doctoral student in business economics at the Harvard Business School, performed numerous research and supervisory tasks for *The Competitive Advantage of Nations*. Paolo Tenti was responsible for the Italian part of research undertaken for the book. He is a consultant in strategy and finance for Monitor Company and Analysis BA. — Milan.

Demand for ceramic tiles within Italy began to grow dramatically in the immediate postwar years, as the reconstruction of Italy triggered a boom in building materials of all kinds. Italian demand for ceramic tiles was particularly great due to the climate, local tastes, and building techniques.

Because Sassuolo was in a relatively prosperous part of Italy, there were many who could combine the modest amount of capital and necessary organizational skills to start a tile company. In 1955, there were 14 Sassuolo area tile companies; by 1962, there were 102.

The new tile companies benefited from a local pool of mechanically trained workers. The region around Sassuolo was home to Ferrari, Maserati, Lamborghini, and other technically sophisticated companies. As the tile industry began to grow and prosper, many engineers and skilled workers gravitated to the successful companies.

The Emerging Italian Tile Cluster

Initially, Italian tile producers were dependent on foreign sources of raw materials and production technology. In the 1950s, the principal raw materials used to make tiles were kaolin (white) clays. Since there were red- but no white-clay deposits near Sassuolo, Italian producers had to import the clays from the United Kingdom. Tile-making equipment was also imported in the 1950s and 1960s: kilns from Germany, America, and France; presses for forming tiles from Germany. Sassuolo tile makers had to import even simple glazing machines.

Over time, the Italian tile producers learned how to modify imported equipment to fit local circumstances: red versus white clays, natural gas versus heavy oil. As process technicians from tile companies left to start their own equipment companies, a local machinery industry arose in Sassuolo. By 1970, Italian companies had emerged as world-class producers of kilns and presses; the earlier situation had exactly reversed: they were exporting their red-clay equipment for foreigners to use with white clays.

The relationship between Italian tile and equipment manufacturers was a mutually supporting one, made even more so by close proximity. In the mid-1980s, there were some 200 Italian equipment manufacturers; more than 60% were located in the Sassuolo area. The equipment manufacturers competed fiercely for local business, and tile manufacturers benefited from better prices and more advanced equipment than their foreign rivals.

As the emerging tile cluster grew and concentrated in the Sassuolo region, a pool of skilled workers and technicians developed, including engineers, production specialists, maintenance workers, service technicians, and design personnel. The industry's geographic concentration encouraged other supporting companies to form, offering molds, packaging materials, glazes, and transportation services. An array of small, specialized consulting companies emerged to give advice to tile producers on plant design, logistics, and commercial, advertising, and fiscal matters.

With its membership concentrated in the Sassuolo area, Assopiastrelle, the ceramic tile industry association, began offering services in areas of common interest: bulk; purchasing, foreign-market research, and consulting on fiscal and legal matters. The growing tile cluster stimulated the formation of a new, specialized factor-creating institution: in 1976, a consortium of the University of Bologna, regional agencies, and the ceramic industry association founded the Centro Ceramico di Bologna, which conducted process research and product analysis.

Sophisticated Home Demand

By the mid-1960s, per-capita tile consumption in Italy was considerably higher than in the rest of the world. The Italian market was also the world's most sophisticated. Italian customers, who were generally the first to adopt new designs and features, and Italian producers, who constantly innovated to improve manufacturing methods and create new designs, progressed in a mutually reinforcing process.

The uniquely sophisticated character of domestic demand also extended to retail outlets. In the 1960s, specialized tile showrooms began opening in Italy. By 1985, there were roughly 7,600 specialized showrooms handling approximately 80 percent of domestic sales, far more than in other nations. In 1976, the Italian company Piemme introduced tiles by famous designers to gain distribution outlets and to build brand name awareness among consumers. This innovation drew on another related industry, design services, in which Italy was world leader, with over $10 billion in exports.

Sassuolo Rivalry

The sheer number of tile companies in the Sassuolo area created intense rivalry. News of product and process innovations spread rapidly, and companies seeking technological, design, and distribution leadership had to improve constantly.

Proximity added a personal note to the intense rivalry. All of the producers were privately held, most were family run. The owners all lived in the same area, knew each other, and were the leading citizens of the same towns.

Pressures to Upgrade

In the early 1970s, faced with intense domestic rivalry, pressure from retail customers, and the shock of the 1973 energy crisis, Italian tile companies struggled to reduce gas and labor costs. These efforts led to a technological breakthrough, the rapid single-firing process, in which the hardening process, material transformation, and glaze-fixing all occurred in one pass through the kiln. A process that took 225 employees using the double-firing method needed only 90 employees using single firing roller kilns. Cycle time dropped from 16 to 20 hours to only 50 to 55 minutes.

The new, smaller, and lighter equipment was also easier to export. By the early 1980s, exports from Italian equipment manufacturers exceeded domestic sales; in 1988, exports represented almost 80 percent of total sales.

Working together, tile manufacturers and equipment manufacturers made the next important breakthrough during the mid- and late 1970s: the development of materials-handling equipment that transformed tile manufacture from a batch process to a continuous process. The innovation reduced high labor costs — which had been a substantial selective factor disadvantage facing Italian tile manufacturers.

The common perception is that Italian labor costs were lower during this period than those in the U.S. and Germany. In those two countries, however, different jobs had widely different wages. In Italy, wages for different skill categories were compressed, and work rules constrained manufacturers from using overtime or multiple shifts. The restriction proved costly: once cool, kilns are expensive to reheat and are best run continuously. Because of this factor disadvantage, the Italian companies were the first to develop continuous, automated production.

Internationalization

By 1970, Italian domestic demand had matured. The stagnant Italian market led companies to step up their efforts to pursue foreign markets. The presence of related and supporting Italian industries helped in the export drive. Individual tile manufacturers began advertising in Italian and foreign home-design and architectural magazines, publications with wide global circulation among architects, designers, and consumers. This heightened awareness reinforced the quality image of Italian tiles. Tile makers were also able to capitalize on Italy's leading world export positions in related industries like marble, building stone, sinks washbasins, furniture, lamps, and home appliances.

Assopiastrelle, the industry association, established trade-promotion offices in the U.S. in 1980, in Germany in 1984, and in France in 1987. It organized elaborate trade shows in cities ranging from Bologna to Miami and ran sophisticated advertising. Between 1980 and 1987, the association spent roughly $8 million to promote Italian tiles in the United States.

4

NEW MODEL: DEBATE

SUMMARY AND KEY POINTS

Since Porter published his book (1990) and the report on Canada's competitiveness (1991), debates have continued over the diamond model and its application in the real world. This chapter summarizes the pros and cons of the Porter model, and highlights the debate between Porter and Rugman. An overall evaluation on the debates will then be provided.

In his first article, "Diamond in the Rough," Rugman argues that Porter's single diamond has two flaws. First, multinational activity is not properly incorporated. Second, the government's role is understated. While he talks primarily about conceptual issues of the diamond model in this article, Rugman discusses more policy issues in his second article, "Porter Takes the Wrong Turn."

Sources:
Moon, H. C., Rugman, A. M. and Verbeke, A. (1997). The new global competitiveness of Korea and the generalized double diamond approach. *The Korean Economic and Business Review*, **Fall**: 48–57.
Rugman, A. M. (1991). Diamond in the rough. *Business Quarterly*, **55**(3): 61–64.
Rugman, A. M. and D'Cruz, J. R. (1993). The double diamond model of international competitiveness: The Canadian experience. *Management International Review*, **33**(2): 17–39.

Porter and Armstrong respond that Rugman fails to distinguish between the geographic scope of competition (for example, North American or global) and the geographic locus of competitive advantage as reflected in the diamond. For example, competition in the automobile industry is global, but Japanese firms use a strong local diamond. Rugman counter-responds that Porter and Armstrong's alleged dichotomy between scope and locus is operationally meaningless. Rugman argues that the appropriate size of the diamond need not be national; it is determined by the strategy of the firm.

The debate in this Chapter, like that in Chapter 2, is sometimes very acute. However, they do not criticize each other personally — just what they say about competitiveness. Anyway, there is no perfect theory. Porter's single diamond model has been extended to the double diamond model (Rugman and D'Cruz), the generalized double diamond model (Moon, Rugman, and Verbeke) and the nine-factor model (Cho). We will discuss these extended models in Chapters 5 and 6.

CONFLICTING PERSPECTIVES

Porter introduced the diamond model when he conducted a four-year study covering 10 nations and 100 industries. The results are documented in *The Competitive Advantage of Nations*, a densely written, 855-page book published in 1990. Here are some quotes about this book.

> *As its title suggests, the book is meant to be a contemporary equivalent of The Wealth of Nations, and the Free Press is marketing the volume as the new-forged version of Adam Smith's world-transforming thunderbolt.*
>
> (Ryan, 1990)

> *This book is long and tough to read. Nevertheless, it is absolutely mandatory. If you read only one book on business this year this should be it.*
> (Thain, 1990)

> *This book is read by aspiring intellectuals and despairing politicians everywhere and has projected Porter into a stratosphere.*
>
> (*The Economist*, October 8, 1994)

Since he published the book *Competitive Strategy* (1980), Porter has been the most famous scholar and is frequently sought by managers and policy makers. Here are some quotes about Porter.

> *Business school professors tend to be an anonymous breed, and their research is often denigrated as a blend of big words and small ideas. Yet Michael Porter of the Harvard Business School stands out as a genuine star.*

When he speaks, people in business and government listen — frequently paying handsomely to do so. (*New York Times*, September 19, 1992)

Professor Porter's extensive contributions to the competitive strategy literature and his unique holistic way of applying economic and strategic concepts to corporate and national strategy have made him an undisputed leader in competitive strategy. (Harvard Business School Bulletin, abstracted from *Business Quarterly*, Spring 1992, p. 12)

Porter is probably the only business academic to have graced the cover of a major magazine — Fortune in November 1987. Indeed, if you were to do a survey of outstanding academics, it would be hard to come up with another name like Porter's (*Management Today*, August 1989)

However, there are criticisms on Porter.

Some people complain that he is forever producing laundry lists of "forces" and "factors" and passing them off as explanations. Others add that his lists, though they are invariably exhaustive, are not always particularly original. (*The Economist*, October 8, 1994)

Porter argues that geographically concentrated clustering can play a significant role for competitiveness. However, Italian tile industry (an example taken by Porter) became internationally competitive using imported machinery. Moreover, any attempt to define which sectors are clustered together is inevitably judgmental and subjective. (Ryan, 1990)

Almost all of Canada's large multinationals rely on sales in the U.S. and other triad markets. Indeed, it could be argued that the U.S. diamond is likely to be more relevant for Canada's industrial multinationals than is Canada's own diamond, since, on average over 70 percent of their sales take place there... This weakness in Porter's model would not only apply to Canadian-based firms but to multinationals from all small open economies, that is, over 90 percent of the world's nations potentially cannot be modelled by the Porter diamond. (Rugman, 1991)

The principle of the diamond may still hold good — but its geographical constituency has to be established on very different criteria (Dunning, 1993). In particular, Porter's single diamond is not much relevant in small economies because their domestic variables are very limited. For example, in the case of

Canada, an integrated North American diamond (including both Canada and the U.S.), not just a Canadian one, is more relevant (Rugman, 1991). Moon and Lee (1995) showed that this is true even in the case of large economies such as the U.S. They found that international variables such as international rivalry and foreign markets are important for the competitiveness of U.S. software firms. The double diamond framework, developed by Rugman and D'Cruz (1993) suggests that managers build upon both domestic and foreign diamonds to become globally competitive in terms of survival, profitability, and growth. Although the Rugman/D'Cruz North American diamond framework fits well for Canada, it does not apply well to other small nations such as Korea. Thus, Moon *et al.* (1995, 1998) developed the framework further, improving its use in analyzing small economies as well as large economies.[1]

The main purpose of this chapter is to compare and contrast debates over the Porter diamond model so that we can correctly understand determinants of international competitiveness in an era of globalization. In particular, the debate between Porter and Rugman will be highlighted. Rugman first criticizes Porter's work, Porter and Armstrong respond, Rugman counter-responds. An overall evaluation on the debates will then be provided.

---

[1]The summary of pros and cons of the Porter model is abstracted from Moon, Rugman, and Verbeke (1997). For more information about the debates between Porter and Rugman, see the following issues of *Business Quarterly*: Winter 1991 (pp. 61–64), Winter 1992 (pp. 59–64), Spring 1992 (pp. 6–10), and Summer 1992 (pp. 7–10).

CRITIC 1: DIAMOND
IN THE ROUGH

In his article, "Diamond in the Rough," Rugman criticizes Porter's work along four dimensions.

THE ECONOMIC SIZE

Porter's work is superficial and plain wrong when applied in Canadian situation. His work needs to be modified in order to analyze the issue of Canada's international competitiveness. Canada is only one-tenth the economic size of the U.S. Since Canada is relatively small, almost all of Canada's large multinationals rely on sales in the U.S. and other triad markets. Indeed, it could be argued that the U.S. diamond is likely to be more relevant for Canada's industrial multinationals than is Canada's own diamond, since, on average over 70 percent of their sales take place there. The Canada–U.S. free trade agreement reinforces this point. This weakness in Porter's model would not only apply to Canadian-based firms but to multinationals from all small open economies, that is, over 90 percent of the world's nations potentially cannot be modeled by the Porter diamond.

FOREIGN DIRECT INVESTMENT

The major conceptual problem with Porter's model is due to the narrow definition that he applies to foreign direct investment (FDI). Porter defines only outward FDI as being valuable in creating competitive advantage. He then states that foreign subsidiaries are not sources of competitive advantage and that inward FDI is "not entirely healthy." He also states that foreign subsidiaries are importers, and that this is a source of competitive disadvantage. All of these statements are questionable and have long ago been refuted by Canadian-based scholars. All have demonstrated that the research and development undertaken by foreign-owned firms is not significantly different from that of Canadian-owned firms. The largest 20 U.S. subsidiaries in Canada export virtually as much as they import. (The ratio of exports to sales is 25 percent while that of imports to sales is 26 percent.)

THE ECONOMIC STAGE

Porter's lack of knowledge of Canada tends to devalue the application of his core model to Canada. Porter's focus on Canada's "home country" diamond cannot explain Canadian competitiveness. Whereas Canada's successful clusters are resource-based, they have value added in them. Porter's statements in his book, to the effect that Canada is a stage one "factor-driven" economy simply are inaccurate and dangerously misleading as policy advice to Canadians. The views expressed by Porter on the role of natural resources are old fashioned and misguided. He argues that reliance on natural resources is as bad as reliance on unskilled labor or simple technology. In fact, Canada has developed a number of successful mega firms that have turned our comparative advantage in natural resources into proprietary firm-specific advantages in resource processing and further refining. These are sources of sustainable competitive advantage. Canada's successful multinationals such as Alcan, Noranda, and Nova, illustrate the methods by which value added has been introduced by the managers of these resource-based companies. Over time, Canada's resource-based industries do, in fact, have sustainable advantages.

TWO OUTSIDE FORCES

The Porter model is based on four country-specific determinants and two external variables: chance and government. Porter's four determinants and two outside forces interact in the diamond of competitive advantage, with the nature of a country's international competitiveness depending upon the type and quality of these interactions. Porter's two outside forces, chance and government, present interesting contrasts. Government is clearly of critical importance as an influence on a home nation's competitive advantage. For example, to penalize foreign firms, government can use tariffs as a direct entry barrier, or it can use subsidies as an indirect vehicle. In both cases domestic firms benefit from short-run competitive advantages. These discriminatory government actions can lead to shelter for domestic firms, where shelter actually prevents the development of sustainable long-run competitive advantages.

According to Rugman, the most serious problem of the Porter model is that it does not incorporate the true significance of multinational activity. However, even Rugman is not sure yet how to incorporate the multinational activity. He says, "It is questionable if multinational activity can actually be added into any, or all, of the four determinants, or included as a third exogenous variable."

CRITIC 2: PORTER TAKES
THE WRONG TURN

While he talks primarily about conceptual issues of the diamond model in his previous article, Rugman discusses more policy issues in his second article on Porter. Rugman's arguments are summarized as follows.

INCOMPATIBLE POLICY RECOMMENDATIONS

The key result of the Porter/Monitor study is the finding that Canada's home "diamond" is weak and leads to an inability of Canadian-based businesses to develop sustainable global competitive advantages, except in resources. But Porter states that resource-based industries are an essential part of Canada's "old economic order," which Porter thinks has no future. He says, in effect, that Canada's diamond is broken and that it needs to be upgraded to improve Canada's lack of international competitiveness. Most of Porter's policy recommendations are sound, especially his call to reduce the budget deficit, upgrade worker and management skills, and improve business–labor–government relations. Yet these policy recommendations are actually incompatible with his analysis. This incompatibility arises because Porter insists on applying his home base diamond analysis to Canada, whereas a much more relevant concept for Canadian managers is that of a North American diamond. This approach, developed by Joe D'Cruz and me in 1991,[2] suggests that to become globally competitive, Canadian managers need to design strategies across both the U.S. and Canadian diamonds. They need to benchmark decisions on a North American basis, not just a Canadian one.

OLD-FASHIONED POLICY RECOMMENDATIONS

Porter's view that multinationals can only succeed with a strong home country base may still be true for the U.S., but it is out of date for Canada. Porter's old-fashioned, naïve, and politically mischievous viewpoint is inconsistent with Canada's support of the free trade agreement, tax reform, constitutional renewal, and other economic, social, and political measures aimed at improving the climate for doing business in a Canadian economy that is interdependent with that of the U.S. It is as if Porter/Monitor had never heard of, or participated in, the divisive free trade election in Canada in 1988. In this the forces of economic nationalism were narrowly defeated by the economic realism and sovereignty considerations underlying the free trade agreement. Porter's strategy would have been suitable in the 1890s, but it is wrong for the 1990s. Instead, to become globally competitive a North American mindset is required for Canadian business decisions.

MISLEADING POLICY RECOMMENDATIONS

After Canadian managers have read Porter's study, they should ask the following questions. First, does Canada need an industrial strategy to mend the broken Canadian diamond? Second, should Canada give up on its resource-based industries and replace them by innovation-driven industries? Third, does Canada need to keep out foreign-owned firms that do not develop product lines using Canada as a home base? The reason these questions are important is that Porter says that Canada's lack of international competitiveness is due to problems in these areas. Yet his analysis fails to provide logical support for his recommendations.

According to Rugman, in sum, Porter's policy recommendations are incompatible, old-fashioned, and misleading. Rugman concludes that Porter took a wrong turning when he crossed the border.

---

[2]Rugman, A. M. and D'Cruz, J. (1991). *Fast Forward: Improving Canada's International Competitiveness*, Toronto: Kodak Canada. It should be noted that Porter does not cite this study correctly in Chapter 3 of his report; instead he cites the study referenced here as number 10.

RESPONSE BY PORTER AND ARMSTRONG

Since Porter and the Monitor company published the report, *Canada at the Crossroads: The Reality of a New Competitive Environment*, there has been a continuing debate on the diamond model among the scholars. After they briefly evaluate several scholars' comments on the validity of the diamond model, Porter and Armstrong highlight their response to Rugman's criticism on Porter. They criticize Rugman along the following points.

GEOGRAPHIC SCOPE AND GEOGRAPHIC LOCUS

Rugman is preoccupied with the North American model and has a lack of understanding of the diamond model. Rugman fails to distinguish between the geographic scope of competition (for example, North American or global) and the geographic locus of competitive advantage, as reflected in the diamond. Competition in the automobile industry is global, but that does not mean there is a "world diamond" for automobile manufacturing and firms based in all nations are equally positioned. The striking competitiveness of Japanese-based firms belies this view. Their success has been fueled by a strong local (Japanese) diamond in which rivalry has been intense, customers demanding and related and supporting industries well developed.

DIFFERENT LEVELS OF ANALYSIS

Regions and even cities register striking differences in economic prosperity. For example, the standard of living within the U.S. varies sharply, and differences have persisted. This refutes any notion that Canada's standard of living is secured by proximity to the U.S. States in the U.S. have different per capita incomes precisely because of differences in their local diamonds. Whereas U.S. states have much in common, their differences are sufficient to strongly influence competitive and income patterns. On a similar note, there are many similarities between Canada and the U.S., but there are also significant differences in institutions, history, culture, government structures and policies, and economic circumstances. Such differences create distinct Canadian diamonds in industries. An example of how competitive fortunes have differed even on opposite sides of the border is provided by the software industries in Vancouver and Seattle. The industry in Seattle is booming. In Vancouver — just 225 kilometers to the north — the industry is far smaller.

BUILDING DOMESTICALLY OR OUTSOURCING ABROAD

Most disturbing about Rugman's North American diamond view is that it apparently leads him to believe that the critical problems we see in Canada in areas of education, training, science, and technology, can be ignored because Canadian firms can source these skills elsewhere. Indeed, Rugman stated in an interview reported in the University of Toronto Bulletin that Canada should look outside its own borders to develop the economy in global context, and not, as we suggest, concentrate first on building up its skills. Canadians must be vitally concerned with the state of their home environment. The Canadian standard of living depends on the particular activities that take place in Canada. The issue is where the most highly productive economic activities, and those that most benefit upgrading in other industries, will be located. These, in turn, will determine the wages that Canadian jobs command and the returns to capital invested there.

Porter and Armstrong conclude that Rugman significantly distorts their views on Canada's competitiveness.

COUNTER-RESPONSE
BY RUGMAN

Rugman is invited to counter-respond to Porter and Armstrong. He focuses on the key question of the practical relevance of Porter's single diamond model versus the "double diamond" approach. His response is as follows.

GEOGRAPHIC SCOPE AND GEOGRAPHIC LOCUS

Porter and Armstrong state that, "Rugman fails to distinguish between the geographic scope of competition (for example, North American or global) and the geographic locus of competitive advantage as reflected in the diamond." Two examples are given to illustrate this point. First, that "competition in the automobile industry is global," but that "Japanese-based firms" use a strong local diamond. Second, that "regions and even countries register striking differences in economic prosperity," which "refutes any notion that Canada's standard of living is secured by proximity to the U.S." Further, "U.S. states...have differences in their local diamonds"... and the software industry in Seattle is booming whereas that in Vancouver is not. Paradoxically, both of these Porter–Armstrong examples offer more support for a double diamond framework than a single diamond. First, Canada's successful auto industry is fully integrated with the one across the U.S. border; the auto pact is an institutionalized double diamond that has worked well for a quarter of a century. Canada is not like Japan with an isolated single diamond; instead the advantages of geography and the economics of the auto pact have let Canada escape from the disadvantages of its own small local diamond. Second, the smaller size of the software industry in Vancouver compared to Seattle is largely explained by Boeing being in Seattle. The real issue is: what U.S. diamond conditions explain Boeing? Why is Boeing in Seattle and not in Vancouver? But this is not a very useful question to ask about the competitiveness of B.C., which surely requires some analysis of forest products and the new, emerging, high tech industries. From the viewpoint of global competitive strategy the locus for Canadian-based businesses must be broader than the national diamond.

DIFFERENT LEVELS OF ANALYSIS

The only point in dispute is the size of the diamond. Does it always have to be a nation? Porter and Armstrong themselves admit that diamonds can go down to state levels. I agree; these are sub-national diamonds. But Porter and Armstrong cannot seem to make a symmetrical logical step and visualize a double diamond that goes up across national borders. Yet for purposes of global strategy, in smaller nations like Canada and New Zealand, this is common. Even in Britain, the E.C. diamond is now impossible to ignore; there is a double diamond for U.K. firms, just as there is for Canadian ones operating in the U.S. The appropriate size of the diamond need not be national; it is determined by the strategy of the firm. The relevant focus is indeed the locus of corporate strategy; for international business, it is an international locus. Multinational firms compete globally, not nationally. Porter and Armstrong's alleged dichotomy between scope and locus is operationally meaningless.

BUILDING DOMESTICALLY OR OUTSOURCING ABROAD

Porter and Armstrong also state that "Rugman's North American diamond view ... apparently leads him to believe that the actual problems we see in Canada in areas of education, training, science and technology, can be ignored because Canadian firms can source these skills elsewhere." Wrong again. The whole point of the double diamond is that it has two diamonds! Therefore I believe very strongly that the elements of the Canadian diamond must be upgraded — they are half of the North American diamond! I have never suggested that Canadian policies for upgrading be ignored; indeed, I wrote that I agree with the Porter report and its recommendations in these cases. It is their analysis that is the subject of dispute. Porter and Armstrong seem to think that my North American diamond is an American-only diamond; it is not — there are two integral and linked components. Having market access to the U.S. for business purposes need not constrain Canadian sovereignty or the need for public policy to upgrade the Canadian diamond. But a limited focus on Canada's diamond alone will fail to lead to the development of globally competitive Canadian businesses.

Rugman concludes, "My articles do not criticize Porter personally — just what he says about Canada; Porter's fame and reputation at Harvard are not in question but his scholarly work on Canada is."

EVALUATION
ON THE DEBATES

In a Dialogue section *Business Quarterly* (Winter, Spring, and Summer 1992) published several articles of pros and cons on Porter's report, *Canada at the Crossroads*. In particular, the debate between Michael Porter and Alan Rugman has called for significant attention both in the business and academic communities. Porter and Rugman are both worldwide distinguished scholars in their own field — Porter in strategic management and Rugman in international business. Exchange of different views will enrich these two academic fields and may lead to marrying these two areas into international strategic management. Some of their insights are keen enough to demand widespread attention. This topic, i.e., the determinants of competitiveness, is a very important issue among scholars and policy makers. Although the debate focuses on the Canadian case, this is a worldwide topic. The inclusion of the New Zealand case is thus appropriate. Business Quarterly should welcome other cases, too. The experience of other countries will benefit Canadian policy makers.

In the debate, Porter appears to be somewhat upset with the provocative articles of Rugman (1991, 1992). However, Porter (1990, especially Chapter 1) is also quite provocative in criticizing the existing economic theories on this issue. The provocative nature of both Porter and Rugman has probably made them the great scholars they are today.

It is noteworthy that there is an important difference in the basic approaches of Porter and Rugman. Understanding this difference will help us understand their current and future debate. As indicated in the titles of his bestselling books such as *Competitive Strategy* and *The Competitive Advantage of Nations*, Porter's approach focuses on competition-based corporate and national strategies. On the other hand, Rugman's basic approach is to understand the rational behavior of multinational firms rather than just to beat the competitors (for example, see Rugman, 1981). According to Rugman, multinational firms frequently utilize foreign markets and resources. Rugman believes that the border for a multinational firm is no longer the nation state. Rugman and other international business scholars may thus feel very uneasy with Porter's diamond model, in which the competitive determinants are fixed on a national level.

Porter (1990) says that nations are most likely to succeed in industries or industry segments where the national "diamond" is the most favorable. The diamond has four broad elements — (1) factor conditions; (2) demand conditions; (3) related and supporting industries; and (4) firm strategy, structure, and rivalry. In his criticisms on the Porter model, Rugman (1991) argues that while most of Porter's analysis would work for large economies such as the U.S., it may not adequately explain small economies such as Canada. The double diamond approach of Rugman (and D'Cruz) says that a Canadian manager needs to consider the U.S. diamond as well as the Canadian and should design across the two diamonds (Rugman, 1992).

The key point of the debate in determining the competitiveness of Canada appears to be whether the diamond is single or double. However, the critical difference between Porter and Rugman on this issue is whether international activities should be included in the model. Rugman's point is that Porter's original model should be extended to encompass international activities. Porter also realizes the importance of international or global activities. However, he refuses to incorporate them, by distinguishing the geographic scope of competition and the geographic locus of competitive advantage (Porter and Armstrong, 1992).

The difference now appears to be pedagogic and minimal, but in fact it is real. In particular, it can have a major impact on policy implications. One extreme example is that if Porter is right, the diamond must be fixed through an appropriate industrial policy; if Rugman is correct, Canada should pursue the North American diamond, and economic integration with the U.S. must be even more aggressively focused (Ballinger, in Porter and Armstrong, 1992). In which direction should Canada go? If the Porter model is taken literally, opportunities would be eliminated because world-class demand and world-class competition do not exist in the national diamond (Stewart, in Porter and Armstrong, 1992).

Another limitation of the single diamond is its poor predictive ability. (Cartwright, in Porter and Armstrong, 1992) says that his New Zealand study cast considerable doubt on the ability of the Porter diamond theory to predict or prescribe the nature of internationally competitive industries that are export-dependent and land-based. Cartwright (Porter and Armstrong, 1992) explains that the home-based diamond model is inadequate because it omits variables that explain international competitiveness.

While criticizing Rugman, Thain (Porter and Armstrong, 1992) also recognizes the importance of international activities, in saying that what we really need to understand is that all national diamonds overlap more or less, and are inextricably linked in a global system. If everybody recognizes the important role of international business in today's global economy, why don't we explicitly incorporate it into the model? The extension and even correction of Porter's original model does not reduce the value of Porter. As long as everybody is talking about his model, Porter remains a big shot. Porter might be surprised to see how his original model could be improved in the future. Still, he has provided the foundation.

Porter's single diamond is not the final answer. Rugman may agree that the double diamond is not, either. In social sciences no theory may survive without being revised and corrected. There will be multiple diamonds, Triad diamond, and even global diamond. Rugman sparked an intelligent and constructive debate that would serve all of us well (Nankivell, in Porter and Armstrong, 1992). The potential value of his ideas will stir up considerable controversy and debate on the issues (Ballinger, in Porter and Armstrong, 1992).

There may be several other areas for further discussion. First, how can we operationalize the model? In other words, how can we practically measure the relative competitiveness of each determinant? Second, the need for internationalization may be different among the determinants. Stewart, for example, argues that two determinants (factor conditions and related industries) may be national, while the other two determinants (demand and rivalry) should be international. However, some multinational firms exploit foreign factors and utilize foreign related industries. This may vary across industries and countries. A more comprehensive discussion can thus be provided. In any case, Stewart has provided another ground for discussion.

Another area of further discussion concerns Porter's two exogenous factors, i.e., chance and government. In particular, the government factor may be integrated into the new model; thus, the shape of the model may be "pentagon" rather than "diamond." Porter (1990, p. 126–127) says that this is not correct because the government's real role in national competitive advantage is in influencing the four determinants. However, all the factors influence one another (see Porter, 1990, Figures 4-1 through 4-4 in Chapter 4). Or government can be placed in the center of the diamond. In any case, it may not be adequate to treat the government merely as an exogenous factor.

Thain (Porter and Armstrong, 1992) suggests that any further debate should focus on the practical realities of how Porter's recommendations can be put into practice. Implementation is very important. However, policy recommendations of Porter's study are based on the single diamond model. If the model is flawed, then the recommendations may not be sound. Here, Rugman has made another important point. Most of Porter's policy recommendations based on it may be sound, but they are incompatible with his analysis (Rugman, 1992, p. 59). We need to continue the analytical debate if the model is still controversial and may be inconsistent with recommendations. Further debate will benefit both scholars and practitioners.

REFERENCES

Dunning, J. H. (1993). Internationalizing Porter's diamond. *Management International Review*, **33**(2): 7–15.

Management Today (1989). Guru on the riverbank, August, pp. 52–56.

Moon, H. C. and Lee, K. C. (1995). Testing the diamond model: Competitiveness of U. S. software firms. *Journal of International Management*, **1**(4): 373–387.

Moon, H. C., Rugman, A. M. and Verbeke. A. (1995). The generalized double diamond approach to international competitiveness, in Rugman, A. M., den Broeck, J. V. and Verbeke, A. (eds.), *Research in Global Strategic Management, Vol. 5: Beyond the Diamond*, Greenwich, CT: JAI Press, pp. 97–114.

Moon, H. C., Rugman, A. M. and Verbeke, A. (1997). The new global competitiveness of Korea and the generalized double diamond approach. *The Korean Economic and Business Review*, Fall: 48–57.

Moon, H. C., Rugman, A. M. and Verbeke, A. (1998). The generalized double diamond approach to global competitiveness of Korea and Singapore. *International Business Review*, 7: 135–150.

New York Times (1992). Economic analyst says U.S. needs long-term investments, 19 September.

Porter, M. E. (1980). *Competitive Strategy: Techniques for Analyzing Industries and Companies*, New York: Free Press.

Porter, M. E. (1990). *The Competitive Advantage of Nations*, New York: Free Press.

Porter, M. E. and The Monitor Company (1991). *Canada at the Crossroads: The Reality of a New Competitive Environment*, Ottawa: Business Council on National Issues and Minister of Supply and Services of the Government of Canada.

Porter, M. E. and Armstrong, J. (1992). Canada at the crossroads: Dialogue (Response by Porter). *Business Quarterly*, 56(4): 6–10.

Rugman, A. M. (1981). *Inside the Multinationals*, New York: Columbia University Press.

Rugman, A. M. (1991). Diamond in the rough. *Business Quarterly*, 55(3): 61–64.

Rugman, A. M. (1992). Porter takes the wrong turn. *Business Quarterly*, 56(3): 59–64.

Rugman, A. M. and D'Cruz, J. R. (1993). The double diamond model of international competitiveness: The Canadian experience. *Management International Review*, 33(2): 17–39.

Ryan, R. (1990). A grand disunity. *National Review*, 42(13): 46–47.

Thain, D. H. (1990). The war without bullets. *Business Quarterly*, 55(1): 13–19.

The Economist (1994). Professor Porter Ph.D., October 8: 75.

Part II

MICHAEL PORTER AND THEORETICAL EXTENSIONS

5

EXTENDED MODEL (1): THE GENERALIZED DOUBLE DIAMOND MODEL

SUMMARY AND KEY POINTS

Porter (1990) proposed the diamond model, and Rugman (1991) pointed out two problems with regard to multinational activity and government. Rugman and D'Cruz (1993) developed a double diamond model. Although this model fits well for Canada, it may not fit well for other nations. Moon *et al.* (1995) extended it to a generalized double diamond that works well for all countries. This generalized model appropriately incorporates multinational activity and government.

In considering multinational activity, Moon *et al.* (1995) emphasized two elements. First, sustainable value added in a country results from both domestically owned and foreign owned firms.

Sources:
Moon, H. C., Rugman, A. M. and Verbeke, A. (1998). A generalized double diamond approach to the international competitiveness of Korea and Singapore. *International Business Review*, 7: 135–150.
Moon, H. C. and Kim, J. Y. (2010). Comparing the competitiveness of Korea and Singapore after ten years of Asian economic crisis. *The Review of Business History*, 25(1): 75–91.

Second, sustainability requires a value added configuration spread over many countries. Thus, multinational activity, whether inbound or outbound, is important for a nation's competitiveness. Since multinational activity affects all the determinants of the diamond, it is not appropriate to treat this variable as one of the determinants. Instead, they incorporate this variable by doubling the diamond.

To test the validity of these two models, this chapter evaluates relevant data for both domestic and international variables in the case of Korea and Singapore. The results generally support the generalized double diamond model. Korea has a "larger" domestic diamond than Singapore, but Singapore has a much "larger" international diamond than Korea. This leads to the conclusion that both domestic and international determinants are important to the competitiveness of Korea and Singapore. Although the data of this chapter are old, the methodology is still valid. For more updated version of this research, refer to Moon and Kim (2010).

INTRODUCTION

In his famous book, *The Competitive Advantage of Nations*, Porter (1990) studied eight developed countries and two newly industrialized countries (NICs). The latter two are Korea and Singapore. Porter is quite optimistic about the future of the Korean economy. He argues that Korea may well reach true advanced status in the next decade (p. 383). In contrast, Porter is less optimistic about Singapore. In his view, Singapore will remain a factor-driven economy (p. 566) which reflects an early stage of economic development. Since the publication of Porter's work, however, Singapore has been more successful than Korea, as will be discussed in this article. This difference in performance raises important questions regarding the validity of Porter's diamond model of a nation's competitiveness.

Porter has used the diamond model when consulting with the governments of Canada (Porter and the Monitor Company, 1991) and New Zealand (Crocombe *et al.*, 1991). While the variables of Porter's diamond model are useful terms of reference when analyzing a nation's competitiveness, a weakness of Porter's work is his exclusive focus on the "home base" concept. In the case of Canada, Porter did not adequately consider the nature of multinational activities (Rugman, 1991). In the case of New Zealand, the Porter model could not explain the success of export-dependent and resource-based industries

(Cartwright, 1993). Therefore, applications of Porter's home-based diamond require careful consideration and appropriate modification.

In Porter's single home-based diamond approach, a firm's capabilities to tap into the location advantages of other nations are viewed as very limited. Rugman (1992, p. 59) has demonstrated that a much more relevant concept prevails in small, open economies, namely the double diamond model. For example, in the case of Canada, an integrated North American diamond (including both Canada and the United States), not just a Canadian one, is more relevant. The double diamond model, developed by Rugman and D'Cruz (1993), suggests that managers build upon both domestic and foreign diamonds to become globally competitive in terms of survival, profitability, and growth. While the Rugman and D'Cruz North American diamond framework fits well for Canada and New Zealand, it does not carry over to all other small nations, including Korea and Singapore. Thus, Moon *et al.* (1995) adapted the double diamond framework to a generalized double diamond which works well for analyzing all small economies. The main purpose of this chapter is to assess the global competitiveness of Korea and Singapore using this new, generalized double diamond framework. It should be emphasized that the comparison between the single diamond approach and the generalized double diamond will be performed at the macro level rather than the level of individual industries. In this context, it should be remembered that Porter himself made statements about Korea and Singapore at the macro level.

This chapter consists of three sections. The first section reviews Porter's (1990) original diamond model and contrasts it with a new framework, the generalized double diamond model (Moon *et al.*, 1995). The second section presents data and analyses the variables. In the subsequent section, the results are discussed.

SINGLE OR DOUBLE DIAMONDS?

Porter (1990, p. 1) raises the basic question of international competitiveness: "Why do some nations succeed and others fail in international competition?" As its title suggests, the book is meant to be a contemporary equivalent of *The Wealth of Nations*, a new-forged version of Adam Smith's opus (Ryan, 1990, p. 46). Porter argues that nations are most likely to succeed in industries or industry segments where the national "diamond" is the most favourable. The diamond has four interrelated components; (1) factor conditions, (2) demand conditions, (3) related and supporting industries, and (4) firm strategy,

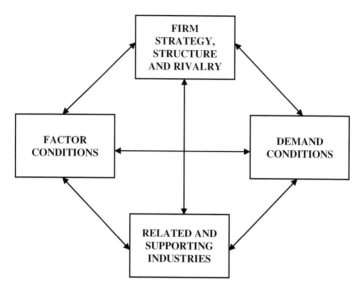

Fig. 5-1 The Home-Based Single Diamond

structure, and rivalry, and two exogenous parameters (1) government and (2) chance, as shown in Figure 5-1.

This model cleverly integrates the important variables determining a nation's competitiveness into one model. Most other models designed for this purpose represent subsets of Porter's comprehensive model. However, substantial ambiguity remains regarding the signs of relationships and the predictive power of the "model" (Grant, 1991). This is mainly because Porter fails to incorporate the effects of multinational activities in his model. To solve this problem, Dunning (1992), for example, treats multinational activities as a third exogenous variable which should be added to Porter's model. In today's global business, however, multinational activities represent much more than just an exogenous variable. Therefore, Porter's original diamond model has been extended to the generalized double diamond model (Moon *et al.*, 1995) whereby multinational activity is formally incorporated into the model.

Firms from small countries such as Korea and Singapore target resources and markets not just in a domestic context, but also in a global context.[1]

---

[1] Global targeting also becomes very important to firms from large economic systems such as the U.S.

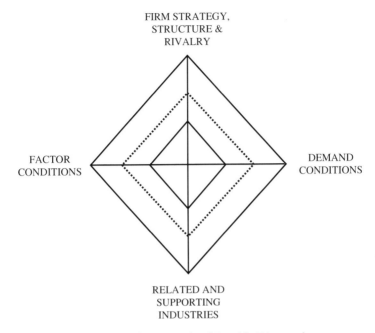

FIRM STRATEGY,
STRUCTURE &
RIVALRY

FACTOR
CONDITIONS

DEMAND
CONDITIONS

RELATED AND
SUPPORTING
INDUSTRIES

Fig. 5-2   The Generalized Double Diamond

Therefore, a nation's competitiveness depends partly upon the domestic diamond and partly upon the "international" diamond relevant to its firms. Figure 5-2 shows the generalized double diamond where the outside one represents a global diamond and the inside one a domestic diamond. The size of the global diamond is fixed within a foreseeable period, but the size of the domestic diamond varies according to the country size and its competitiveness. The diamond of dotted lines, between these two diamonds, is an international diamond which represents the nation's competitiveness as determined by both domestic and international parameters. The difference between the international diamond and the domestic diamond thus represents international or multinational activities. The multinational activities include both outbound and inbound foreign direct investment (FDI).

In the generalized double diamond model, national competitiveness is defined as the capability of firms engaged in value added activities in a specific industry in a particular country to sustain this value added over long periods of time in spite of international competition. Theoretically, two methodological differences between Porter and this new model are important. First, sustainable value added in a specific country may result from both domestically owned and foreign owned firms. Porter, however, does not incorporate foreign activities into his model as he makes a distinction between geographic scope of competition and the geographic locus of competitive advantage (Porter and Armstrong, 1992). Second, sustainability may require a geographic configuration spanning many countries, whereby firm specific and location advantages present in several nations may complement each other. In contrast, Porter (1986, 1990) argues that the most effective global strategy is to concentrate as many activities as possible in one country and to serve the world from this home base. Porter's global firm is just an exporter and his methodology does not take into account the organizational complexities of true global operations by multinational firms (Moon, 1994).

Porter's narrow view on multinational activities has led him to underestimate the potential of Singapore's economy. Porter (1990, p. 566) argues that Singapore is largely a production base for foreign multinationals, attracted by Singapore's relatively low-cost, well-educated workforce and efficient infrastructure including roads, ports, airports, and telecommunications. According to Porter, the primary sources of competitive advantage of Singapore are basic factors such as location and unskilled/semi-skilled labor which are not very important to national competitive advantage. In actual fact, Singapore has been the most successful economy among the NICs. Singapore's success is mainly due to inbound FDI by foreign multinational enterprises in Singapore, as well as outbound FDI by Singapore firms in foreign countries. The inbound FDI brings foreign capital and technology; whereas outbound FDI allows Singapore to gain access to cheap labor and natural resources. It is the combination of domestic and international diamond determinants that leads to a sustainable competitive advantage in many Singaporean industries.

Multinational activities are also important in explaining Korea's competitiveness. The most important comparative advantage of Korea is its human resources which have been inexpensive and well disciplined. However, Korea has recently experienced severe labor problems. Its labor is no longer cheap and controllable. Major increases in the wages in Korea were awarded to a newly militant labor force in 1987–1990, which lifted average earnings in manufacturing by 11.6 percent in 1987, 19.6 percent in 1988, 25 percent in 1989 and 20.2 percent in 1990 (The Economist Intelligence Unit, 1992). Korea's wage level is now comparable to that of the United Kingdom, but the quality of its products has not kept pace. For the last several years, Korea's wage increases have been significantly higher than those in other NICs and three or four times as high as those in other developed countries (*Chungang Daily Newspaper*, February 25, 1995). Faced with a deteriorating labor advantage, Korean firms have two choices: (1) go abroad to find cheap labor; (2) enhance their production capabilities by introducing advanced technology from developed countries. In both cases, the implementation of these choices requires the development of multinational activities.

To sum up, multinational activities are very important when analyzing the global competitiveness of Korea and Singapore. In fact the most important difference between the single diamond model (Porter, 1990) and the generalized double diamond model (Moon *et al.*, 1995) is the successful incorporation of multinational activities in the latter. In the next section, we will assess the Porter versus the generalized double diamond models using data for both domestic and international determinants in the cases of Korea and Singapore.

DIAMOND VARIABLES AND DATA

Dependent Variables

The dependent variable of the diamond model is a nation's competitiveness. Porter (1990) argues that the only meaningful concept of competitiveness at the national level is national productivity (p. 6), although he uses exports and outbound FDI as proxies for competitiveness (p. 25). In our view, the two latter variables should be regarded as explanatory variables and not as proxy for the dependent variable. Table 5-1 lists possible proxy variables for the dependent variable of the diamond model in the cases of Korea and Singapore.

Table 5-1   Dependent Variables of the Diamond Model

	Korea	Singapore
Productivity		
GNP per capita ($), 1993	7,660	19,850
GDP per energy kg (oil equil) ($), 1993	2.6	3.6
Managers' Perception		
Strong economy as a whole (% agreed), 1992	14.1	58.8
Strong manufacturing base (% agreed), 1992	27.1	57.5

Sources:
International Monetary Fund (1996). *International Financial Statistics*, February;
The World Bank (1995). *World Development Report 1995*;
IMD (1992). *The World Competitiveness Report*, Lausanne, Switzerland.

Productivity variables include output per capita and output per unit of energy consumption. Managers' perception variables include the strength of the general economy and manufacturing base. While these variables are used for illustrative purposes only, they suggest that Singapore is more competitive than Korea.

Independent Variables

As discussed, the most important debate over the diamond model is whether the international variables should be incorporated into the model or not. We will assess the model, first with the domestic variables only, and then with both the domestic and international variables. Table 5-2 lists the domestic

Table 5-2 Domestic Independent Variables of the Diamond Model

	Korea	Singapore
Factor Conditions		
Basic	Wages in manufacturing (USA = 100.0), 1994	
	37.0	37.0
Advanced	Scientists & technicians (1,000 persons), 1986–1991	
	45.9	22.9
Demand Conditions		
Size	Average annual growth (%), 1980–1993	
	8.2	6.1
Sophistication	Education index (literacy + schooling), 1992	
	2.6	2.1
Related & Supporting Industries		
Transportation	Paved roads (km/million persons), 1992	
	1,090.0	993.0
Communication	Telephones (per 100 persons), 1990–1992	
	41.4	39.2
Firm Strategy, Structure & Rivalry		
Rivalry	Unequal treatment of foreigners (% agreed), 1992	
	43.7	37.2

Sources:
U.S. Department of Commerce (1995). *Statistical Abstract of the U.S. 1995*, September;
United Nations Development Programme (1994). *Human Development Report 1994*;
The World Bank (1995). *World Development Report*;
IMD (1992). *The World Competitiveness Report*, Lausanne, Switzerland.

Table 5-3 International Independent Variables of the Diamond Model

	Korea	Singapore
Factor Conditions		
Basic	Outbound FDI per capita ($), 1994	
	56.7	743.0
Advanced	Inbound FDI per capita ($), 1994	
	18.2	1,907.2
Demand Conditions		
Size	Export dependency (% of GNP), 1994	
	25.5	140.5
Sophistication	Export diversification (% of exp. without top 3), 1992	
	53.5	58.6
Related & Supporting Industries		
Transportation	Good air transport system (% agreed), 1992	
	70.6	97.8
Communication	International telex traffic (outgoing traffic in minutes per capita), 1990	
	0.2	7.7
Firm Strategy, Structure & Rivalry		
Rivalry	Openness to foreign products (% agreed), 1992	
	57.5	87.7

Sources:
International Monetary Fund (1996). *International Financial Statistics*, February;
Europa Publications Limited (1995). *The Europa World Year Book 1995*, London, England: Europa Publications Limited;
IMD (1992). *The World Competitiveness Report*, Lausanne, Switzerland.

independent variables and Table 5-3 lists the international independent variables. These variables do not constitute a full set of all relevant parameters but represent acceptable proxies to illustrate the "value added" of incorporating international elements in the diamond model.

Factor conditions

Porter distinguishes between basic factors and advanced factors. Basic factors include natural resources, climate, location, unskilled and semiskilled labor, and debt capital. Advanced factors include modern communications infrastructure and highly educated personnel such as engineers and scientists. Porter (1990, p. 77) argues that advanced factors are now the most significant ones for competitive advantage. Since Korea and Singapore are not yet fully developed countries, however, basic factors remain important for their competitiveness. In this study, we choose to measure basic factors by wages in manufacturing and advanced factors are measured by the number of the technical staff per 1,000 persons as shown in Table 5-2 which reports domestic independent variables.[2] Since wages are rapidly increasing in these countries, Korea and Singapore are investing in other countries such as China and the Southeast Asian countries where labor is cheap. Yet Korea and Singapore still need to attract multinational firms from advanced countries, as this may be one way to obtain access to modern technologies. In short, both inbound and outbound FDI are important in enhancing these countries' factor conditions. These international determinants are reported as international independent variables in Table 5-3.

Demand conditions

The rate of growth of home demand can be more important to competitive advantage than its absolute size. Rapid domestic growth leads a nation's firms to adopt new technologies faster, with less fear that such technologies would make existing investments redundant, and to build large, efficient facilities with the confidence that they will be utilized (Porter, 1990, p. 94). In addition, a nation's firms gain competitive advantage if domestic buyers are sophisticated and demanding as regards the product or service (Porter, 1990, p. 89). It can be hypothesized that a higher level of education of the consumers increases demand sophistication. The size and sophistication of demand conditions are measured by average annual growth and an education index, respectively in Table 5-2.[3]

For both Korea and Singapore, however, domestic markets are relatively small so global economies of scale cannot be achieved. The most successful firms in these countries target international, rather than domestic markets.[4] The export market measured as a percentage of GNP can serve as a proxy for the relative importance of international demand. If a country's exports

---

[2] Both Korea and Singapore are natural resource-poor countries. Therefore, only labour, but not natural resources, is considered as a determinant for the state of the factor conditions.

[3] See United Nations Development Programme (1994, p. 108) for the calculation of the education index.

[4] For example, Korea's export market at the beginning of internationalization was larger than the domestic market (Cho et al., 1994).

depend on just a few foreign countries, however, its export markets are not diversified and are thus not sophisticated. The diversification of export markets serves a proxy for the sophistication of international demand faced by a nation's firms. It is hypothesized that a high ratio of exports, excluding the top three destination countries, *vis-à-vis* total exports, reflects a more diversified and more sophisticated international demand. These data for proxies for international demand are shown in Table 5-3.

Related and supporting industries

Related and supporting industries are those whereby firms coordinate or share activities in the value chain or those which involve products that are complementary to the firms of a given nation. These industries may have strong backward and forward linkages with the firms in a given sector. Since we are testing the competitiveness of manufacturing industries in general in Korea and Singapore, however, the information on general infrastructure such as transportation and communication is important. Transportation is measured by paved roads (km/million persons) and communication is measured by telephone lines (per 100 persons) as shown in Table 5-2. We recognize that modern physical infrastructure could be regarded as an advanced factor, but we did not incorporate it in our earlier section on factor conditions as we believe that it is better to incorporate physical infrastructure as a related and supporting industry.

Again, both Korea and Singapore depend heavily on international business. In today's global business, it is neither efficient nor desirable to rely solely on home-based related and supporting industries.[5] The infrastructure for international business is important. The infrastructure for international transportation is measured by the extent to which international air transport infrastructure meets business requirements. The infrastructure for international communication is measured by the international telex traffic in terms of traffic in minutes per capita. The relevant data reflecting these variables are shown in Table 5-3. We recognize that other proxy variables could be used, such as seaport infrastructure, but we have chosen these proxies for convenience of illustration.

---

[5] Porter (1990, p. 103) argues that foreign suppliers (and related industries) rarely represent a valid substitute for home-based ones. However, when a firm cannot compensate for the disadvantages (e.g., technology) in the home country, the firm will seek this factor in the foreign country (Moon and Roehl, 1993).

Firm strategy, structure, and rivalry

The final determinant of a nation's competitiveness reflects the context in which firms are created, organized, and managed. National advantage may result from a good match among these variables. However, Porter (1990) finds that no one managerial system is universally appropriate (p. 108). Instead, he expresses a strong preference in favor of vigorous domestic rivalry for creating and sustaining competitive advantage in an industry (p. 117). In this study we attempt to measure whether rivalry, as well as strategy and structure, is domestically oriented or not. This is difficult to do and we choose to measure it by the extent to which foreigners are treated unequally as compared to domestic citizens as shown in Table 5-2. It is hypothesized that a high level of unequal treatment of foreigners is xenophobic and it is correlated with a high domestic orientation of rivalry and firm strategy and structure.

Porter (1990, p. 117) argues that domestic rivalry is superior to rivalry with foreign competitors. This argument may be true in large economies such as the United States, but not in small economies such as Canada (Rugman, 1990), Korea, and Singapore. The successful firms in Korea and Singapore are more concerned about international rivalry than about domestic rivalry. International rivalry can be measured by the openness to foreign products which is the extent to which national protectionism does not prevent competitive products from being imported as shown in Table 5-3.

EMPIRICAL RESULTS OF THE DIAMOND TESTS

The data for domestic independent variables in Table 5-2 and international independent variables in Table 5-3 are transformed into "competitiveness indices" in Table 5-4. It should again be emphasized that these are used for illustrative purposes only, as indications that Porter's single diamond model lead to wrong conclusions. To calculate the competitiveness index, for each variable, a maximum value "100" is given to the country which has the higher value and a relative ratio in terms of percentage is given to the other country which has the lower value. If a variable is measured by two elements, one half weight is given to each element. For example, in Table 5-2, both basic and advanced factor conditions of Korea have equal or higher values than those of Singapore so that maximum value "100" is given to each of the two factor conditions of Korea. Thus, the competitive index of Korea's domestic factor conditions is

$$100/2 + 100/2 = 100.0$$

Table 5-4   Competitiveness Index of the Diamond Model

	Korea	Singapore
Factor Conditions		
Domestic Variables	100.0	75.0
International Variables	4.3	100.0
Demand Conditions		
Domestic Variables	100.0	77.6
International Variables	54.7	100.0
Related & Supporting Industries		
Domestic Variables	100.0	92.9
International Variables	37.4	100.0
Firm Strategy, Structure & Rivalry		
Domestic Variables	100.0	85.1
International Variables	65.6	100.0

Singapore's basic factor conditions have the same value (37.0) as that of Korea. The maximum value "100" is given to Singapore for this element. However, Singapore's advanced factor has the value (22.9) which represents 49.9% of that (45.9) of Korea's advanced factor. Thus, the competitive index of Singapore's domestic factor conditions is

$$100/2 + 49.9/2 = 75.0$$

Table 5-4 shows that for all four determinants of the diamond model Korea has higher competitive indices for domestic variables, but Singapore has higher competitive indices for international variables. This difference is clearly visualized in Figures 5-3 and 5-4. Korea's domestic diamond consisting of solid lines and its international diamond consisting of dotted lines are shown in Figure 5-3. Similarly, Singapore's domestic and international diamonds are shown in Figure 5-4. The international diamond is constructed by adding the international competitiveness index to the domestic competitiveness index for each variable. In Figure 5-3, for example, domestic competitiveness index (D1d) for factor conditions is "100.0" By adding the international competitiveness index "4.3" to this value, the coordinate "D1i" represents "104.3". Therefore, the international diamond represents domestic plus international determinants. It can thus be said that the difference between

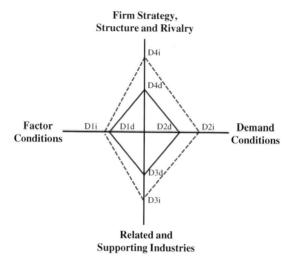

Fig. 5-3   The Competitiveness of Korea

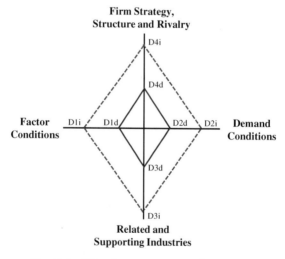

Fig. 5-4   The Competitiveness of Singapore

the international diamond and domestic diamond is the international or multinational determinants of the nation's competitiveness.

Three interesting points can be made when comparing the domestic and international diamonds in Figures 5-3 and 5-4. First, Korea has a "larger" domestic diamond than Singapore, but Singapore has a "larger" international diamond than Korea.[6] This result implies that Korea is more competitive than Singapore when considering only domestic determinants, but less competitive than Singapore when considering both domestic and international determinants. As shown in Table 5-1, Korea is less competitive than Singapore according to several parameters. This leads to the conclusion that both domestic and international determinants are important to the competitiveness of Korea and Singapore.

Second, compared with that of Singapore, Korea's international diamond appears to be almost identical to its domestic one with respect to factor conditions. This implies that Korea is relatively weak as regards the international portion of the factor conditions. Singapore has actively pursued outbound FDI to compensate for a shortage of domestic labor and inbound FDI to obtain access to foreign capital and technology. However, Korea has not been as active as Singapore in these multinational activities. In contrast, Porter's work reflects a lack of knowledge of the Korean economy and leads to an incorrect suggestion. Porter (1990) claims that Korea's competitive advantage has thus far rested largely on basic factor conditions (p. 477), but that its future depends upon (domestic) demand conditions, related and supporting industries, and vigorous (domestic) rivalry (p. 479).[7] These variables represent three corners of the diamond, yet neglect one — factor conditions. As can be seen in Figure 5-3, the future of the Korean economy depends more on factor conditions than anything else.

Third, the government factor is very important in influencing a nation's competitive advantage. Governments frequently pursue interventionist trade and industrial strategies (Rugman and Verbeke, 1990). For example, the thirty years of Korea's economic growth have been marked by a number of different phases and in each period government intervention in economic and business affairs has been high (Moon, 1992). Facing a new global environment, the Korean government is now taking various steps to enhance Korea's competitiveness. For related and supporting industries, the government brings together research institutions, universities, and private companies in a

---

[6] Figure 5-3 and Figure 5-4 are drawn on the same scale.

[7] In 1994, one of Korea's leading business newspapers, *Mae-il-kyung-jai* (Daily Economic Review), invited several world-famous scholars to express their opinions on Korea's competitiveness. Porter received special attention, thanks to his diamond model. Porter (1994) suggested a similar policy to this, but neglected a possible solution to the problem of factor conditions through multinational activities.

Table 5-5 Information Sources of the Variables

Dependent Variables		
Productivity		
GNP per capita ($), 1993	WB, p. 163	
GDP per energy kg (oil equil) ($), 1993	WB, p. 171	
Managers' Perception		
Strong economy as a whole (% agreed), 1992	IMD, p. 1.26	
Strong manufacturing base (% agreed), 1992	IMD, p. 1.28	

Independent Variables	Domestic	International
Factor Conditions		
Basic	USDC, p. 865	IMF, p. 344, 508
Advanced	UNDP, p. 138	IMF, p. 344, 508
Demand Conditions		
Size	WB, p. 163	IMF, p. 344, 508
Sophistication	UNDP, p. 129	EPL, p. 1789, 2697
Related & Supporting Industries		
Transportation	WB, p. 225	IMD, p. 5.20
Communication	UNDP, p. 160	IMD, p. 5.27
Firm Strategy, Structure & Rivalry		
Rivalry	IMD, p. 2.39	IMD, p. 2.37

Sources:
International Monetary Fund (IMF) (1996). *International Financial Statistics*, February;
The World Bank (WB) (1995). *World Development Report 1995*;
IMD (1992). *The World Competitiveness Report*, Lausanne, Switzerland;
U.S. Department of Commerce (USDC) (1995). *Statistical Abstract of the U.S. 1995*;
United Nations Development Programme (UNDP) (1994). *Human Development Report 1994*;
Europa Publications Limited (EPL) (1995). *The Europa World Year Book 1995*, Europa Publications Limited.

joint effort to create science parks.[8] As regards demand conditions, Korea pushes global demand because of the relatively small size of its domestic market. The government also emphasizes globalization in the area of firm strategy, structure, and rivalry. Korea has unveiled plans to privatize or merge many state-funded companies. Recent efforts to alleviate entry barriers against foreign companies are also examples of public effort to achieve a globalization of industry structure and rivalry.

Yet as shown in Figure 5-3, the most important determinant of Korea's global competitiveness lies in factor conditions. Korean firms are no longer cost competitive in overseas markets because the Southeast Asian countries have cheaper sources of labor. On the other hand, Korean firms' technology does not match that of developed countries such as the U.S. and Japan. The implications for Korea's competitiveness are now clear: to find cheap labor and to increase technological capability. In order to obtain access to cheap labor, Korean firms need to invest in Southeast Asian countries and China. For technological improvement, Korean firms need to invest more in R&D and specialize in the most competitive sectors. However, this is a risky and very long-term strategy. The most practical means of compensating for the country's lack of advanced technology is to import foreign technology. To conclude, both inbound and outbound FDI are important to maintain Korea's competitive edge regarding factor conditions. At the current stage of economic development, the crucial role of the Korean government is to relax various regulations and to provide a favorable environment for both inbound and outbound FDI.

CONCLUSION

The concept of globalization has become both a buzzword and a crucial long-term goal in many small economies such as Korea and Singapore. Globalization represents both a challenge and an opportunity for these countries. However, this concept is extremely complex and it is not clear how to increase global competitiveness. Porter's diamond model is a good starting paradigm for analyzing important determinants of global competitiveness. However, Porter's

---

[8] For example, Daedok Science Town includes 13 government institutes, three private research institutes, and three universities on a 53-sq. km area. The primary goal of the science parks is to develop their own indigenous technologies. These parks are also playing major roles in the transfer of technology from the West. For a comparison of science parks of NICs, see Gwynne (1993).

original diamond model is incomplete, mainly because he did not adequately incorporate multinational activities.

A new model, the generalized double diamond model, developed and extended in this chapter, has led to three important extensions to Porter's original framework. First, the new model explicitly incorporates multinational activities, whereas Porter's original diamond considers mainly the impact of traditional home-based activities. Second, the new approach easily allows us to operationalize the competitiveness paradigm, whereas Porter's original approach is hard to operationalize. In the generalized double diamond approach, a comparison of the sizes and shapes of the domestic and international diamonds reveals major strategic differences. Third, the new model includes government, not as an exogenous parameter, but as an important variable which influences the four determinants of the diamond model.

All of these three extensions are important when analyzing the global competitiveness of Korea and Singapore. First, as discussed above, both outbound and inbound FDI, i.e., multinational activities, are crucial to a nation's competitiveness. Second, by comparing the sizes and shapes of both domestic and international diamonds of Korea and Singapore, the most important variable requiring policy intervention can be identified (i.e., factor conditions in the case of Korea). Third, the government factor in small economies such as Korea and Singapore is more important than anything else in affecting the other variables. This does not mean that the government should intervene in every aspect of business affairs, but that the government should be very careful when intervening, considering its potentially large impact on competitiveness.

REFERENCES

Cartwright, W. R. (1993). Multiple linked diamonds: New Zealand's experience. *Management International Review*, **33**(2): 55–70.

Cho, D. S., Choi, J. and Yi, Y. (1994). International advertising strategies by NIC multinationals: The case of a Korean firm. *International Journal of Advertising*, **13**: 77–92.

Chungang Daily Newspaper (1995). Wages of Korea and other major countries, February.

Crocombe, F. T., Enright, M. J. and Porter, M. E. (1991). *Upgrading New Zealand's Competitive Advantage*, Auckland: Oxford University Press.

Dunning, J. H. (1992). The competitive advantage of countries and the activities of transnational corporations. *Transnational Corporations*, **1**(1): 135–168.

Europa Publications Limited (1995). *The Europa World Year Book 1995*, London, England: Europa Publications Limited.

Grant, R. M. (1991). Porter's competitive advantage of nations: An assessment. *Strategic Management Journal*, **12**(7): 535–548.

Gwynne, P. (1993). Directing technology in Asia's dragons. *Research Technology Management*, **32**(2): 12–15.

IMD (1992). *The World Competitiveness Report*, Lausanne, Switzerland.

International Monetary Fund (1996). *International Financial Statistics*, February.

Moon, H. C. (1992). New challenges for Korean conglomerates, in Chen, T., Choi, Y. B and Lee, S. (eds.), *Economic and Political Reforms in Asia*, New York: St. John's University Press.

Moon, H. C. (1994). A revised framework of global strategy: Extending the coordination-configuration framework. *The International Executive*, **36**(5): 557–574.

Moon, H. C. and Roehl, T. W. (1993). An imbalance theory of foreign direct investment. *Multinational Business Review*, **1**(1): 56–65.

Moon, H. C. and Kim, J. Y. (2010). Comparing the competitiveness of Korea and Singapore after ten years of Asian economic crisis. *The Review of Business History*, **25**(1): 75–91.

Moon, H. C., Rugman, A. M. and Verbeke, A. (1995). The generalized double diamond approach to international competitiveness, in Rugman, A., den Broeck, J. V. and Verbeke, A. (eds.), *Research in Global Strategic Management, Vol. 5: Beyond The Diamond*, Greenwich, CT: JAI Press, pp. 97–114.

Porter, M. E. (1986). Competition in global industries: A conceptual framework, in Porter, M. E. (ed.), *Competition in Global Industries*, Boston: Harvard Business School Press, pp. 15–60.

Porter, M. E. (1990). *The Competitive Advantage of Nations*, New York: Free Press.

Porter, M. E. (1994). Competitiveness of the Korean economy. *Mae-il-kyung-jai (Daily Economic Review)*.

Porter, M. E. and Armstrong, J. (1992). Canada at the crossroads: Dialogue (Response by Porter). *Business Quarterly*, **56**(4): 6–10.

Porter, M. E. and The Monitor Company (1991). *Canada at the Crossroads: The Reality of A New Competitive Environment*. Ottawa: Business Council on National Issues and Minister of Supply and Services of the Government of Canada.

Rugman, A. M. (1990). *Multinationals and Canada-United States Free Trade*, Columbia: University of South Carolina Press.

Rugman, A. M. (1991). Diamond in the rough. *Business Quarterly*, **55**(3): 61–64.

Rugman, A. M. (1992). Porter takes the wrong turn. *Business Quarterly*, **56**(3): 59–64.

Rugman, A. M. and D'Cruz, J. R. (1993). The double diamond model of international competitiveness: The Canadian experience. *Management International Review*, **33**(2): 17–39.

Rugman, A. M. and Verbeke, A. (1990). *Global Corporate Strategy and Trade Policy.* London, New York: Croom Helm, Routledge.

Ryan, R. (1990). A grand disunity. *National Review*, **42**(13): 46–47.

The Economist Intelligence Unit (1992). *South Korea 1992–93: Annual Survey of Political and Economic Background*, EIU Country Profile.

World Bank (1995). *World Development Report: Workers in An Integrating World*, Oxford: Oxford University Press.

United Nations Development Programme (1994). *Human Development Report 1994*, New York: Oxford University Press.

United States Department of Commerce (1995). *Statistical Abstract of The United States 1995.*

6

EXTENDED MODEL (2):
THE NINE-FACTOR MODEL

SUMMARY AND KEY POINTS

Cho (1994) argues that Porter's original model is limited in its application to developing countries such as Korea. He emphasizes different groups of human factors and different types of physical factors in explaining a nation's competitiveness. Human factors include workers, politicians and bureaucrats, entrepreneurs, and professionals. Physical factors include endowed resources, domestic demand, related and supporting industries, and other business environment. An external factor, chance, is added to these eight internal factors to make a new paradigm, the nine-factor model.

The differences between the nine-factor model and Porter's diamond model are in the distinction between physical and human determinants, and in the separation of chance events. The diamond model includes both natural resources and labor in factor conditions, but the nine-factor model places natural resources under endowed resources, while labor is included within the category of workers.

Source:
Cho, D. S. (1994). A dynamic approach to international competitiveness: The case of Korea. *Journal of Far Eastern Business*, **1**(1): 17–36.

Human factors mobilize the physical factors, and people combine and arrange the physical factors with the aim of obtaining international competitiveness.

The role of human variables is particularly important in explaining the development pattern of developing countries because physical factors are not sufficiently developed at this developing stage. It is thus the human factors, rather than physical factors, which can create competitive industries and related infrastructure to expedite the nation's economic growth. The nine-factor model is further developed by incorporating the international dimension of competitiveness, which will be discussed in the next chapter.

INTRODUCTION

Michael Porter's recent work helps explain the sources of international competitiveness possessed by the economies of advanced nations, but has a limited application when it comes to explaining the levels and dynamic changes of economies in less developed or developing countries. The experience of Korea's economic development in the past three decades reveals how groups of well-educated, motivated, and dedicated people have played a central role in not only shaping the nation's competitiveness but also moving the nation dynamically from a less developed stage to an advanced one. If we modify Porter's diamond model to take account of the Korean experience, we are left with a new paradigm of international competitiveness. It divides sources of international competitiveness into two broad categories: "physical" factors and "human" factors. By "physical" factors, we refer to endowed resources, the business environment, related and supporting industries, and domestic demand, which together determine the level of international competitiveness of a given nation at a given time. Human factors include workers, politicians and bureaucrats, entrepreneurs, and professional managers and engineers. By creating, motivating, and controlling the four physical elements, these human factors drive the national economy from one stage of international competitiveness to the next. An external factor of pure chance is added to these eight internal factors to make the new paradigm a nine-factor model. As we shall see, this new framework can elucidate the sources of economic growth in less developed countries as well as those dynamic changes in international competitiveness that are associated with economic growth. The relative importance of each of the eight physical and human factors changes as the national economy moves from a less developed stage to a developing stage, to a semi-developed stage, and, finally, to a fully developed stage.

When a nation's trade balance swings from surplus to deficit, its people begin to worry about an economic decline and associate it with a diminution in the nation's international competitiveness. Governments can point to uncontrollable or external factors such as a slowdown in the international economy or high exchange rates as the cause of trade deficits and weakened international competitiveness. Businessmen would take advantage of this occasion to demand tax cuts and the imposition of import barriers as corrective measures. However, trade balance and international competitiveness are not the same. There are nations which suffer from weak international competitiveness, whilst possessing balanced trade accounts or even, as a result of import controls, trade surpluses. Some nations have demonstrable international competitiveness, but reveal occasional trade deficits. Lastly, international competitiveness is not determined by external factors alone. Under the same global economic environment, some nations gain market share at the expense of others. In this chapter, the term "international competitiveness" is defined in a way that systematically explains the long-term resilience of a nation's economy. Next, a new paradigm is formulated, and it is composed of the nine factors which determine the international competitiveness of a nation as it moves from a less developed stage to a developing stage, to a semi-developed stage, and finally to a developed stage. Then, the model is applied to Korea and to the development of its four major industries at different stages of international competitiveness. The final part of this chapter looks at policies to improve international competitiveness.

THE THEORETICAL BACKGROUND TO INTERNATIONAL COMPETITIVENESS

A Definition of International Competitiveness

One misconception of international competitiveness is based on the notion that it depends on a plentiful supply of labor, capital, and natural resources at low prices (Porter, 1990a, p. 84–85). This economic theory mistakenly links a nation's international competitiveness to its factor endowments. Endowed resources are only a part of many determinant factors. There are countries with plentiful resources but a weak economy. In a world in which raw materials, capital, and even labor move across national borders, the possession of endowed resources alone does not determine international competitiveness. Another misconception is to measure a nation's international competitiveness by its share of world markets (Brown and Sheriff, 1978). While a useful indicator, it is often misleading because a nation's share of world markets can rise regardless of its international competitiveness. A nation may arbitrarily raise its market share by lowering export prices below production costs, sometimes through government subsidies, but its international competitiveness is not necessarily strengthened. As we have seen, trade balances have limited value in this debate (HMSO, 1985). Some nations register large temporary trade deficits, despite their maintaining competitiveness when they are confronted with political or international difficulties. A good illustration is the Federal Republic of Germany in the early 1990s which had to carry trade deficits while undergoing unification with East Germany. On the other hand, Middle East nations showed extravagant trade surpluses during the energy crises of the 1970s, but their industries generally lacked international competitiveness. Trading accounts are inappropriate indicators, at least in the short term, of industrial strength. One widespread misconception is to divide international competitiveness into two categories: price competitiveness, such as nominal wages, exchange rates and labor productivity; and non-price competitiveness, such as quality, marketing, service and market differentiation (Francis and Tharakan, 1989). In order to gauge price competitiveness, export price, production cost, and consumer or wholesale price indices are used. Rising prices are seen as weakening a nation's international competitiveness. In reality there are cases in which nations with strong international competitiveness can and do raise the price of their products. Quality status, durability, design, and consumer satisfaction are used to evaluate non-price competitiveness, but there are no empirical studies to prove their influence. Price and non-price factors are not the causes but the results of a nation's international competitiveness.

In summary, traditional views cover only a part of many factors determining the level of international competitiveness, or mistake results for causes (Baker and Hart, 1989, p. 5–8). A new definition of international competitiveness is required and it should include all of the major factors in a holistic, systematic manner if the causal relations between the factors and the resulting level of a nation's competitiveness are to be discovered. The international competitiveness of a national industry can be defined by its having a superior market position through high profits and constant growth when compared to competitors. A country cannot possess international competitiveness simply because it has one or two successful industries. Sri Lanka has a well-developed trade in tea growing and processing, and Iceland is the center of a strong fish processing industry, yet few would argue that these two nations have international competitiveness. A nation needs to have a multitude of industries with strong competitiveness. Nor can a nation be regarded as internationally competitive if her industries are strong because of some external factors. The U.S., in the 1945–1970 period, enjoyed an uncontested position in most of the industries which were reliant upon high levels of technology and vast domestic markets. A nation needs the sources of competitiveness which can be applied to a number of industries. A nation, then, is internationally competitive when it has many industries with competitive advantage based on common domestic sources of competitiveness.

Existing Studies on Determinants of International Competitiveness

Studies on determinants of international competitiveness are mostly predicated on theories of international trade which focus on the comparative cost of production, natural resources, and technologies (Leontief, 1956). Since each nation has different comparative advantages, scholars have not succeeded in finding a general theory that can explain the economic fortune of countries with a small number of generic, universally applicable factors. In the early 1960s, economists began to recognize how a nation's international competitiveness could be affected not only by its trade, but also by overseas direct investment undertaken by multinational enterprises. Theories of FDI subsequently proliferated. Concepts of monopolistic advantages have identified ownership-specific advantages such as technology, marketing know-how, management skills, financial resources, and scale economies as the sources of competitiveness uniquely possessed by multinationals (Kindleberger, 1969, p. 13). On the other hand, industrial organization theory has demonstrated market imperfections or failures to be the main spur of FDI and the origins of the advantages exercised by multinational enterprises (Buckley and Casson, 1976, p. 33–65). By concentrating on a particular type of business organization, both approaches failed to explain the sources of national competitive advantage in a comprehensive and systematic manner. Dunning integrated these independently evolved theories in order to explain comprehensively all the advantages possessed of multinational enterprises. He outlined the changing investment patterns which a nation may undergo as it moves from one stage of development to the next. But he does not deal with the importance of international competitiveness in relation to stages of national development (Dunning, 1981, p. 80–81, 109–137; 1988, p. 140–165). Buckley and

Casson have discussed the evolving role of specific factors which determine the success of multinational enterprises operating in foreign markets, but their discussion is limited to issues of geography and entrepreneurial culture (Buckley and Casson, 1991, p. 27–55). In answer to these shortcomings new more systematic studies on international competitiveness have been produced by Kogut, Goldsmith and Clutterbuck and Yamazawa. They have presented the determinants of international competitiveness at the level of individual companies, but they do not show how these develop into the macro-level advantages of a nation or industry (Kogut, 1985, p. 15–28; Goldsmith and Clutterbuck, 1984; Yamazawa, 1970, p. 61–90).

The link was first demonstrated by Porter. He pointed out that classical trade theories based on comparative advantage did not satisfactorily explain the trade patterns of resource-poor countries like Japan. Then he presented his model of international competitiveness, based on the "diamond" (Porter, 1990b, p. 69–130). The model is composed of four determinants: factor conditions; firm strategy, structure, and rivalry; related and supporting industries and demand conditions. Besides these four, Porter cites chance and government as additional factors. In essence, this model shows how an industry can maintain international competitiveness when these determinants are in place, but it must be said that Porter's theory primarily explains the economies of advanced nations. His model needs to be modified for it to be applied to developing or less developed nations, because the countries have to create international competitiveness without necessarily having any of the four determinants in place. Porter's analysis cannot explain the success which Korea and Taiwan have achieved in the second half of the twentieth century. A new model will serve two objectives: one is better to evaluate which elements have contributed to the international competitiveness of less developed economies; the other is to show how a nation can improve its national advantage.

A NEW MODEL OF INTERNATIONAL COMPETITIVENESS FOR LESS DEVELOPED COUNTRIES

The Nine-Factor Model

In order to assess Korea's international competitiveness, two major considerations should be addressed. Government and businesses had to introduce capital and technology from foreign countries or create resources and other factors influencing economic growth from their initial stages. The key engine of Korea's economic growth has been an abundant and diverse group of people with generally high levels of education, motivation, and dedication to work. Korea's population can be grouped into four: workers; politicians and bureaucrats who formulate and implement economic plans; entrepreneurs who make investment decisions despite high risks; and professional managers who are in charge of operations and engineers who implement new technologies. To appreciate their contribution to Korea's development, a nine-factor model is required. There are four physical determinants of international competitiveness, namely endowed resources, the business environment, related and supporting industries, and domestic demand; there are also four human factors namely workers, politicians and bureaucrats, entrepreneurs, and professional managers and engineers. External chance events should be noted as the ninth factor (see Figure 6-1).

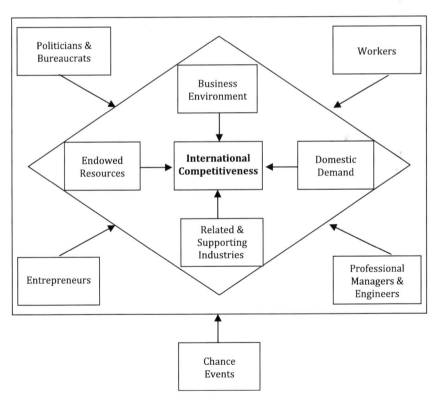

Fig. 6-1 A New Paradigm of International Competitiveness

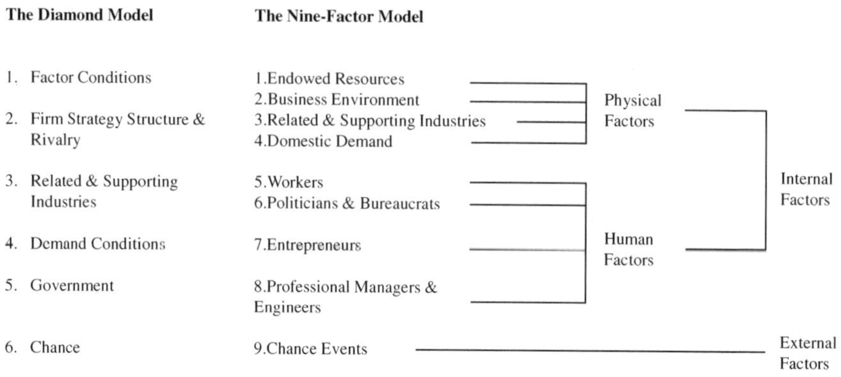

The Diamond Model	The Nine-Factor Model		
1. Factor Conditions	1.Endowed Resources 2.Business Environment 3.Related & Supporting Industries 4.Domestic Demand	Physical Factors	
2. Firm Strategy Structure & Rivalry			Internal Factors
3. Related & Supporting Industries	5.Workers 6.Politicians & Bureaucrats		
4. Demand Conditions	7.Entrepreneurs	Human Factors	
5. Government	8.Professional Managers & Engineers		
6. Chance	9.Chance Events		External Factors

Fig. 6-2 Comparison of the Diamond and the Nine-Factor Model

The difference between the new model and Porter's diamond model is to be found as much in the division of factors as in the addition of new ones (see Figure 6-2). The diamond included both natural resources and labor in factor conditions, but the nine-factor model places natural resources under endowed resources, while labor is included within the category of workers. A detailed investigation of the nine factors of international competitiveness is needed.

Physical factors

(a) *Endowed resources* can be divided into mineral, agricultural, forestry, fishery, and environmental resources. Mineral resources are depletable, and energy resources such as coal, oil, and natural gas can be distinguished from non-energy resources such as iron ore, gold, and silver. Agriculture, forests, and fish stocks are renewable and environmental factors are composed of land, weather, water and other natural advantages (Shin, 1988, p. 9–11). All these resources can form inputs into economic activities, and they may add to a nation's international competitiveness.

(b) *Business environment.* The business environment should be viewed at the levels of nation, industry, and company. At the national level, there are visible and invisible components: the first includes roads, ports, telecommunications, and other forms of infrastructure; the second is concerned with the people's acceptance of competitive values and market mechanisms and the commitment of producers, merchants, consumers, and other participants in the economy to the legitimacy and obligations of commercial deals and credit. At an industrial level, the business environment is determined by the number and size of competitors, the type, and height of entry barriers; the degree of product differentiation; and other factors shaping the nature of rivalry and economic activity. At a company level, the strategy and organization of businesses and the attitudes and behavior of individuals and groups within enterprises are major considerations (Porter, 1990b, p. 107–124).

(c) *Related and supporting industries.* Related industries can be divided into vertically related industries and horizontally related industries. While one encompasses the influence of upstream and downstream stages of production, the other is concerned with industries that use the same technology, raw materials, distribution networks or marketing activities. Supporting industries include financial, insurance, information, transportation, and other service sectors (Porter, 1990b, p. 100–106).

(d) *Domestic demand* includes both quantitative and qualitative aspects. The size of domestic market determines minimum economies of scale for indigenous companies, as well as the stability of demand. The home economy acts as a test market for products that can be shipped overseas, and the risks of international commerce are reduced. Greater benefits can be gained from the qualitative dimensions. The expectations of consumers can stimulate competitiveness, and, in a nation where consumers have sophisticated and strict standards on product quality in addition to a high degree of consumerism, its businesses can accrue international advantages in the course of satisfying demanding home conditions (Porter, 1990b, p. 86–100).

Human factors

It is the human factors which mobilize the above-mentioned physical factors. People combine and arrange the physical factors with the aim of obtaining international competitiveness. Workers, politicians and bureaucrats, entrepreneurs, and professional managers and engineers have to be considered.

(a) *Workers.* The most easily identified measure of the worth of workers is the wage level, yet it is only one of the many attributes which directly or indirectly affect labor productivity. Others are levels of education, a sense of belonging to an organization, acceptance of authority, a work ethic, and the size of the labor pool. The traditional explanation of Korea's comparative advantage in cheap labor from the 1960s to the mid-1980s overlooked more fundamental factors such as high education levels, discipline, and the work ethic.

(b) *Politicians and bureaucrats.* Politicians seek to win and maintain power, and economic development is one of the many routes they can choose for achieving their primary objective. Nations governed by politicians that are committed to growth and success can assist in the creation of international competitiveness. China in the late 1980s and 1990s is a manifestation of how a national economy can benefit from leaders that appreciate the value of economic development, even under a Communistic system. In general, an efficient and non-corrupt bureaucracy can assist the application of state policy, and can make a substantial addition to international competitiveness.

(c) *Entrepreneurs.* As entrepreneurs venture on new businesses despite a high degree of risk, they are distinct from ordinary businessmen. They are essential to any nation at an early stage of economic development. Over time, a country's competitiveness is strengthened by their efforts to diminish risks and maximize returns.

(d) *Professional managers and engineers.* When international competition necessitates fierce price cutting and a search for enhanced service, risk-taking attitude alone will not bring deeply entrenched competitiveness. The dedicated work of professional managers in reducing production costs by even small fractions and the cutting of delivery times determines the future of nations as well as individual businesses.

The external factor: Chance events

Chance events are unpredictable changes in the environment, often unassociated with the international business system. They include unexpected breakthroughs in new technologies or products, oil shocks, sharp fluctuations in world capital markets or foreign exchange rates, changes in the policies of foreign governments, movements in international demands, and the outbreak of war. Physical and human factors have in many cases to be reconfigured if a nation is to maintain competitiveness, or take the opportunity to improve competitive advantage.

THE LIFE CYCLE OF NATIONAL COMPETITIVENESS

We can evaluate a nation's international competitiveness by judging the influence which the nine factors may have, and we can similarly begin to understand its development. A nation's economic status is determined by its international competitiveness and the nine factors have varying weights as a

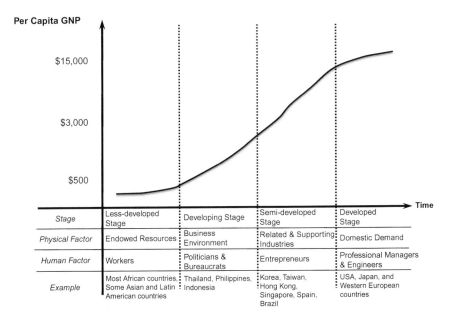

Fig. 6-3 Life Cycle of National Competitiveness

country moves from a less-developed stage to a developing stage, then to a semi-developed stage, and finally to a developed stage.[1] A model framework of the life cycle of national competitiveness is shown in Figure 6-3, and a review of the characteristics prevalent in each stage and the major sources of competitive advantage at each juncture will be valuable.

Less Developed Stage

Countries prior to economic development have only limited endowed and labor resources, and they tend to lack the management know-how and technology which can put these assets into production processes that can generate value-added. It follows that they lack international competitiveness, and nations with a per capita income of less than $500 in 1990 are to be found in this category, a number of African and Southwest Asian nations

---

[1]The per capita GNP standard measuring each nation's economic status differs from one scholar to another. In this research, the standards dividing less-developed nations, developing nations, semi-developed nations and developed nations were set at $500, $3,000, and $15,000. Please refer to Keegan (1989, pp. 86–89).

being exemplary. Although most of the Central and South American nations have per capita incomes of more than $500, a few do belong to this group. These nations cannot implement stable economic policies because of frequent changes of power and other political uncertainties, although they do possess considerable natural resources and quite sizable labor pools.

Developing Stage

The developing stage, when a nation is at the early period of development, sees the inertia of a less developed economy being overcome by politicians beginning to fulfill political ambition through policies of growth and construction. In the process, they mobilize bureaucrats to carry out industrial policies, and enhance the business environment through the creation of financial markets and social infrastructures. Sometimes, endowed resources and available workforces are channeled into government-run enterprises, and a nation has its first opportunity to strengthen international competitiveness. Businesses tend to introduce production technology from foreign countries and they also depend on foreign markets for the sale of products. As a result, a nation's international competitiveness in this stage largely rests on changes in the international business environment, including foreign exchange rates and the prices of raw materials. Because businesses are still establishing organizational capacity and facing strong competition in world markets, the government frequently allocates scarce resources to one or two companies in each industry. Most industries at this stage of development are monopolized by a single or a few enterprises.

The process of founding international competitiveness through collaboration between politicians and bureaucrats can be seen in the case of Korea during the 1960s. President Park Chung-Hee, who assumed power as a result of a military coup, had to cope with the abrupt suspension of economic assistance from the U.S., which disapproved of his military regime. Park believed that to keep power he had to reduce huge trade deficits. He formulated and implemented a series of Five-Year Economic Development Plans from 1962 onward, designed to invest resources in selected strategic industries, and, in order to improve the business environment, highways, ports, subways, and other essential social infrastructure were built. Companies were encouraged to develop manufacturing facilities in textiles, footwear, steel, electronics, machinery, and automobiles, and received financial support and payment guarantees from the government. Nations at the developing stage show a per capita income of between $500 and $3,000, and include Korea and Taiwan in the 1960s through to the early 1970s, and Thailand, Malaysia, Indonesia, and the Philippines in the 1990s.

Semi-Developed Stage

As economic development passes the early period, a capitalist system may allow entrepreneurs to make bold investments despite associated high risks, and they begin to reduce their dependence on the government. In other words, monopoly rents do not accrue only to state-supported enterprises, and the business environment has become favorable to the process of active investment. Entrepreneurs are prepared to invest and seek to achieve economies of scale. If necessary, they borrow resources from overseas. While nations with abundant natural resources will take advantage of them, those at a semi-developed stage may secure essential in-puts at low prices through long-term contracts or direct resource development. As a result of these efforts, the latter's international competitiveness can become stronger than that of the former. The human factors which form the main source of international competitiveness include risk-taking entrepreneurs. An oligopolistic pattern of competition appears amongst businesses at the semi-developed stage, and companies tend to diversify into new areas from their initial, successful base, resulting in the further development of related and supporting industries. The international competitiveness of industries is enhanced by the strengthening of these linkages. Nations at this stage have a per capita income in the range of $3,000 to $15,000, and are evidenced by Japan in the 1960s and the so-called newly industrializing economies of Korea, Taiwan, Hong Kong, and Singapore in the 1990s.

Developed Stage

Following the innovation of manufacturing processes, products and business organizations in the semi-developed stage, the connections among horizontally and vertically related and supporting industries are further enhanced. The goods and services of these industries can enter competitive international markets on equal terms with those from advanced countries. Manufacturing processes become more sophisticated, product quality is improved, and a balanced development between upstream and downstream areas is achieved. The role of entrepreneurs becomes less important, as professional managers and engineers develop their businesses and increase efficiency. Sectors that are horizontally and vertically related to initially successful industries become internationally competitive, and government controls such as the artificial allocation of funds, market protection, and the payment of subsidies, are gradually phased out. The wage pressures from workers do intensify, as does competition from innovations in marketing, product quality, and sales service. As income levels rise, consumers make more demands for better quality and services. Per capita incomes of more than $15,000 are apparent in developed nations, which comprise the U.S., Japan, Germany, and other West European countries.

THE LIFE CYCLE OF INDUSTRIAL COMPETITIVENESS

As can be seen from the above analysis, international competitiveness is determined by four physical factors — endowed resources, the business environment, related and supporting industries and domestic demand and these are created, mobilized and controlled by the four human factors — workers, politicians and bureaucrats, entrepreneurs, and professional managers and engineers. These eight factors play different roles in the different stages of a nation's economic development. Each nation's economy also consists of primary, secondary and tertiary sectors, and the balance of activity between them differs between different stages of development. The stage and speed of each industry's development differs according to the nation's overall business environment. In order to appreciate each nation's international competitiveness more fully, an analysis of industries is needed to supplement the macroperspective. An industry's international competitiveness is strengthened or weakened according to changes in the business environment and the specific responses of human actors. A static approach using the nine factors requires a dynamic analysis based on the life cycle of industrial competitiveness. Industries move from an early stage to a growth stage, to a maturing stage, and finally to a declining stage (Smallwood, 1984, p. 84–192). The physical and human factors of international competitiveness have varying influences as each industry passes through different phases.

Early Stage

In general, an industry is at an early stage if its sources of competition are limited to endowed resources, such as abundant mineral resources and ample and fertile land. Despite their availability, some countries cannot utilize their given attributes due to insufficient know-how and technology. An industry gains growth potential by making lower priced products and using unprocessed resources and labor.

Growth Stage

To transfer from the early stage to a growth stage, industries need politicians and bureaucrats who are willing to support businesses systematically. Politicians and bureaucrats create a business environment favorable to active investment, select certain industries for advancement, provide administrative and financial support, tax credits, insurance, and information services, and payment guarantees to chosen entrepreneurs. They sometimes protect particular industries until enough demand becomes captive or until access to foreign technology has been won. The market is organized on monopolistic or oligopolistic lines.

Maturing Stage

Innovation occurs in manufacturing processes, product development, and business organization. Connections among horizontally and vertically related industries become stronger at this stage, and businesses which pursue a balanced development in both downstream and upstream areas remain competitive in international markets. Entrepreneurs take a leading role in a system reliant on active investment. This stage comes at a time when an industry's international competitiveness is extended to horizontally and vertically related industries, and government measures, such as the artificial allocation of investment capital, market protection, and the payment of subsidies, are phased out. Industries embrace full competition from both domestic and foreign firms and the ensuing competition stimulates product development and quality improvements.

Declining Stage

An industry that passes through the maturing stage and fails to maintain innovation naturally enters a declining stage. Markets are saturated at this point, and consumers' expectations for product quality are high. Production costs rise if businesses try to meet sophisticated consumer demands, resulting in a fast decline in their international competitiveness. Industries can correct these problems if professional managers and engineers cooperate to achieve organizational and technological innovations.[2]

---

[2]Japanese shipbuilding industry provides an example. Japanese shipbuilding industry fell into a declining stage in the early 1980s due in the main to the cost leadership possessed by developing countries such as Korea and Brazil. Since the mid-1980s, however, Japan has drastically changed the nature of the industry by introducing robotization into manufacturing processes, thereby recovering their cost competitiveness.

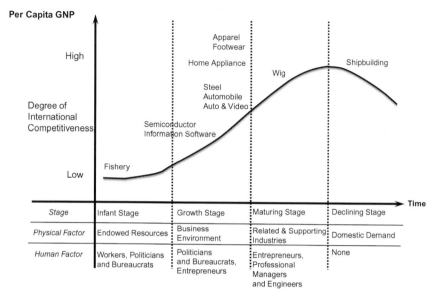

Fig. 6-4   Life Cycle of Industrial Competitiveness

CASE STUDIES: KOREA'S MAJOR INDUSTRIES

Figure 6-4 illustrates the above-mentioned life cycle of industrial competitiveness as applied to Korean industries which have had, presently possess, or are expected to achieve international competitiveness. The four cases studied were made to represent each stage of the industry life cycle: semiconductors belong to the early stage; automobiles to the growth stage, steel to a maturing stage, and apparel to a declining stage.

The Semiconductor Industry

Korea's semiconductor industry began in 1965 with the establishment of a joint venture called Komy Semiconductor. The string of factories established by U.S. or Japanese firms to assemble simple transistors performed simple assembly processes requiring little technological input (Korea Electronic Industries Promotion Institute, 1989, p. 9). The only source of international competitiveness at this early phase was various labor attributes such as low wages, work discipline, and an abundant supply of skilled manpower. Many workers had been previously employed and trained by companies in the apparel and home electronics industries, and they quickly adapted to semiconductors. Various tax incentive schemes and direct financial support from government attracted foreign investment in this sector. In the growth period since 1978, Korea's semiconductor industry has been assisted by a variety of advantages: basic technologies were made available through joint ventures with foreign companies; Korean engineers, educated and trained in the U.S. and other advanced countries, returned; the government designated the industry to be strategically important, and provided companies with incentives for expansion and for research and development. Byung-Cheol Lee of the Samsung Group initiated a major investment in the industry at a time when nobody was sure of its success; and the spirit of rivalry amongst Samsung, Hyundai, and Goldstar prompted additional developments in production and technology. The temporary shortage of electronic parts during the energy crisis of 1979 and the opportunities opened by the U.S.–Japan Semiconductor Agreement in the U.S. market benefited Korean semiconductor makers.

The Automobile Industry

Korea's automobile industry was founded in 1962 with a complete knockdown or kit mode of production with parts supplied by Honda and Toyota, and it reached a semi-knock-down stage in 1967. Soon, General Motors moved into Korea with a local assembly plant to tap the growing Korean market. Major sources of international competitiveness during this early stage were the skilled labor force, geographic proximity to the Japanese companies which Korean firms were emulating, and industrial policies banning the importation of assembled cars and providing indigenous exporters with tax incentives. In essence, Korea's automobile industry gained its growth potential through the correct combination of foreign capital and technologies, joint international ventures, and government industrial policy. In 1975, a new company entered the industry. It was the Hyundai Motor Company, which chose a strategy very different from the existing manufacturers. Instead of depending on the foreign capital and technology being offered through a joint venture proposed by Ford, Chairman Ju-Young Chung of the Hyundai Group decided that the company should construct its own plant with the money earned from construction and shipbuilding. It was a bold attempt with high risks, but in return it provided the company with the invaluable asset of independence and autonomy at a point when it was beginning to penetrate overseas markets. Unlike Mazda and Ford-affiliated Kia or GM-affiliated Daewoo, Hyundai could move into and export to any part of the world. In the 1980s, Hyundai made inroads into the American and European markets and firmly established itself as one of the major automobile makers of the world.

Major sources of competitive advantage in the growth stage since the mid-1970s came from Chung's aggressive investment in production facilities and overseas marketing, the integration of subcontractors into the Hyundai family business and the development of indigenous technologies and original models. Although the government in 1980 disrupted the automobile industry by unsuccessfully mandating a merger between Hyundai and Daewoo and the closing of Kia, it later provided generous assistance in research and development and continued to protect the domestic market from an invasion of Japanese models. Other major factors underpinning expansion included the concurrent development of related industries such as steel, electricals, electronics, and machinery, as well as a growth in aggregate domestic demand (KIET, 1987).

The Steel Industry

The history of Korea's steel industry has been the history of Pohang Iron and Steel Co. (POSCO). The industry's foundations are to be found before the First Five-Year Economic Development Plan in 1962, but it was not until the first phase of steel mill construction was completed in Ulsan in 1973 that the industry was firmly established. From that point, POSCO moved rapidly through the early stage. The industry was developed through an abundant labor force possessing skills and work discipline, foreign capital, the transfer of technologies from Western European countries, and government assistance as exemplified most notably by the Steel Industry Promotion Law. The increase in steel demand was induced by the series of economic development plans, and the then President, Park Chung-Hee, was convinced that the industry was fundamental to a number of related industries like automobiles, shipbuilding, electrics and electronics, and machinery. Chairman T.J. Park of POSCO was another important influence in his company's and industry's success.

The growth stage began after the second phase of construction at the Ulsan steel mill in 1978, when advanced steel-making countries were reducing their production capacities and modernizing facilities. Major sources of international competitiveness during this stage were state industrial policies, the rise in domestic demand, and relative cost increases in U.S. and Japanese firms. Most importantly, it was Chairman Park's leadership that drove POSCO's continued expansion, including the second steel plant at Kwangyang Bay, and he was determined to create a globally renowned company committed to product quality and managerial excellence. The maturing stage started in 1988 when major competitors in Japan, the U.S., and Europe had completed their rationalization programs and concentrated on high value-added steel products. Korea sustained its international competitiveness in basic steel products, but its position in special steel categories was weakened. In response, POSCO increased efficiency and developed more expensive goods. Diversification strategies into telecommunications and other related and non-related industries were led by professional managers of POSCO in an attempt to broaden the company's commercial base.

The Apparel Industry

The apparel industry was one of Korea's earliest successful industries, and, in its early stage in the 1950s, major sources of competitiveness were found in a plentiful, cheap, and dexterous labor force, post-war reconstruction projects by the government, state support for foreign loans, and technology imports, and the knowledge already possessed in long-established firms. As the industry entered its growth stage in the 1960s, sources of advantage shifted to the high education levels of workers and their ability to adapt to new technologies, export-driven industrial policies, financial and tax benefits through the Textile Industry Promotion Law, investment and construction by entrepreneurs, and the growth in original engineering manufacture-based exports. Apparel makers transformed themselves into general trading companies such as Sunkyong, Hyosung, and Hanil,[3] and they assisted the penetration of foreign markets. A developing petrochemical industry then supplied high-quality artificial materials at competitive prices.

In the maturing stage of the 1980s, the U.S. enforced quotas on apparel imports, and the Korean government shifted priorities from light goods industries to heavy machinery, chemicals, and electronics. Wage levels increased in the course of Korea's rapid economic growth. The apparel industry had to face full and open competition, and mergers and acquisitions occurred. Independently or in partnership with general trading companies, manufacturers moved their plants to East Asian countries and the Caribbean islands, where production costs were lower and barriers to the U.S. market could be avoided. Marketing subsidiaries were established overseas to facilitate and diversify export markets, and managerial policies have sustained the industry's competitiveness in the 1990s. Yet there are three areas of weakness:

---

[3] Hanil Synthetic Fiber Co. Ltd. lost the title of general trading company in 1981.

most sophisticated textile machines have to be imported; many closely related industries such as dyeing and fashion design are not internationally competitive; and, as a consequence, technologies and know-how in the manufacturing of top-quality apparel are lacking. Unless these deficiencies are remedied, the apparel industry will enter the declining stage.

CONCLUSION
A Comparison of Four Industries

If we compare the historical evolution of four industries, it is possible to identify the fact that major sources of competitiveness were identical at each stage of the industrial life cycle regardless of industry type. Major sources of advantage in the early stage of all four industries were the workers and politicians and bureaucrats. In the semiconductor industry, it was the labor content of production that persuaded foreign investors to establish a whole industry. In automobiles, it was the skilled workers and state industrial policies that attracted overseas interest and, in the steel industry, it was employee skills and disciplines and the commitment of the political leader. In apparel, an abundant supply of cheap and dexterous labor and the government's reconstruction objectives were determinant. The state remains a major source of competitiveness in the growth stage, but entrepreneurs become more influential than workers. In the semiconductor industry, the government designated it to be strategically important, providing incentives and subsidies for research and development, while the leadership of Chairman Lee of Samsung was critical. In automobiles, Japanese automobiles faced import barriers, and Chairman Chung established the Hyundai Motor as a major international producer. Government's policies and the management of Chairman Park turned POSCO into a global leader. In the apparel industry, the government provided financial assistance through an export promotion policy, while a number of entrepreneurs like Chairman Chey of Sunkyong created general trading companies.

As an industry moves to a maturing stage, the entrepreneurs continue to be crucial sources of strength, but government's influence is less determinant than that of professional managers and engineers. The professional managers of POSCO slowly but steadily enhanced efficiency and diversified the business, while engineers led the development of high value-added products. In apparels, professional managers also brought about diversification in export markets, invested abroad, and penetrated local markets.

Implications for the Korean Economy

The Korean economy possesses international competitiveness because it has a number of industries in the growth and maturing stages and common sources of advantage. In the life cycle of national competitiveness, it can be placed in the semi-developed stage category (see Figure 6-3), moving toward a developed stage. Nevertheless, Korea has been experiencing a major crisis in recent years, because the real wage level has more than doubled in just four years, the trade balance has evolved into a big deficit since 1989, and the rate of economic growth has slowed from a 10 percent level to less than 6 percent in 1992. Koreans are very concerned about their economy deterioration before it reaches a par with advanced nations. What is the model telling us about Korea and its ability to reach a developed phase?

Workers and politicians and bureaucrats — the main forces of economic growth until now — should enable entrepreneurs and professional managers and engineers to take a lead. As the sources of economic growth moved from workers to government, and from government to entrepreneurs, Korea has been transformed from a less developed country into a developing country and then into a semi-developed country. In becoming a developed country, wages will inevitably be raised until they meet the marginal cost of capital needed to automate production processes, and, as democracy develops, government cannot so definitively promote certain industries at the expense of others. Korean companies cannot compete with counterparts from advanced nations by venturing into risky investments, because increased competition has lowered industry-wide marginal profits and major losses are more likely. So, if Korea is to become an advanced nation, professional managers and engineers must have a prominent role, yet workers too will have to cooperate with efforts to improve productivity. The government needs to stabilize the business environment so that planning can be conducted with greater certainty, and entrepreneurs and powerful family-business groups must bestow responsibilities and authority on corporate managers.

Implications for Other Nations

This analysis has indicated the roles which workers, politicians and technocrats, entrepreneurs, and professional managers and engineers must perform if international competitiveness is to be strengthened. Industries at an early stage of development need to invest in endowed resources; those at a growth stage must improve the business environment; those at a maturing stage must build synergy with related and supporting industries. Governments should determine their policies towards different industries based on the proper understanding of their level of international competitiveness. A comprehensive industrial policy should reinforce mutually supportive links between industries, but governments should appreciate when its active engagement is desirable and when it becomes less beneficial. Entrepreneurs, professional managers and engineers should also appreciate their varying roles in an industry's life cycle, and the organization of firms and the setting of policy have to adjust.

Limitations of the Study and Suggestions for Future Research

This research attempted to analyze the international competitiveness of a nation from static and dynamic perspectives, by using the nine-factor and the life cycle models. Caution is needed in the generalization of the nine-factor model because it has only been to Korea and the industrial life cycle approach has been tested against four Korean industries. The findings in this study need to be validated by similar and parallel work on other nations and industries.

REFERENCES

Baker, M. J. and Hart, S. J. (1989). *Marketing and Competitive Success*, New York: Philip Allan, pp. 5–8.

Brown, C. and Sheriff, T. D. (1978). De-industrialization: A background paper, in Blackaby, F. (ed.), *De-industrialization*, London: Heinemann.

Buckley, P. J. and Casson, M. C. (1976). *The Future of the Multinational Enterprise*, London: MacMillan, pp. 33–65.

Buckley, P. J. and Casson, M. C. (1991). Multinational enterprises in less developed countries: Cultural and economic interactions, in Buckley, P. J. and Clegg, J. (eds.), *Multinational Enterprises in Less Developed Countries*, Chap. 2, London: MacMillan, pp. 27–55.

Dunning, J. H. (1981). *International Production and the Multinational Enterprise*, London: George Allen & Unwin.

Francis, A. and Tharakan, P. K. M. (eds.) (1989). *The Competitiveness of European Industry*, London and NY: Routledge, pp. 5–20.

Goldsmith, W. and Clutterbuck, D. (1984). *The Winning Streak: Britain's Top Companies Reveal Their Formulas for Success*, Weidenfeld & Nicolson.

HMSO (1985). *Report from the Select Committee of the House of Lords on Overseas Trade*, The Aldington Report.

Keegan, W. J. (1989). *Global Marketing Management*, 4th Edn., Englewood Cliffs, NJ: Prentice-Hall, pp. 86–89.

KIET (1987). Future picture of automobile industries, *Series of Future Industries*.

Kindleberger, C. P. (1969). *American Business Abroad*, New Haven: Yale University Press.

Kogut, B. (1985). Designing global strategies: Comparative and competitive value-added chains. *Sloan Management Review*, **Summer**: 15–28.

Korea Electronic Industries Promotion Institute (1989). Prospect for Long-term Development of Electronic Industries, p. 9.

Leontief, W. (1956). Factor proportions and structure of American trade: Further theoretical and empirical analysis. *Review of Economics and Statistics*, **38**(4): 386–407.

Porter, M. E. (1990a). The competitive advantage of nations. *Harvard Business Review*, **March–April**: 73–93.

Porter, M. E. (1990b). *The Competitive Advantage of Nations*, New York: Free Press.

Smallwood, J. E. (1984). The product life cycle: A key to strategic marketing planning, in Weitz, B. A. and Wensley, R. (eds.), *Strategic Marketing: Planning Implementation and Control*, Boston, MA: Kent Publishing Company, pp. 184–192.

Shin, U. S. (1988). *Resource Economics*, South Korea: Park-Young Sa, pp. 9–11.

Yamazawa, I. (1970). Intensity analysis of world trade flow. *Hitotsubashi Journal of Economics*, **10**(2): 61–90.

7

EXTENDED MODEL (3): DOUBLE-DIAMOND-BASED NINE-FACTOR MODEL

SUMMARY AND KEY POINTS

We have seen the generalized double diamond (GDD) model in Chapter 5, and the nine-factor (NF) model in Chapter 6 as extended models of Michael Porter's single diamond model in explaining national competitiveness. This chapter (Cho *et al.*, 2008) introduces an integrated framework of these two models, the "dual double diamond" (DDD) model, as a new approach to analyze country-specific advantages (CSAs) with various characteristics.

In addition, this chapter empirically tests the explanatory power of each of the four related models, namely, the single diamond model, the GDD model, the NF model, and the DDD model. The results show that the GDD and NF models have better explanatory power than the single diamond when assessing CSAs of countries with high international connectivity and high human-factor dependency,

Sources:
Cho, D. S., Moon, H. C. and Kim, M. Y. (2009). Does one size fit all? A dual double diamond approach to country-specific advantages. *Asian Business & Management*, 8(1): 83–102.

respectively, and that the DDD model is more comprehensive than the GDD and NF models in explaining CSAs of countries with heterogeneous attributes.

This chapter also discusses the implications of the DDD model for investments by multinational corporations (MNCs) in Asian countries. As countries with different characteristics need different models to appropriately assess their national competitiveness, it is critical for MNCs to employ a proper model when analyzing the CSAs of countries in which they are planning to invest. In this light, the DDD model, or double-diamond-based nine-factor model, can provide a better framework than other models to evaluate the investment environment of nations.

INTRODUCTION

In this era of globalization, countries bear critical importance, especially to multinational corporations (MNCs), in that country-specific advantages (CSAs) (Rugman and Verbeke, 1992) are sources from which MNCs sustain or create their competitive advantages. In this regard, an accurate analysis of CSAs is imperative and, therefore, the location variable is no longer exogenous to MNCs.

A clear understanding of CSAs should be based on a rigorous analysis of national competitiveness, which is a comprehensive representation of various aspects comprising the business environment of each country. In other words, for the successful implementation of global expansion via foreign direct investment (FDI), MNCs should be equipped with a robust tool to measure and analyze national competitiveness, with which MNCs can have an accurate analysis of the CSAs of both home and host countries and, consequently, can make appropriate location choices for FDI, because it is the combination of CSAs of both home and host countries that constitutes the sources of MNCs' competitiveness.

One important point in assessing national competitiveness is that countries differ from one another in many aspects: countries differ, *inter alia*, in the size and status of their economic development; countries also differ in their sources and scopes of competitiveness. Therefore, when analyzing the competitiveness of countries with various attributes, one size does not fit all: different countries require different criteria. Those different criteria, however, should be framed in a systematic way so that MNCs can have a comprehensive understanding of the competitiveness of countries around the world and correctly assess the information of their CSAs.

For this purpose, this chapter introduces the "dual double diamond" (DDD) model as a new model that measures and analyzes more comprehensively than existing models the national competitiveness of countries with various characteristics, and empirically evaluates existing models on national competitiveness in terms of their explanatory power over different sources and scopes of national competitiveness. The results first show that the "generalized double diamond" (GDD) model and the nine-factor (NF) model have better explanatory power than Porter's diamond model when assessing the national competitiveness of countries with high international connectivity and high human-factor dependency, respectively, and that the DDD model is more comprehensive than the GDD and NF models in explaining the national competitiveness of countries with heterogeneous attributes.

This chapter is structured as follows: The first section will discuss the validity of Porter's single diamond model and its extended models, and then introduce the DDD model. The remainder of the chapter will be devoted to empirical tests on the explanatory power of the models and the adequacy of the DDD model as a new model of national competitiveness.

PREVIOUS LITERATURE ON NATIONAL COMPETITIVENESS

Although capital, labor, and natural resources have been regarded as sources of national competitiveness, it is not difficult to find counter-examples to these traditional theories: some countries flourish without blessed factor endowments, whereas others languish with abundant resources. In an effort to explain these contradictions, Porter (1990), on the basis of a four-year study of 10 countries, introduced the diamond model as a new approach to the analysis of national competitiveness. Porter's diamond model systematically incorporates many important variables into a single model, together with the production factor conditions that most traditional theorists employ to explain national competitiveness. Therefore, this model is comprehensive and its explanatory power was revolutionary (Ryan, 1990; Thain, 1990). Porter's diamond model consists of endogenous and exogenous variables. The endogenous variables are composed of *Factor Conditions, Firm Strategy, Structure, and Rivalry, Related and Supporting Industries*, and *Demand Conditions. Government* and *Chance* comprise the exogenous variables.

Although Porter's diamond model contributed to the revolutionary development of explanations on national competitiveness, it has not been free from criticism and has been extended from the perspective of scopes and sources of national competitiveness. For the scopes of national competitiveness, the (generalized) double diamond model extends Porter's diamond from the domestic into the international context by incorporating multinational activities into the original model (Rugman, 1991; Rugman and D'Cruz, 1993; Moon *et al.*, 1995, 1998; Dunning, 2003). As criticized in several studies (Cartwright, 1993; Dunning, 1993; Hodgetts, 1993, *inter alia*), Porter's diamond model, which focuses on the *home-base* of a country, needs consideration of the international context to fully explain the national competitiveness of small and open countries.

For this purpose, Rugman and D'Cruz (1993) introduced the "double diamond" model, linking the domestic diamond of each country to that of a relevant "triad," thus incorporating the international context of national competitiveness. In this era of ever-increasing globalization, however, the double diamond model approach faces a structural limitation in that countries participating in the global economy utilize not only triad but also non-triad diamonds. Linking both the triad diamonds and non-triad diamonds to the domestic diamond of each country would resemble a bunch of grapes, making it difficult to appreciate the competitiveness of each country (Kim, 2006).

Therefore, we need to generalize the double diamond model in order to effectively analyze and operationalize both the domestic diamond and the international diamond, including triad and non-triad countries interacting in the global economy. For the generalization of the double diamond model, Moon *et al.* (1995, 1998) further extended the model into the GDD model, which is composed of a domestic diamond and an international diamond. The domestic diamond of the GDD model assesses the extent to which a country enhances competitiveness by utilizing its domestic resources, whereas the international diamond evaluates the extent to which the country enhances its competitiveness by aggregating all of the non-domestic diamonds. Therefore, the GDD model considers the four factors of Porter's single diamond model in both domestic and international contexts.

Regarding the sources of national competitiveness, Porter's diamond model has been extended to better explain the dynamic role of the human factors in national competitiveness through the introduction of the "NF" model (Cho, 1994; Cho and Moon, 2000). As the focus of Porter's diamond model is primarily on physical factors, mixed with some human factors, it cannot appropriately explain the national competitiveness of countries, in particular developing countries, whose major sources for enhancing national competitiveness are human rather than physical factors. In other words, Porter's diamond model is mainly designed to explain the sources of national competitiveness possessed by the economies of advanced nations, but is limited in its applicability when explaining the levels and dynamics of national competitiveness in less developed or developing countries. Moreover, although the title of Porter's book, *The Competitive Advantage of Nations* (1990), incorporates "nation," he actually analyzes national competitiveness at industry level and, consequently, treats government as an exogenous variable. For a more appropriate analysis of CSAs, however, government, one of the most important factors influencing national competitiveness, should be incorporated as an endogenous variable.

In order to provide a better explanation of the dynamic role of human factors and government, the NF model divides the sources of national competitiveness into *physical* (that is, non-human) *factors* and *human factors* (The variable "firm strategy, structure, and rivalry," included among the four variables, is not precisely physical but rather a non-human variable). For this purpose, in addition to the four physical factors of Porter's single diamond, the NF model incorporates four human factors (*Workers, Politicians and Bureaucrats, Entrepreneurs*, and *Professionals*) and one exogenous variable, *Chance Events*. The human factors in the NF model drive the national economy forward by creating, motivating and controlling the four physical factors in Porter's diamond model.

THE DUAL DOUBLE DIAMOND MODEL

Shortcomings in Existing Models

Porter's diamond model largely focuses on the physical factors in the domestic context when explaining national competitiveness. In order to provide a better explanation of the competitiveness of countries with different attributes, Porter's diamond model has been extended into the GDD and NF models, incorporating the international context and human factors, respectively. In order to have a comprehensive understanding of the national competitiveness of countries with various characteristics, however, it is necessary to integrate existing models and to explicitly consider international human factors. First, the extended models need to be integrated into a single model. As both scopes and sources of national competitiveness simultaneously interact, national competitiveness should be analyzed from both of these perspectives. The existing models, however, consider only one of these two criteria.

Second, none of the existing models explicitly analyze the role of the international human factors. A careful reader would find that neither Porter's diamond nor its extended models take into consideration the role of international human factors. In this era of globalization, as represented in the increasing concerns about phenomena such as the "brain drain," the role of international human factors in enhancing national competitiveness is far greater than ever before and must be considered as one of the most important factors in explaining national competitiveness.

Therefore, in order to provide a comprehensive analysis of national competitiveness, it is necessary to integrate the existing models into a single model, while explicitly considering the international human factors, a model covering four dimensions of *domestic physical factors, domestic human factors, international physical factors* and *international human factors.*

The Dual Double Diamond Model

In order to fully understand the competitiveness of countries with a variety of characteristics, this chapter introduces the DDD model as a new model on national competitiveness that integrates the four dimensions of national competitiveness into a single framework. Figure 7-1 illustrates the studies on Porter's diamond model and its extended models, and the structure of each model. The horizontal axis represents the extension to Porter's diamond model in terms of sources of national competitiveness, whereas the vertical axis shows the extension from the perspective of scopes of national competitiveness.

Each of the extended models to Porter's diamond model can double it in its own way. The GDD model (Model 3) doubles Porter's diamond by imposing an international diamond on the existing domestic diamond. On the other hand, the NF model (Model 2) doubles Porter's diamond by introducing a diamond of human factors to the existing diamond of physical factors. Thus, the integration of these two extensions and incorporation of international human factors into a single framework results in a "dual double diamond" (DDD), which lies at the lower right-hand corner of Figure 7-1.

The DDD model provides a comprehensive analysis of the competitiveness of countries with heterogeneous attributes, encompassing the four dimensions of national competitiveness: *physical* and *human factors* in *domestic* and *international* contexts. The DDD model measures the physical factors of national competitiveness with four factors — *Factor Conditions, Firm*

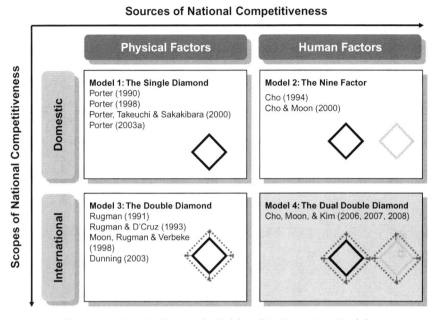

Fig. 7-1 Porter's Diamond Model and Its Extension Models

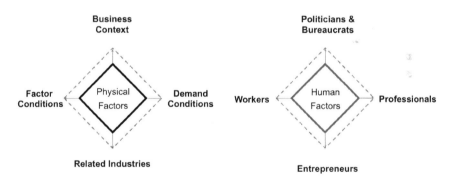

Fig. 7-2 The Dual Double Diamond Model

Strategy, Structure, and Rivalry, Related and Supporting Industries, and *Demand Conditions* — in domestic and international contexts. For the human factors, the model also analyzes national competitiveness with four factors — *Workers, Politicians and Bureaucrats, Entrepreneurs*, and *Professionals* — in domestic and international contexts. Figure 7-2 expounds the structure of the DDD model.

MODELING

For a clear demonstration of the structure and coverage of each model on national competitiveness, we organize the models as follows on the basis of the original intentions of each model, utilizing each of the four parts of national competitiveness illustrated in Figure 7-1: *domestic physical factors, domestic human factors, international physical factors* and *international human factors*.

Model 1 (M1): Porter's Diamond Model = DP
Model 2 (M2): The NF Model = DP + DH
Model 3 (M3): The GDD Model = DP + IP
Model 4 (M4): The DDD Model = DP + IP + DH + IH

where

DP = domestic physical factors (upper-left corner of Figure 7-1)
DH = domestic human factors (upper-right corner of Figure 7-1)
IP = international physical factors (lower-left corner of Figure 7-1)
IH = international human factors (lower-right corner of Figure 7-1)

For the DP factors, variables including, but not limited to, natural resources, market size, infrastructure, and governance structure in the domestic context are selected as proxies. The DH factors include domestic wage, government officials, domestic entrepreneurs, and professionals. On the other hand, variables such as foreign direct investment, trade openness, international network and global standard are selected for the IP factors, whereas the openness of the labor market and professional jobs are used for IH factors.

HYPOTHESES

As each of the extended models is developed to complement missing or disregarded parts of the previous models, it is expected that, when statistically compared with previous models, the extended models will have better explanatory power in the criteria they focus on. For the empirical analysis of the validity and explanatory power of the four models on national competitiveness, we test the following four hypotheses:

Porter's Diamond Model Versus the Generalized Double Diamond Model

The GDD model introduces the international context into the analysis of national competitiveness, an important criterion that Porter's diamond model lacks in assessing national competitiveness. Equipped with the international context, the GDD model is expected to provide a more appropriate analysis of the national competitiveness of countries with high international connectivity than Porter's diamond model.

Hypothesis 1: *The GDD model has better explanatory power than Porter's diamond model in measuring the national competitiveness of countries with high international connectivity.*

If this hypothesis is accepted, the result would support the assertion that Porter's diamond model is to be reserved for countries with a strong home-base and that the GDD model is more appropriate for explaining the national competitiveness of countries with higher international connectivity.

Porter's Diamond Model Versus the Nine-Factor Model

The NF model is designed to more accurately assess the national competitiveness of countries where human factors greatly contribute to enhancing national competitiveness. Therefore, the NF model is expected to provide better results when analyzing the national competitiveness of countries with high human-factor dependency than Porter's diamond model.

Hypothesis 2: *The NF model has better explanatory power than Porter's diamond model in measuring the national competitiveness of countries with high human-factor dependency.*

The results of this test will show whether Porter's diamond is essentially a physical-factor–oriented model and whether the NF model is more suitable in explaining the national competitiveness of countries with higher dependency on human factors than on physical factors.

The Generalized Double Diamond Model Versus the Dual Double Diamond Model

Although the GDD model incorporates an international context into its analysis of national competitiveness, the model can be extended further by distinguishing human factors from physical factors. Considering human factors in addition to the international context, the DDD model is expected to yield a better analysis of the national competitiveness of countries with high human-factor dependency than the GDD model.

Hypothesis 3: *The DDD model has better explanatory power than the GDD model in explaining the national competitiveness of the countries with high human-factor dependency.*

The Nine-Factor Model Versus the Dual Double Diamond Model

Like Porter's diamond model, the NF model focuses on the domestic context of national competitiveness. Because the DDD model analyzes physical and human factors in both domestic and international contexts, it would be a better method than the NF model in understanding the national competitiveness of countries with high international connectivity.

Hypothesis 4: *The DDD model has better explanatory power than the NF model in explaining the national competitiveness of the countries with high international connectivity*

RESEARCH DESIGN

The Model

In order to test each of the four hypotheses, we suggest a general hypothesis as follows:

$$\textit{General Hypothesis: } \bar{d}_{\text{low}} < \bar{d}_{\text{high}}$$

where

$$\bar{d}_g = \left(\sum_{i=1}^{n_g} \left(M_{\text{extended}}(g_i) - M_{\text{previous}}(g_i) \right) \right) / n_g ;$$

$M_{\text{extended}}(g_i)$ $(M_{\text{previous}}(g_i))$ = national competitiveness index of the ith country in each country group g measured with the extended (previous) model; and

$$n_g = \text{number of countries in each country group } g.$$

More specifically, we first classified the countries into two country groups (g: *low* or *high*) according to each country's score in *international connectivity* and *human-factor dependency*, respectively, thus resulting in four country groups of *high international connectivity*, *low international connectivity*, *high human-factor dependency*, and *low human-factor dependency*. We then calculate, in each country group, the difference score of each country between its national

Table 7-1 Variables for Each Hypothesis

Hypotheses	Country Groups	$M_{extended}$	$M_{previous}$
H_1	International Connectivity (low or high)	M_3: GDD	M_1: SD
H_2	Human-Factor Dependency (low or high)	M_2: NF	M_1: SD
H_3	Human-Factor Dependency (low or high)	M_4: DDD	M_3: GDD
H_4	International Connectivity (low or high)	M_4: DDD	M_2: NF

Note: SD: Porter's single diamond model; NF: nine-factor model; GDD: generalized double diamond model; DDD: dual double diamond model.

competitiveness indices measured with the extended model ($M_{extended}(g_i)$) and its previous model ($M_{previous}(g_i)$). The sum of the difference scores of countries in each country group is then divided by the number of countries in each country group (n_g), thus yielding the mean of difference scores ($\bar{d}_g$). Finally, each hypothesis statistically compares each group's mean of difference scores ($\bar{d}_{low}$ and $\bar{d}_{high}$). A higher mean of difference scores in the high group would represent the underestimated portion of national competitiveness when measured with the previous model, thus supporting the better explanatory power of the extended model.

For each hypothesis, we use the variables listed in Table 7-1. To test the impact of the scopes of national competitiveness, H_1 (H_4) analyzes the discrepancy between the GDD model and Porter's single diamond model (the DDD model and the NF model) from the perspective of international connectivity. Likewise, H_2 (H_3) examines the impact of the sources of national competitiveness by calculating the discrepancy between the NF model and Porter's single diamond model (the DDD model and the GDD model) with the criterion of human-factor dependency.

Data

For the empirical test of the four models on national competitiveness, we reorganize the statistical data in the *IPS National Competitiveness Research* (IPS, 2006) in compliance with the structures of the four models with full consideration of the original intentions of each model. The report measures and analyzes the national competitiveness of 66 countries with 275 criteria comprising physical factors and human factors in both domestic and international contexts. The 275 criteria are composed of the most recent 137 hard data collected through various statistical sources published by international or government organizations, and 138 soft data collected by the Korea Trade-Investment Promotion Agency (KOTRA), which has 100 offices spread over 73 countries.

Among the 275 criteria used in the report, four criteria comprising the exogenous factor (Chance Event) and supplementary information (Supplementary Data) are not included in the process of calculating national competitiveness. As 55 criteria in the remaining 271 criteria are used for informative purposes (background information), we select 216 criteria for the calculation of the national competitiveness index of the 66 countries. Each factor is calculated as an average of its sub-factors, and each of the 23 sub-factors is also calculated as an average of its elements or criteria. Table 7-A1 in Appendix lists the factors, sub-factors, and the number of criteria employed in the study. For further information on the criteria, refer to the IPS (2006) report.

Measures and Method

To test the four hypotheses, the 66 countries studied in the IPS report are classified into four sub-groups by two criteria, *international connectivity* and *human-factor dependency*. For international connectivity, *FDI openness* calculated as (Outward FDI (stock) + Inward FDI (stock))/(GDP × 2) can be a good proxy variable. As the international connectivity of a country implies the relationship between a country and MNCs through which the country can enhance and sustain its sources of competitiveness on a global scale, FDI that transfers intangible assets through MNCs' exploration and exploitation activities can effectively achieve the goal of securing sources abroad for enhancing and sustaining competitiveness. Consequently, a high proportion of both inward and outward FDI to GDP would represent a high level of the connection to the outside of a country for enhancing national competitiveness.

As human factors enhance national competitiveness by creating, motivating, and controlling physical factors, high performance per a given factor endowment can be attributed to high efficiency in utilizing human factors. Therefore, *GDP per Land Area*[1] can be a proxy to categorize countries into

---

[1] High correlation coefficients between the land area and major natural resources show that land area can be employed as a proxy variable for factor endowments (natural resources): Aluminum production: $r = 0.81$; Natural gas production: $r = 0.74$; Round wood production: $r = 0.72$; Oil

a high human-factor-dependent group and a low human-factor-dependent group.

Each sub-group is composed of 33 countries in accordance with each country's score in international connectivity or human-factor dependency. Table 7-A2 in Appendix shows the name of countries studied in this article and their positions in the sub-groups. Hong Kong and Singapore, for example, are classified into the high group in both international connectivity and human-factor dependency, while China and India are classified into the low group.

As the dependent variable varies across hypotheses, neither the analysis of variance (ANOVA) nor the multivariate analysis of variance (MANOVA) techniques would be applicable to the tests. Therefore, before comparing the mean of the difference scores of each group with that of the other group in each hypothesis, we employ the independent t-test to statistically test the validity of country grouping. In order to prevent the inflated Type I error from multiple comparisons, the α-level of each hypothesis is set to 0.01.[2]

RESULTS

Table 7-2 demonstrates the changing rankings of countries when analyzed by the different models of national competitiveness. As expected, countries with high international connectivity and/or human-factor dependency boast higher rankings in the DDD model than those measured by Porter's single diamond model. For example, Switzerland, Singapore, Belgium, Hong Kong, United Kingdom, and Taiwan — countries with both high international connectivity and high human-factor dependency — witness increases in their rankings, while China, India, Russia, Jordan, and Saudi Arabia — countries with both low international connectivity and low human-factor dependency — experience decreasing rankings.

Table 7-3 summarizes the results of the statistical analyses conducted on the four hypotheses. All of the hypotheses are supported at the 0.001 level: t-statistics with high statistical significance demonstrate the validity

---

production: $r = 0.53$; Coal production: $r = 0.51$; Pig iron and crude steel production: $r = 0.48$; Cement production: $r = 0.37$ (All the correlations are significant at the 0.01 level (2-tailed)).

[2]As the probability of committing at least one Type I error in the set of K independent comparisons is calculated as $p = 1 - (1 - \alpha)^K$ (Glass and Hopkins, 1996), in order to employ a significance level of 0.05 for the complete set of multiple comparisons, we adopt a significance level of 0.01 for each comparison.

Table 7-2 Changing Rankings of National Competitiveness

Country	SD	NF	GDD	DDD	Country	SD	NF	GDD	DDD
U.S.	1	1	1	1	Argentina	34	53	32	47
Netherlands	2	2	2	2	Philippines	35	31	36	35
Canada	3	3	4	4	Saudi Arabia	36	39	47	43
Denmark	4	4	3	3	Colombia	37	36	38	37
Sweden	5	5	5	7	Thailand	38	32	33	30
Finland	6	6	12	16	Portugal	39	34	34	28
Norway	7	7	10	10	Brazil	40	40	46	45
Australia	8	8	17	11	India	41	35	50	49
Japan	9	14	13	18	South Africa	42	46	44	51
Israel	10	9	14	12	Hungary	43	38	40	36
Switzerland	11	10	9	9	Czech Republic	44	42	37	39
Austria	12	16	16	17	Pakistan	45	47	43	42
New Zealand	13	17	19	21	Oman	46	48	48	50
Singapore	14	11	7	6	Malaysia	47	37	35	34
Belgium	15	12	11	8	Croatia	48	50	41	52
Germany	16	19	8	13	Romania	49	44	45	41
Hong Kong	17	13	6	5	Dominican Republic	50	51	51	44
France	18	15	15	15	Vietnam	51	43	52	40
Kuwait	19	26	21	23	Cambodia	52	57	53	57
Chile	20	21	20	20	Panama	53	49	49	38
United Kingdom	21	18	18	14	Guatemala	54	52	54	46
Italy	22	24	25	24	Egypt	55	54	55	54
Korea	23	22	26	27	Indonesia	56	55	58	55
Spain	24	23	22	22	Ukraine	57	63	61	63
China	25	27	23	26	Nigeria	58	62	57	59
Taiwan	26	20	24	19	Sri Lanka	59	56	56	56
Greece	27	28	31	33	Peru	60	59	60	60
Russia	28	41	39	48	Morocco	61	58	59	58
Mexico	29	29	28	25	Turkey	62	61	62	62
Jordan	30	25	30	31	Libya	63	65	65	65
U.A.E.	31	33	27	29	Kenya	64	60	63	61
Venezuela	32	45	42	53	Iran	65	66	64	66
Poland	33	30	29	32	Bangladesh	66	64	66	64

Note: SD: Porter's single diamond model; NF: nine-factor model; GDD: generalized double diamond model; DDD: dual double diamond model;
Countries are listed in the order of rankings measured by Porter's single diamond model.

Table 7-3   Results of Statistical Analyses

Hypotheses	Groups	N	$\bar{d}_g$	t	df
			Descriptive Statistics	t-test	
H1	High	33	45.686	3.913	64
	Low	33	28.887		
H2	High	33	67.804	4.774	64
	Low	33	49.014		
H3	High	33	133.928	4.401	64
	Low	33	102.743		
H4	High	33	112.033	4.102	64
	Low	33	82.393		

Note: All the *t*-statistics are significant at the 0.001 level (2-tailed).

of the country groupings and all the high groups have higher means of the difference scores ($\bar{d}_g$) than lower groups. As each hypothesis is supported at the 0.001 level, the probability of committing a Type I error in the multiple comparisons is less than 0.05 ($p = 1 - (1 - 0.01)^2 = 0.0199$) (Glass and Hopkins, 1996). These results statistically support that the GDD and the NF models have better explanatory power than Porter's diamond model in terms of scopes and sources of national competitiveness, respectively. Furthermore, the results also corroborate that the DDD model is better than the GDD model and the NF model in explaining the national competitiveness of countries with various characteristics: not only the competitiveness of countries with developed economies and a strong home-base, but also that of countries with high foreign-dependency and/or fewer factor endowments.

DISCUSSION

The results of the statistical analyses support the rationales provided for each extended model of Porter's diamond model. The higher mean of the difference scores of the countries with high international connectivity illustrates the underestimated competitiveness of countries with high international connectivity when analyzed with Porter's diamond model, and supports the rationale of introducing the international context into Porter's home-based diamond. In a similar vein, the higher mean of the difference scores of the countries with high performance per given factor endowments demonstrates the neglected portion of national competitiveness of countries with high human-factor dependency, and supports the necessity of considering the human factors to better assess national competitiveness.

Compared with the DDD model, however, the GDD model and the NF model reveal their innate limitations as one-way extended models. Although the GDD model incorporates the international context, it still misses the human factors of national competitiveness. Likewise, the NF model lacks the international context of national competitiveness. Furthermore, none of the two extended models can explain the impact of the international human factors on national competitiveness. Integrating both extensions to Porter's diamond model, i.e., *scopes* and *sources*, and incorporating the international human factors, the DDD model presents an analytical tool to assess more comprehensively than existing models the competitiveness of countries with various characteristics.

As MNCs are different bundles of resources and capabilities with strong influences from country effects (Shan and Hamilton, 1991; Makino *et al.*, 2004), each MNC needs different sets of CSAs with which it can enhance its competitiveness. In their strategic consideration of the locations to invest in, MNCs analyze CSAs of candidate countries to determine the best location, with simultaneous considerations of the CSAs of their home countries. Here, it is critical for MNCs to correctly choose an appropriate analytical model, because different models, as shown in the results of the empirical analyses, yield different assessments for the same countries: a wrong choice of the analytical model for CSAs could result in a fatal strategic error.

As a matter of fact, Porter (1990) considered a country's diamond as a platform mainly for outbound FDI (OFDI) and this perspective was one of the main criticisms on Porter (1990) by other scholars, including Rugman (1991, 1992). There are other works (e.g., Reich, 1990) emphasizing the role of inbound FDI (IFDI) in enhancing national competitiveness. Later, Porter himself actually changed his perspective and acknowledged the importance of IFDI, by saying that prosperity in a county is a reflection of what both domestic and foreign firms choose to do in that country (Porter, 2000, p. 16), and that productivity is the goal, regardless of whether firms operating in that country are domestic or foreign owned (Porter, 2003b, p. 31). Accordingly, the criteria of the diamond model can readily be applied not only to the analysis of CSAs in OFDI but also to that in IFDI (Foster and Wang, 2007). The DDD model, incorporating the rationale of the (generalized) double diamond model, acknowledges both IFDI and OFDI as sources for enhancing national competitiveness and, therefore, allows us to have a more comprehensive model when analyzing CSAs of both home and host countries.

If MNCs were to only consider the CSAs of large developed countries like the U.S. into their analyses for investment, Porter's single diamond model might be sufficient in providing a systematic analysis of the CSAs and the rest of the extended models would be redundant. Location factors of MNCs, however, are composed not only of large developed countries but also of less developed and developing countries of various sizes and characteristics. Then, the corollary is that Porter's diamond model does not satisfactorily fit. In this era of increasing global competition, MNCs are forced to seek out every corner of the world for favorable CSAs and, therefore, their location portfolios are full of countries with various sizes and characteristics. In this light, the DDD model can provide a more comprehensive and integrated analysis of MNCs' heterogeneous location portfolios.

This is especially true for countries in Asia, an area in dynamics. Consider *CHINDIA* (China and India) and the *Four Asian Tigers* (Hong Kong, Singapore, Taiwan, and Korea). As shown in Table 7-2, countries in these two groups show different trends in their changes of rankings. To begin with, there is generally little change in the rankings of CHINDIA, regardless of the models. The rankings of the Four Asian Tigers, however, show drastic changes with the application of different models, although Korea seems to be an exception. Singapore rises from 14th place to 6th, Hong Kong from 17th to 5th, and Taiwan from 26th to 19th. As the Four Asian Tigers have overcome their comparative disadvantages with the strategic utilization of human resources and active openness, their rankings rise when analyzed with the DDD model. In other words, as the Four Asian Tigers have overcome the adversity in their domestic physical factors and developed their national competitiveness through the intensive use of global physical factors and human factors in both domestic and international scopes, we can have a better assessment of their CSAs with the DDD model that comprehensively analyzes the physical and human factors of national competitiveness in both domestic and international scopes. In CHINDIA, however, openness and human factors are not as critical as they are for the Four Asian Tigers and, therefore, different models do not yield large differences in rankings.

In sum, as countries with different characteristics need different models to appropriately assess their national competitiveness, it is critical for MNCs to employ a proper model when analyzing the CSAs of countries in which they are planning to invest. In this light, the DDD model provides a better framework than existing models to comprehensively analyze the national competitiveness of countries with heterogeneous attributes.

CONCLUSION

This article presents the DDD model as a more comprehensive model to measure and analyze the national competitiveness of countries with heterogeneous characteristics, by integrating Porter's diamond model and its extended models, and incorporating international human factors into a single framework. Empirical tests on the validity of Porter's diamond model, the GDD model, the NF model, and the DDD model show that the DDD model has more comprehensive explanatory power on national competitiveness than existing models.

The contributions of this article can be summarized as follows. First, this article introduces the DDD model as a new model on national competitiveness. The DDD model can measure and analyze more comprehensively the national competitiveness of countries with a variety of characteristics. As CSAs consist of various aspects of a country and are comprehensively represented in national competitiveness, the DDD model provides a better strategic framework for MNCs to exhaustively analyze the CSAs of the countries with various attributes and thus to efficiently implement a global expansion strategy. Secondly, this article empirically tests the validity of Porter's diamond model and each of its extended models. Statistical analyses demonstrate the limits of the existing models and the adequacy of the DDD model.

In country sub-groupings, this article employs international connectivity and human-factor dependency as proxy variables classifying countries. Other proxy variables, based on careful interpretation of the original intentions in each model, can enhance our understanding of each model's contribution, and test the validity of the DDD model in different ways. In addition, a more detailed study on the relationship among the models would allow us to have a better insight on national competitiveness.

REFERENCES

Cartwright, W. R. (1993). Multiple linked diamonds: New Zealand's experience. *Management International Review*, 33(2): 55–70.

Cho, D. S. (1994). A dynamic approach to international competitiveness: The case of Korea. *Journal of Far Eastern Business*, 1(1): 17–36.

Cho, D. S. and Moon, H. C. (2000). *From Adam Smith to Michael Porter*, Singapore: World Scientific.

Cho, D. S., Moon, H. C. and Kim, M. Y. (2006). Competitive strategy to enhance national competitiveness. *Proceedings of the Academy of International Business 2006 Annual Meeting*, Beijing, China, 23–26 June.

Cho, D. S., Moon, H. C. and Kim, M. Y. (2007). Beyond Porter's single diamond: A dual double diamond model approach to national competitiveness. *Proceedings of the Academy of International Business 2007 Annual Meeting*, Indianapolis, Indiana, 25–28 June.

Cho, D. S., Moon, H. C. and Kim, M. Y. (2008). Characterizing international competitiveness in international business research: A MASI approach to national competitiveness. *Research in International Business and Finance*, 22(2): 175–192.

Dunning, J. H. (1993). Internationalizing Porter's diamond. *Management International Review*, 33(2): 7–15.

Dunning, J. H. (2003). The role of foreign direct investment in upgrading China's competitiveness. *Journal of International Business and Economy*, 4(1): 1–13.

Foster, M. J. and Wang, Z. (2007). Nanjing's performance as China's FDI inflows grow. *International Journal of Management and Decision Making*, 8(2): 426–439.

Glass, G. V. and Hopkins, K. D. (1996). *Statistical Methods in Education and Psychology*, 3rd Edn., Needham Heights, MA: Allyn and Bacon.

Hodgetts, R. M. (1993). Porter's diamond framework in a Mexican context. *Management International Review*, 33(2): 41–54.

IPS (2006). IPS National Competitiveness Research 2006 Report, Seoul: IPS and IPS-NaC.

Kim, M. Y. (2006). Inequality in globalization: An extension of the Gini index from the perspective of national competitiveness. *Journal of International Business and Economy*, 7(1): 119–140.

Makino, S., Isobe, T. and Chan, C. M. (2004). Does country matter? *Strategic Management Journal*, 25(10): 1027–1043.

Moon, H. C., Rugman, A. M. and Verbeke, A. (1995). The generalized double diamond approach to international competitiveness, in Rugman, A. M., den Broeck, J. V. and Verbeke, A. (eds.), *Research in Global Strategic Management, Vol. 5: Beyond the Diamond*, Greenwich, CT: JAI Press, pp. 97–114.

Moon, H. C., Rugman, A. M. and Verbeke, A. (1998). A generalized double diamond approach to the global competitiveness of Korea and Singapore. *International Business Review*, 7: 135–150.

Porter, M. E. (1990). *The Competitive Advantage of Nations*, New York: Free Press.

Porter, M. E. (1998). Clusters and the new economics of competition. *Harvard Business Review*, 76(6): 77–90.

Porter, M. E. (2000). Attitudes, values, beliefs, and the microeconomics of prosperity, in Harrison, L. E. and Huntington, S. P. (eds.), *Culture Matters*, New York: Basic Books, pp. 14–28.

Porter, M. E. (2003a). *Malaysia's Competitiveness: Moving to the Next Stage*, Kuala Lumpur, Malaysia (Presentation slides).

Porter, M. E. (2003b). Building the microeconomic foundations of prosperity: Findings from the business competitiveness index, in World Economic Forum, *The Global Competitiveness Report*, Oxford and New York: Oxford University Press, pp. 29–56.

Porter, M. E., Takeuchi, H. and Sakakibara, M. (2000). *Can Japan Compete?* Cambridge, MA: Perseus Publishing.

Reich, R. B. (1990). Who is us? *Harvard Business Review*, **68**(1): 53–64.

Rugman, A. M. (1991). Diamond in the rough. *Business Quarterly*, **55**(3): 61–64.

Rugman, A. M. (1992). Porter takes the wrong turn. *Business Quarterly*, **56**(3): 59–64.

Rugman, A. M. and D'Cruz, J. R. (1993). The double diamond model of international competitiveness: The Canadian experience. *Management International Review*, **33**(2): 17–39.

Rugman, A. M. and Verbeke, A. (1992). A note on the transnational solution and the transaction cost theory of multinational strategic management. *Journal of International Business Studies*, **23**(4): 761–771.

Ryan, R. (1990). A grand disunity. *National Review*, **42**(13): 46–47.

Shan, W. and Hamilton, W. (1991). Country-specific advantage and international cooperation. *Strategic Management Journal*, **12**(6): 419–432.

Thain, D. H. (1990). The war without bullets. *Business Quarterly*, **55**(1): 13–19.

APPENDIX

Table 7A-1   List of Factors, Sub-Factors, and the Number of Criteria

Factors	Sub-Factors	NCR	B.I.	Input
Factor Conditions	Energy Resources	6	0	6
	Other Resources	17	8	9
Demand Conditions	Demand Size	22	11	11
	Demand Quality	8	0	8
Related & Supporting Industries	Transportation	10	1	9
	Communication	11	1	10
	Finance	23	0	23
	Education	10	1	9
	Science & Technology	9	2	7
	Cluster Development	3	0	3
	Overall Living Environment	16	1	15
Business Context	Strategy & Structure	5	0	5
	Global Mindset	5	0	5
	Business Culture	7	0	7
	Foreign Investment	29	18	11
Workers	Quantity of Labor Force	10	4	6
	Quality of Labor Force	6	1	5
Politicians & Bureaucrats	Politicians	11	0	11
	Bureaucrats	39	7	32
Entrepreneurs	Personal Competence	6	0	6
	Social Context	5	0	5
Professionals	Personal Competence	7	0	7
	Social Context	6	0	6
	Total:	271	55	216

Note: NCR: the number of criteria in the IPS National Competitiveness Research Report;
B.I.: the number of criteria used as background information;
Input: the number of criteria used in this study.

Table 7A-2   Countries Studied and Their Positions in the Country Sub-Groups

No	Country	International Connectivity	Human Factor Dependency	No	Country	International Connectivity	Human Factor Dependency
1	Argentina	H	L	34	Libya	L	L
2	Australia	H	L	35	Malaysia	H	H
3	Austria	H	H	36	Mexico	L	L
4	Bangladesh	L	H	37	Morocco	H	L
5	Belgium	H	H	38	Netherlands	H	H
6	Brazil	H	L	39	New Zealand	H	H
7	Cambodia	H	L	40	Nigeria	H	L
8	Canada	H	L	41	Norway	H	H
9	Chile	H	L	42	Oman	L	L
10	China	L	L	43	Pakistan	L	L
11	Colombia	L	L	44	Panama	H	L
12	Croatia	H	H	45	Peru	L	L
13	Czech Republic	H	H	46	Philippines	L	L
14	Denmark	H	H	47	Poland	L	H
15	Dominican Republic	L	H	48	Portugal	H	H
16	Egypt	L	L	49	Romania	L	L
17	Finland	H	H	50	Russia	L	L
18	France	H	H	51	Saudi Arabia	L	L
19	Germany	H	H	52	Singapore	H	H
20	Greece	L	H	53	South Africa	H	L
21	Guatemala	L	L	54	Spain	H	H
22	Hong Kong	H	H	55	Sri Lanka	L	L
23	Hungary	H	H	56	Sweden	H	H
24	India	L	L	57	Switzerland	H	H
25	Indonesia	L	L	58	Taiwan	H	H
26	Iran	L	L	59	Thailand	L	L
27	Israel	H	H	60	Turkey	L	H
28	Italy	L	H	61	U.A.E	L	H
29	Japan	L	H	62	Ukraine	L	L
30	Jordan	L	L	63	United Kingdom	H	H
31	Kenya	L	L	64	United States	L	H
32	Korea	L	H	65	Venezuela	H	L
33	Kuwait	L	H	66	Vietnam	L	L

Note: H: high; L: low;

International Connectivity = (Outward FDI (stock) + Inward FDI (stock))/(GDP × 2);

Human-Factor Dependency = (GDP/Land Area);

Countries are listed in alphabetical order.

8

METHODOLOGY FOR
NATIONAL COMPETITIVENESS
ANALYSIS

SUMMARY AND KEY POINTS

This chapter (Cho *et al.*, 2008) introduces the MASI methodology which is a step-by-step approach to the analysis of national competitiveness and provides specific guidelines for enhancing competitiveness of both nations and multinational corporations (MNCs). Empirical analyses with the data of 66 countries are also conducted to test this methodology. The MASI methodology designed for national competitiveness suggests valuable implications to multinational corporations because much of MNCs' competitiveness comes from host countries.

The MASI approach provides (1) the dual double diamond model for measuring national competitiveness (Measure); (2) the 3 × 3 framework for classifying country groups (Analyze); (3) an application of business strategy models (cost versus differentiation) to the analysis

Source:
Cho, D. S., Moon, H. C. and Kim, M. Y. (2008). Characterizing international competitiveness in international business research: A MASI approach to national competitiveness. *Research in International Business and Finance*, **22**(2): 175–192.

of national competitiveness (Simulate); (4) a series of viable strategies to enhance national competitiveness (Implement).

From a rigorous theoretical and empirical analysis, some important implications are derived. First, in the measurement, the dual double diamond model presents a more sophisticated analysis than other models. Second, country groupings allow MNCs to analyze more relevantly the competitive positions of candidate host countries for investment. Third, from strategy simulation, MNCs can find out strategic leverages (e.g., cost or differentiation) of countries. Lastly, implementation procedure of the MASI methodology shows dynamic aspects of countries, allowing MNCs to plan long-term strategy.

INTRODUCTION

Multinational corporations (MNCs) have played a major role in this era of globalized economy. In this regard, it is natural that the unit of analysis in the field of international business has principally been MNCs. However, instead of focusing only on firm-specific factors, the scope of our analysis should be extended to include location factors that play a vital role in determining a firm's competitiveness: as MNCs and countries are two main players in the game of international business, a clear understanding of the mechanism driving competitiveness of countries, which has not been given much attention by scholars in international business, is of great importance for establishing and implementing viable strategy for MNCs.

To understand and enhance national competitiveness as a source of competitive advantage, this article introduces a systematic methodology called MASI (Measure-Analyze-Simulate-Implement), which contains (1) the dual double diamond (DDD) model for measuring national competitiveness (Measure); (2) the 3 × 3 framework for classifying country groups (Analyze); (3) an application of business strategy models (cost versus differentiation) to the analysis of national competitiveness (Simulate); and (4) a series of viable strategies to enhance national competitiveness (Implement). Empirical application of the methodology to data of 66 countries shows general principles of national competitiveness and strategic implications to enhance competitive advantages of both countries and MNCs. This new framework helps scholars of international business understand mechanisms governing competitiveness of countries and implications for establishing and implementing global strategy of MNCs.

This article consists of two parts: *theoretical development of the MASI methodology* and *its empirical application*. In the first part of the article, each of the four components comprising the MASI methodology will be developed and discussed in a theoretical perspective. Then, the methodology will be applied to empirical analyses utilizing more than 200 statistical data of 66 countries in the world.

THEORETICAL DEVELOPMENT

Measure: What is National Competitiveness?

Previous studies on national competitiveness

Traditional trade theorists have considered capital, labor, and natural resources as sources of national competitiveness. In reality, however, there are numerous counterexamples that disprove the arguments of traditional theorists. Criticizing the conventional model, whose origins date back to Adam Smith and David Ricardo, for being at best incomplete and at worst incorrect, Porter (1990) introduced the diamond model in his book, *The Competitive Advantage of Nations*. As the title implies, this book is meant to replace *The Wealth of Nations* (Smith, 1776). In this book, Porter argues that national prosperity is created, not inherited. Thus, his model is dynamic. In addition, this model is comprehensive because it creates a single model by incorporating the production factor conditions that most traditional theorists have employed with other important variables to explain national competitiveness. Therefore, the explanatory power of the diamond model was revolutionary (Ryan, 1990; Thain, 1990). Porter's single diamond model consists of two parts: *endogenous variables* and *exogenous variables*. The endogenous variables of the model are composed of Factor Conditions, Firm Strategy, Structure, and Rivalry, Related and Supporting Industries, and Demand Conditions, while the exogenous variables consist of Government and Chances.

Porter's single diamond model, however, was not free from criticism and has been extended in two directions. The first was the incorporation of multinational activities through the introduction of the double diamond model (Rugman, 1991; Rugman and D'Cruz, 1993; Moon *et al.*, 1998; Dunning, 2003). While the variables of Porter's single diamond model are useful when analyzing a nation's competitiveness, the model is narrowly focused on the home-base. Therefore, in order to broaden the domestic focus of Porter's single diamond into an international context, the double diamond model was introduced as an extension to Porter's single diamond model by incorporating an international diamond into the single diamond model.

Another extension to Porter's original model was the nine-factor model (Cho, 1994; Cho and Moon, 2000). In addition to the four physical determinants of Porter's single diamond, this model adds four additional human variables: Workers; Politicians and Bureaucrats; Entrepreneurs; and Professionals. There are two advantages of the nine-factor model over Porter's single model. First, although Porter's single diamond already includes some of these human variables, treating the human variables separately from the physical variables provides a clearer perspective on sources of competitiveness, especially in the case of countries with limited factor endowments. Second, the government variable, which is treated as exogenous in Porter's single model, is incorporated as endogenous in the nine-factor model. Although the title of the book is about the nation, Porter's single diamond model was actually designed for industry analysis, thereby treating the government factor as exogenous. If we are interested in the analysis at the national level, however, the government factor should be treated as endogenous since the government is the main factor for a nation's competitiveness.

Moreover, as Porter's single diamond model is mainly designed to explain the sources of national competitiveness possessed by the economies of advanced nations, the model is limited in its applicability when explaining the levels and dynamic changes of economies in less developed or developing countries. The human factors in the nine-factor model drive the national economy forward by creating, motivating, and controlling the four physical factors in Porter's diamond model and, therefore, play an important role in explaining national competitiveness.

A new model: The dual double diamond (DDD) model

A good theory should be comprehensive enough to capture the most important independent variables to explain a dependent variable. Although Porter's single diamond includes several important variables, it is not comprehensive enough to be used in explaining today's complicated economy. Specifically, the single diamond cannot be used in an international context because it is limited to a domestic scope. In this globalized world, international factors must be considered in order to appropriately assess a nation's competitiveness (Rugman, 1991; Rugman and D'Cruz, 1993; Moon et al., 1998). Furthermore, the single diamond model does not distinguish human factors from physical factors. In reality, the roles of different groups of people are important for explaining different types of economic development (Cho, 1994; Cho and Moon, 2000).

Although the double diamond model and the nine-factor model enhance the explanatory power of Porter's single diamond model in terms of the sources (physical/human) and the scopes (domestic/international) of national competitiveness, there are still two unsettled problems. First, these extension models are not integrated into a single framework. As both the sources and the scopes are vital for a comprehensive understanding of national competitiveness, the two criteria should be considered in a single framework simultaneously, not in two separated models.

Second, none of the two extension models explicitly consider the importance of international human factors: the double diamond model focuses only on the physical factors, while the nine-factor model considers only the domestic context of national competitiveness. In the era of globalization, the importance of international human factors well represented in such issues as brain drainage cannot be emphasized enough. Consequently, a framework on national competitiveness should be comprehensive enough to take international human factors into consideration. To resolve these problems in the existing models, we need a new model integrating the extension models into a single framework with consideration of international human factors.

Figure 8-1 illustrates the studies on Porter's single diamond model and its extensions. The horizontal axis shows the extension to the diamond model in terms of sources of national competitiveness. The vertical axis, on the other hand, demonstrates the extension with regard to the scopes of national competitiveness. As the sources (physical/human factors) and the scopes (domestic/international contexts) interact together to determine a nation's competitiveness, a model that integrates the sources and scopes of national competitiveness into a single framework can more thoroughly explain national competitiveness.

The two existing extensions double the original single diamond in two distinct ways. Model 2 in Figure 8-1 introduces a new diamond of human factors as an extension to the sources of national competitiveness. On the other hand, Model 3 doubles its original diamond as an extension to the scopes of national competitiveness, from a domestic context to international context. Thus, the integration of these two extensions into a single framework results in a dual double diamond (DDD). At the lower right hand corner of Figure 8-1 is the DDD model, encompassing the previous extensions. The DDD model considers both physical and human factors in both domestic and international

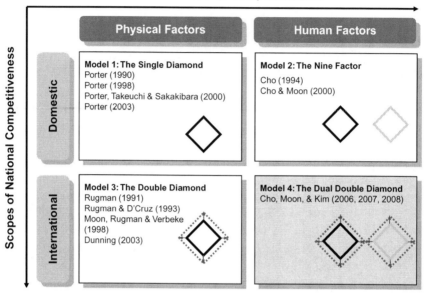

Fig. 8-1   Extensions to the Diamond Model

contexts and, consequently, is expected to provide a more comprehensive explanation for national competitiveness than the existing models.

Analyze: Classifying Nations

A nation's competitiveness is more meaningful when it is assessed among nations with similar characteristics competing in similar industries because competitiveness implies a relative position among competitors in the same competitive group. For example, it is more useful to compare Austria and Belgium than Austria and Australia, because the first two countries have more comparable characteristics than the latter two. Therefore, in order to derive meaningful implications, we should analyze the distinctiveness of the competitive situation in which a country competes with other countries and, for this, it is necessary to classify countries into groups of similar characteristics, as well as to locate a country's overall competitive position by sorting countries in accordance with its competitiveness among all countries.

As for the characteristics of countries, both comparative advantages and competitive advantages should be considered. To take into account both aspects of country characteristics, we classify countries according to size and

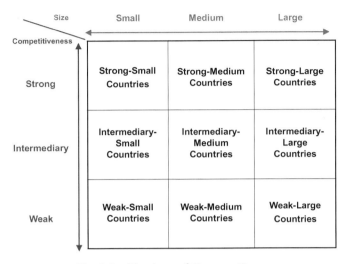

Fig. 8-2   Typology of Country Groups

competitiveness. In terms of size, countries are grouped into three different categories of large, medium, and small according to their population and land size. For competitiveness, countries are classified as strong, intermediary, and weak by a composite index of variables comprising the DDD model. A 3 × 3 matrix of country groups is illustrated in Figure 8-2.

Simulate: Applying Business Models to the National Level

Assuming that a country, like a firm, is an organization that tries to enhance and sustain competitiveness with its resources and capabilities to provide a higher living standard and better environment for industrial development, we can apply business strategy to the analysis of national competitiveness and determine strategic implications. In this light, we apply the classical distinction between two generic strategies (Porter, 1980, 1996) at the corporate level, *cost strategy* and *differentiation strategy*, to the national level. At the national level, the competitive advantage of a cost strategy is "low cost and high efficiency," which mainly utilizes cheap Factor Conditions and Workers in the less developed stage. In contrast, a differentiation strategy refers to "high cost but high value," and focuses on Demand Conditions and Professionals in the more developed stage. Figure 8-3 illustrates the different focuses of the cost strategy and the differentiation strategy on the variables comprising the DDD model.

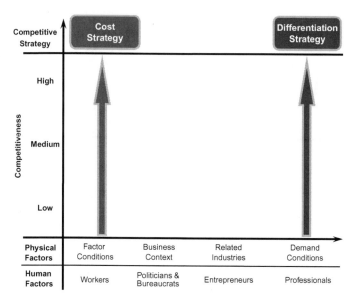

Fig. 8-3   Competitive Strategies on Nations

In order to determine the relative competitive positions for the two different strategies, we have given different weights to the competitiveness variables comprising the DDD model. To derive appropriate weight schemes on each of the two strategic alternatives in a scientific and logical manner, we employ an analytic hierarchy process (AHP), a mathematical decision-making technique designed to determine the relative importance of a set of alternatives (Saaty, 1980). Much of business literature acknowledges the usefulness of the AHP technique as a multi-criteria decision-making tool (Sureshchandar and Leisten, 2006).

For the cost strategy, equal weights (50%) are given to the physical and human factors. However, the variables and sub-variables have different weights, with a larger emphasis placed on Factor Conditions and Workers. Likewise, for the differentiation strategy, equal weights (50%) are given to the physical and human factors, and the variables and sub-variables are not weighted equally. However, unlike the cost strategy, a larger emphasis is given on Demand Conditions and Professionals. Table 8-1 demonstrates in detail the weighting schemes for the cost strategy and the differentiation strategy, respectively.

By interpreting the changes of national competitiveness through strategic simulation, we can understand competitive structures of countries and derive strategic implications for further development of national competitiveness.

Table 8-1   Weights for Cost Strategy and Differentiation Strategy

Main Factors		Weights C	Weights D	Sub-factors	Weights C	Weights D
Physical Factors	Factor Conditions	32/120	4/120	Energy Resources	1/2	1/2
				Other Resources	1/2	1/2
	Business Context	16/120	8/120	Strategy & Structure	1/4	1/4
				Global Mindset	1/4	1/4
				Business Culture	1/4	1/4
				Foreign Investment	1/4	1/4
	Related & Supporting Industries	8/120	16/120	Transportation	1/7	1/7
				Communication	1/7	1/7
				Finance	1/7	1/7
				Education	1/7	1/7
				Science & Technology	1/7	1/7
				Overall Living Environment	1/7	1/7
				Cluster Development	1/7	1/7
	Demand Conditions	4/120	32/120	Demand Quantity	3/4	1/4
				Demand Quality	1/4	3/4
Human Factors	Workers	32/120	4/120	Quantity of Labor force	3/4	1/4
				Quality of Labor force	1/4	3/4
	Politicians & Bureaucrats	16/120	8/120	Politicians	3/4	1/4
				Bureaucrats	1/4	3/4
	Entrepreneurs	8/120	16/120	Personal Competence	3/4	1/4
				Social Context	1/4	3/4
	Professionals	4/120	32/120	Personal Competence	3/4	1/4
				Social Context	1/4	3/4

Note: C: Cost strategy; D: Differentiation strategy.

For example, if a country witnesses augmentation of national competitiveness when applied with the differentiation strategy, we can conclude that the country has a competitive structure in which high value-added factors among variables comprising national competitiveness have much more potential for further development of national competitiveness. Namely, in this competitive structure, Related and Supporting Industries and Demand Conditions in the physical factors, and Entrepreneurs and Professionals in the human factors contribute more to the development of national competitiveness than the rest of the components. Therefore, we can derive an implication that resources and capabilities in countries must be utilized in a manner to enhance competitiveness of high value-added factors detected through strategy simulation.

Implement: Optimal Strategic Mix

Once the competitive position, competitiveness structure, and strategic implications of national competitiveness are clarified, a series of concrete strategies suitable to needs of each country in different stages of economic development should be followed to guarantee further successful development. As countries in different competitive positions and with different competitive structures need different strategies and focuses, we introduce a transitional matrix with different strategies in each of eight factors comprising the DDD model, with which countries can implement optimal strategic mix tailored for each country.

The eight factors comprising the DDD model can have different weight schemes according to the status of economic development. As discussed in the strategy simulation section, the cost strategy primarily focuses on Factor Conditions and Workers, while the differentiation strategy basically emphasizes Demand Conditions and Professionals. In addition, according to the results of the strategy simulation that will be discussed in the application section of this article, the viable strategy to enhance national competitiveness should transit from the cost strategy to the differentiation strategy as countries move into higher stages of economic development. Therefore, in the early stage of national competitiveness development, the viable strategy should be the cost strategy with focuses on Factor Conditions and Workers. As countries move into a higher stage of national competitiveness development, the strategic focus should gradually move from the cost strategy to the differentiation strategy in every factor comprising the DDD model. In the final stage, countries should employ the differentiation strategy to enhance national competitiveness with an emphasis on Demand Conditions and Professionals. Figure 8-4 depicts

Factor \ Stage	Developing	Transitional	Developed
Factor Conditions	Resource-based	Manufacturing -based	Knowledge -based
Business Context	Protectionism	Efficiency	Competition
Related Industries	Physical Infrastructure (Roads & Ports)	Industrial Cluster	Regional Integration
Demand Conditions	Quantity	Quality	Sophistication

(Physical Factors)

☐ Differentiation Strategy ■ Cost Strategy

Factor \ Stage	Developing	Transitional	Developed
Workers	Cheap	Motivated	Skilled
Politicians & Bureaucrats	Facilitation	Support & Regulation	Advice
Entrepreneurs	Risk Taking	Efficiency Developing	Value Creating
Professionals	Operational	Managerial	Strategic

(Human Factors)

☐ Differentiation Strategy ■ Cost Strategy

Fig. 8-4   Implementation of Optimal Strategic Mix

the optimal strategic mix to enhance national competitiveness with changing strategies and focuses.

In the optimal strategic mix, a country can locate its competitive position and derive strategies necessary to develop national competitiveness further in each factor of the DDD model. For example, a country with national competitiveness in Demand Conditions less than a third among all countries finds its status of Demand Conditions in "Developing" stage and focuses on enhancing "Quantity" of its demand conditions to advance to "Transitional" stage where it should implement "Quality"-based strategy.

DATA AND APPLICATION

Data

Data for empirical analyses are selected from the *IPS National Competitiveness Research 2005 Report* (IPS, 2005), published annually by the Institute for Industrial Policy Studies. The report covers 66 countries and collects statistical data for 275 criteria comprising physical and human factors in both the domestic and international contexts.

The report uses the most up-to-date 137 hard data collected through various statistical sources published by international or government organizations, and 138 soft data collected by the Korea Trade-Investment Promotion Agency (KOTRA), which has 105 offices abroad. Among the 275 criteria, 63 criteria are used as background information and not included in the calculation of the national competitiveness index. The selection of the countries in the report depends largely on the availability of the statistical data of countries. The list of countries studied in this article can be found in Figure 8-6. Refer to the IPS report (IPS, 2005) for further information.

Application

Measure: the validity of the DDD model

To prove the validity of the DDD model as a comprehensive model for explaining national competitiveness, we conduct two kinds of analyses: a case study in which the national competitiveness of Korea and Singapore are compared to contrast the differences among the four models, and a formal statistical correlation analysis of data covering 66 countries in the world to determine general characteristics and explanatory power of the models. Korea and Singapore are selected in the case study because these countries can contrast the characteristics of each of the four models effectively: as the incorporation of the international context is designed to explain the competitiveness of those countries with small and open economies and the extension toward the human factors intends to explain the competitiveness of those countries with limited factor endowments but much dynamics, Korea and Singapore are expected to effectively depict the characteristics of the four models.

In both of the two empirical analyses, the national competitiveness indices are calculated by reorganizing variables comprising national competitiveness in accordance with the intended purpose of each model. For domestic physical factors, variables such as natural resources, market size, infrastructure, and governance structure in the domestic context are selected. International physical factors include foreign direct investment, trade openness, international network, and global standard. On the other hand, variables such as domestic wage, government officials, domestic entrepreneurs, and professionals are selected for the domestic human factors, and openness of labor market and professional job's openness are utilized as international human factors.

The index of the single diamond model (Model 1 in Figure 8-1) is calculated by using only the criteria in domestic physical factors. To calculate the index of the nine-factor model (Model 2 in Figure 8-1), both physical and human factors in the domestic context are selected. For the index of the double diamond model (Model 3 in Figure 8-1), physical factors in both domestic and international contexts are used. Finally, for the index of the DDD model (Model 4 in Figure 8-1), both physical and human factors in both domestic and international contexts are considered.

Figure 8-5 illustrates the variations of national competitiveness between Korea and Singapore when analyzed with each of the four models. In Model 1, among 66 countries, Korea ranks 23rd and Singapore 17th making the difference 6. A closer look at the diamond shows that Singapore is more competitive than Korea in all factors except Demand Conditions.

In Model 3, on the other hand, Korea ranks 25th while Singapore 13th, with a difference of 12 in ranking. Compared with Model 1, Korea falls and Singapore moves up in its ranking when international variables are considered. This demonstrates that Korea has a relatively weak competitiveness structure in the international context. In addition, Singapore exceeds Korea in Demand Conditions that is less competitive than that of Korea when considering only the domestic context. This implies that Singapore successfully solves its weakness in Demand Conditions through internationalization. Furthermore, the gap between Korea and Singapore increases in Business Context and Related & Supporting Industries. This consequently represents that the

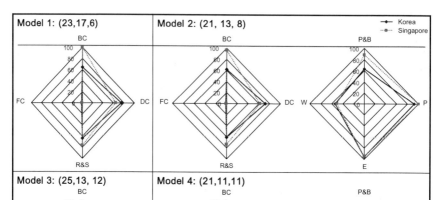

Fig. 8-5 Variations on National Competitiveness: Korea vs. Singapore
Note: National competitiveness rankings of Korea and Singapore among 66 countries and the difference between the rankings of these two countries are listed in the parenthesis with the order of the rankings of Korea, Singapore, and their difference. Indices in each model are internally standardized by taking the maximum value of the model as 100. FC: Factor Conditions, BC: Business Context, DC: Demand Conditions, R&S: Related and Supporting Industries. W: Workers, P&B: Politicians and Bureaucrats, E: Entrepreneurs, P: Professionals.

addition of the international context recognizes the national competitiveness of the two countries with much more clarity.

Model 2 shows the national competitiveness of Korea and Singapore with an additional diamond of the human factors. In Model 2, Korea ranks 21st and Singapore 13th with a difference of 8 in ranking, which is larger than that of Model 1. Singapore demonstrates more competitiveness in all the human factors except Workers, in which it shows almost the same level of competitiveness compared with that of Korea. Both Korea and Singapore gain competitiveness in ranking when including the human factors in addition to the physical factors. However, Singapore's larger diamond in the human factors expounds that Singapore is more competitive than Korea in its human resource management.

Model 4 contrasts the two countries in the DDD model. While Korea's ranking remains the same compared with that of Model 2, Singapore's ranking shows an increase of two places, thus implying that Singapore is more competitive in the international context. Physical factors in Model 4 have the same features as mentioned in Model 3. In human factors of Model 4, Singapore exceeds Korea in every corner of the diamond, even in Workers which has a similar level of competitiveness with that of Korea when confined only to the domestic context. In addition, the gap between the two diamonds in human factors also increases.

All of these analyses demonstrate that the DDD model is more comprehensive and thus is better at explaining both the sources and the scopes of national competitiveness than other models. The DDD model is particularly useful for explaining small, open, and dynamic economies such as Singapore, whose national competitiveness otherwise cannot be fully understood.

The correlation analysis contrasts the statistical validity of the four models by comparing the relationship between economic variables and national competitiveness indices measured with each of the four models. The national competitiveness indices for the correlation analysis consist of two groups. The first one is composed of the indices of national competitiveness calculated by the four models (Model 1 through Model 4 in Figure 8-1). The other one is composed of the discrepancies between the index calculated with Porter's single diamond model (Model 1) and those with the other three models (Models 2, 3, and 4) to determine the distinctive features of the latter three models in comparison with Porter's single diamond model. For economic variables, the analysis considers country's size and its economic development. Specifically, the land size and land per capita are selected for the size of nations; GDP, annual growth rate of GDP, and GDP per capita are chosen for the level of economic development.

Table 8-2 displays the results of the correlation analysis. None of the national competitiveness indices measured with the four models show a statistically significant correlation with Land and Land per capita, but the indices show a strong correlation with GDP, Annual Growth Rate of GDP, and GDP per capita. Considering a positive correlation with high statistical significance between Land and Natural Resources[1] ($r = 0.831$), and Land

---

[1] "Natural Resources" was calculated as a composite index of "Energy Resources" and "Other Resources" (IPS, 2005).

Table 8-2   Correlation Analysis for Different Models with Some Economic Variables

	Land	Land per Capita	GDP	AGR[a] of GDP	GDP per Capita
Model 1:	0.162	0.110	0.440**	−0.378**	0.875**
The Single	0.097	0.190	0.000	0.001	0.000
Diamond	66	66	66	66	66
Model 2:	0.085	0.043	0.376**	−0.384**	0.847**
The	0.249	0.366	0.001	0.001	0.000
Nine-Factor	66	66	66	66	66
Model 3:	0.188	0.088	0.479**	−0.357**	0.867**
The Double	0.066	0.242	0.000	0.002	0.000
Diamond	66	66	66	66	66
Model 4:	0.087	0.024	0.383**	−0.370**	0.842**
The Dual	0.243	0.425	0.001	0.001	0.000
Double Diamond	66	66	66	66	66
Model 2 —	−0.348**	−0.306**	−0.269*	−0.055	−0.071
Model 1[b]	0.002	0.006	0.014	0.331	0.286
	66	66	66	66	66
Model 3 —	−0.005	−0.172	−0.152	0.361**	−0.659**
Model 1[c]	0.483	0.084	0.112	0.001	0.000
	66	66	66	66	66
Model 4 —	−0.316**	−0.351**	−0.303**	0.103	−0.293**
Model 1[d]	0.005	0.002	0.007	0.205	0.008
	66	66	66	66	66

Note: [a] AGR: Annual Growth Rate;
[b] The index of the nine-factor model — the index of the diamond model;
[c] The index of the double diamond model — the index of the diamond model;
[d] The index of the dual double diamond model — the index of the diamond model;
Data are arranged in the order of "Pearson correlation, Sig. (1-tailed), Numbers of data"
$**p < 0.01$; $*p < 0.05$; all one-tailed tests.

per capita and Natural Resources $(r = 0.534)$, we can understand that natural resources, which have previously been regarded as important factors comprising national competitiveness, have no direct correlation with national competitiveness. In other words, in contrast to what economists have argued, factor endowments do not have a critical impact on national competitiveness.

GDP and GDP per capita show positive correlations with all four models. Annual Growth Rate of GDP, however, has a negative correlation with all four models. Considering that developing countries have relatively higher rates of economic growth than developed countries, the negative correlation between Annual Growth Rate of GDP and the competitiveness indices also support the argument that level of economic development has a positive correlation with national competitiveness.

The discrepancies between indices measured with the single diamond model and the other three extended models reveal important implications. The effects of human factors on national competitiveness (Model 2–Model 1) show negative correlations with Land, Land per capita, and GDP, implying that the role of human factors is more closely associated with smaller countries and less developed economies. On the other hand, the effects of multinational activities (Model 3–Model 1) have a positive correlation with Annual Growth Rate of GDP and a negative correlation with GDP per capita, indicating that multinational activities are more important for rapidly growing but relatively less developed economies. All of these findings considered, Porter's single diamond may be useful in explaining large and/or developed economies, but not the small and/or developing economies.

By integrating the human factors and the international context into Porter's single diamond, a more comprehensive analysis can be made. The combined effects of human factors and multinational activities (Model 4–Model 1) have statistically significant correlations with all the variables except Annual Growth Rate of GDP, while the effects of human factors (Model 2–Model 1) demonstrate statistical significance with the first three variables of Land, Land per capita, and GDP, and the effects of multinational activities (Model 3–Model 1) with the last two variables of the Annual Growth Rate of GDP and GDP per capita. In other words, the DDD model can comprehensively explain in a single framework the national competitiveness of not only large and/or developed countries but also small and/or developing countries. Therefore, it is clearly proven that the DDD model, an extension in both sources and scopes of competitiveness, is more comprehensive and thereby has more explanatory power in measuring national competitiveness than other models.

Analyze: 3 × 3 country groups

We grouped countries into 3 × 3 framework with the cluster analysis technique. Cluster analysis is a statistical technique that classifies objects into clusters

Table 8-3   ANOVA for Grouping Countries

	Cluster		Error			
	Mean Square	df	Mean Square	df	F	Sig.
Population & Land Area[a]	2182.228	11	0.633	52	3449.844	0.000
National Competitiveness[b]	4212.107	2	17.428	63	241.691	0.000

Note: [a]The size of each country is calculated as a summation of two indices: the index of population and the index of land size as listed in the IPS 2005 report; [b]National Competitiveness is measured with the DDD model.

according to the characteristics of the objects. Objects in the same cluster share significant homogeneity, while there is significant heterogeneity among objects in different clusters (Hair et al., 1998). The size and competitiveness are used as two criteria of country groupings. The size of each country is calculated as a summation of two indices: the index of population and the index of land size listed in the IPS 2005 report. Competitiveness is measured with the DDD model (IPS, 2005). Table 8-3 displays the results of an ANOVA test on the criteria for grouping countries. The country groupings are statistically significant with p-values of two criteria less than 0.001.

A total of 66 countries are categorized into 9 country groups according to the results of the cluster analysis, as illustrated in Figure 8-6. Austria and Belgium are classified into the Strong-Small Countries, while Australia in Strong-Large Countries. As discussed, therefore, it is more relevant to compare Austria with Belgium than with Australia. By simultaneously considering the size and competitiveness, we can now compare and contrast the relative competitiveness of nations more systematically: a country can figure out with whom to compete and the characteristics of its competitors more clearly.

Simulate: changing landscape of competition and competitive structure

To determine the changing landscape of competition, competitive structures of countries, and general implications of competitive strategy, we first calculate and compare three different indices according to strategic alternatives, and then conduct correlation analyses with the indices. The three different indices

Small Group — Country (19) (overall: Small)

Level	Country
Strong	Austria
	Belgium
	Denmark
	Hong Kong
	Israel
	Netherlands
	Singapore
	Switzerland
Intermediary	Croatia
	Czech Republic
	Greece
	Hungary
	Jordan
	Kuwait
	Panama
	Portugal
	U.A.E.
Weak	Dominican Republic
	Guatemala

Medium Group — Country (23) (overall: Medium)

Level	Country
Strong	Finland
	France
	New Zealand
	Norway
	Sweden
	Taiwan
	United Kingdom
Intermediary	Chile
	Italy
	Korea
	Malaysia
	Philippines
	Poland
	Romania
	Spain
	Thailand
Weak	Cambodia
	Kenya
	Morocco
	Oman
	Sri Lanka
	Ukraine
	Venezuela

Large Group — Country (24) (overall: Large)

Level	Country
Strong	Australia
	Canada
	Germany
	Japan
	United States
Intermediary	Brazil
	China
	Colombia
	Mexico
	Russia
	Saudi Arabia
Weak	Argentina
	Bangladesh
	Egypt
	India
	Indonesia
	Iran
	Libya
	Nigeria
	Pakistan
	Peru
	South Africa
	Turkey
	Vietnam

Fig. 8-6 Country Groups

Note: Countries are sorted by alphabetical order in each country group. Values in parenthesis indicate number of countries in the group.

are No Strategy Index (NSI), Cost Strategy Index (CSI), and Differentiation Strategy Index (DSI). NSI is an original index of each country's national competitiveness measured with the DDD model and has an equal weight scheme over the factors and sub-factors comprising the DDD model, to which different weight schemes listed in Table 8-1 are applied to generate CSI and DSI. CSI is a modified index by applying the weight scheme of the cost strategy in Table 8-1. Likewise, we can calculate DSI with the weight scheme of the differentiation strategy to NSI.

Findings from strategy simulation can be summarized into four categories. First, each competitive strategy changes the landscape of competition. Figure 8-7 shows the changing competitiveness of 66 countries when applied the cost strategy and the differentiation strategy to the original national competitiveness indices that are represented as no strategy. The figure demonstrates a unique pattern and suggests interesting findings. First, there are large differences in the indices among the high ranking nations, but very small differences among the low ranking nations. This implies that a nation has to be more careful in choosing strategies as it

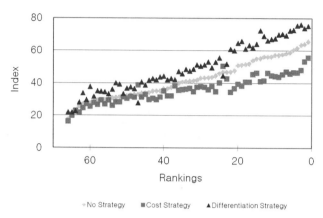

Fig. 8-7   Changing Indices with Different Strategies

becomes more competitive: strategic alternatives cause more drastic results as national competitiveness of countries enhances. Second, in most cases, the appropriate strategic choice is differentiation strategy. This is especially true of those countries with high competitiveness. Finally, there is no clear superior strategy for those countries in lower rankings because the indices do not change much with different strategies. This implies that countries with low competitiveness should radically change their current economic or social structure in order to enhance their national competitiveness. These findings suggest that competitive strategy might have an immense impact on the landscape in which countries compete to enhance national competitiveness and, therefore, should be taken into consideration when designing national strategy to enhance national competitiveness.

Second, countries differ in competitive structures from others. For example, Japan's NSI is 51.18 (19th place). However, if Japan pursues the cost strategy, its index becomes 38.36 (CSI) and its ranking falls to 37th place. On the contrary, if Japan pursues the differentiation strategy, the country will have an index of 65.75 (DSI) and will top the rankings. On the other hand, India is the opposite case. India's NSI of 33.01 (47th place) will go up to 38.87 (38th place) with the cost strategy but will go down to 27.72 (59th place) with the differentiation strategy.

A close look at these changing indices and rankings would reveal the competitive structure of countries. As the index and ranking of Japan increases when applied with the differentiation strategy, we can figure out that Japan has a competitive structure suitable to the differentiation strategy. Likewise, we

Table 8-4   Correlation between Strategic Changes and Economic Variables

		CSI–NSI[a]	DSI–NSI[b]
SIZE	Pearson Correlation	0.375**	−0.394**
	Sig. (2-tailed)	0.002	0.001
	N	66	66
Competitiveness (NSI[c])	Pearson Correlation	−0.843**	0.695**
	Sig. (2-tailed)	0.000	0.000
	N	66	66

Note: [a] CSI–NSI: Cost Strategy Index — No Strategy Index;
[b] DSI–NSI: Differentiation Strategy Index—No Strategy Index;
[c] NSI: No Strategy Index;
** $p < 0.01$; * $p < 0.05$; all two-tailed tests.

can understand that India has a competitive structure appropriate for the cost strategy. Therefore, countries have to pursue appropriate strategies in accordance with their competitive structures to maximize their competitiveness.

Third, the cost strategy is appropriate for a large-sized country with low competitiveness, while the differentiation strategy is suitable for a small-sized country with high competitiveness. Table 8-4 shows the results of correlation analyses between the effects of strategy changes (CSI–NSI: the discrepancy between CSI and NSI, DSI–NSI: the discrepancy between DSI and NSI) and some economic variables (size and competitiveness). From theses correlation analyses, we can derive important implications. Overall, the analyses demonstrate that the cost strategy is more viable to those countries that are larger and have a lower competitiveness, while the differentiation strategy is better suited for those countries that are smaller and have a higher competitiveness. The positive correlation coefficient between Size and CSI–NSI indicates that the larger the Size, the better the performance of CSI in comparison with NSI. On the other hand, the negative relationship between NSI and CSI–NSI implies that the higher the competitiveness, the worse the CSI performs in comparison with NSI. Therefore, the cost strategy is appropriate for a large-sized country with low competitiveness. The exact opposite results are found in the case of the differentiation strategy. Consequently, the differentiation strategy is suitable for a small-sized country with high competitiveness.

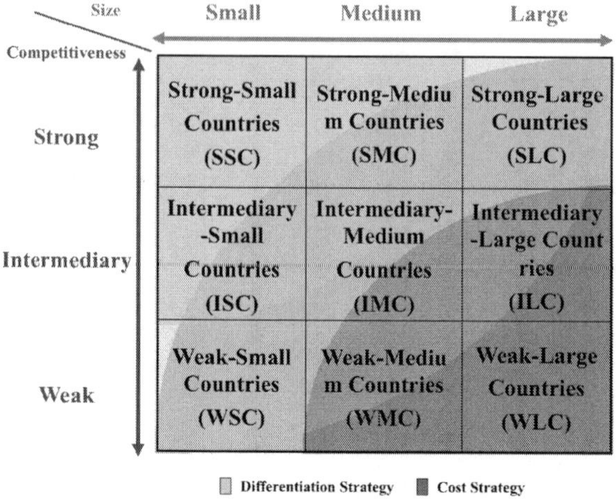

	Small	Medium	Large
Strong	Strong-Small Countries (SSC)	Strong-Medium Countries (SMC)	Strong-Large Countries (SLC)
Intermediary	Intermediary-Small Countries (ISC)	Intermediary-Medium Countries (IMC)	Intermediary-Large Countries (ILC)
Weak	Weak-Small Countries (WSC)	Weak-Medium Countries (WMC)	Weak-Large Countries (WLC)

☐ Differentiation Strategy   ■ Cost Strategy

Fig. 8-8   Viable Strategies for Different Country Groups

Lastly, only one of the cost strategy or the differentiation strategy is viable for a country. By comparing discrepancies among the indices, we found that NSI of each country is less than either CSI or DSI of the country. This reveals that a country must employ either cost or differentiation as its optimum strategy to enhance its competitiveness. In addition, CSI–NSI and DSI–NSI has a negative correlation ($r = -0.899$) with high statistical significance ($p < 0.001$). This indicates that the cost strategy and differentiation strategies have a complementary distribution, implying that once one of the two strategies is chosen, the other must be abandoned.

All these findings can be systematically illustrated in Figure 8-8, which shows viable strategies for different country groups. As distinguished by different degrees of shades, the cost strategy is better for the countries located in the lower right area, and the differentiation strategy performs better with the countries located in the upper left area.

Implement: toward higher competitiveness

The strategic resources and capabilities of the country should be focused on advancing national competitiveness to the next stages in the optimal strategy mix. For example, in 2005, Korea ranked 22nd among 66 countries in overall national competitiveness and 32nd in Business Context (Firm Strategy, Structure, and Rivalry). Therefore, the competitive position of the Korean Business Context can be located approximately in the middle among

66 countries, which is the Transitional stage in Figure 8-4. In other words, the current source of competitiveness in the Korean Business Context is efficiency. To enhance competitiveness of the Business Context of Korea, strategic resources and capabilities should focus on achieving a business environment that promotes competition, as represented in the Developed stage in Figure 8-4. As competition results in competitiveness, national strategy to advance the competitive position of the Korean Business Context from the Transitional stage into the Developed stage should lay its basis on competition.

It is important to consider the inertia of national competitiveness when establishing and implementing strategy to enhance national competitiveness. A time-series analysis on the national competitiveness shows that countries have different inertia in their development of national competitiveness (IPS, 2005). Consequently, some countries accomplish the development of national competitiveness in a much shorter time than others, while other countries lag behind or even witness retrogression. In this light, the strategy and focuses suggested above are not applicable to all countries indiscriminately. Some countries can drive to the next stage much faster than others, even skipping some stages while other countries may stand still in a stage without any progress for a long time. The implementation of strategies to enhance national competitiveness should, therefore, take the inertia of national competitiveness into consideration.

DISCUSSION

The MASI methodology designed for countries also suggests valuable implications to MNCs. In the globalized economy, a comprehensive analysis of national competitiveness and a systemic methodology to enhance it can reveal sources of competitive advantages to MNCs because much of MNCs' competitiveness comes from host countries.

In the measurement, the DDD model presents a more sophisticated analysis of the location-specific advantages (LSAs) than existing models. Extended into both the scopes and the sources of national competitiveness, the DDD model can provide a more comprehensive understanding of the competitive sources, structures, and positions of countries. As LSAs are one of the most important sources of competitiveness in MNCs, together with firm-specific advantages (FSAs), MNCs can establish more comprehensive and fine-tuned competitive strategy with the DDD model analysis.

Country groupings allow MNCs to analyze more relevantly the competitive positions of candidate host countries into which MNCs are planning to invest. By locating and comparing countries in the country groups, MNCs can have a much clearer understanding of would-be host countries and, consequently, can detect alternative host countries that would otherwise be neglected: MNCs can effectively evaluate the validity in choosing a specific country and its opportunity cost.

From strategy simulation, MNCs can find out strategic leverages of countries. Instead of regarding countries as bundles of homogeneous resources to be uniformly exploited by MNCs, the competitive structure analyzed through strategy simulation allows MNCs to recognize countries' strategic values with which MNCs can leverage their investment. In addition, by providing complementary capabilities and resources necessary to enhance competitiveness of host countries, MNCs can secure dominant positions in negotiating the conditions of investments.

Implementation procedure of the MASI methodology shows dynamic aspects of countries, allowing MNCs to plan long-term strategy. Understanding the current position and further strategic focus of countries in the optimal strategic mix would help MNCs design their global expansion strategy in accordance not only with the current competitiveness of the countries but also with the future competitiveness changed by implementation of competitive strategy. As globalization has brought dynamics into every corner of the world, understanding dynamic aspects of LSAs, especially in terms of strategic choices, would allow MNCs to devise more viable strategy.

MNCs and countries depend on each other. As MNCs and countries are closely interconnected, the MASI methodology to enhance national competitiveness can also be used for MNCs to improve their competitiveness.

CONCLUSIONS

This chapter introduces a MASI methodology for a comprehensive study of national competitiveness: *what is national competitiveness and how to enhance it?* In the first stage, national competitiveness is comprehensively measured with the DDD model (Measure). In the next stage, the results are analyzed with the 3×3 framework of country groups (Analyze). Then, implications for enhancing national competitiveness are derived through the application of business strategy models to the national level (Simulate). In the final stage, a series of detailed strategies to enhance the national competitiveness in different stages of economic development are suggested (Implement).

Empirical analyses with the MASI methodology demonstrate the validity of the DDD model as a new comprehensive model measuring competitiveness of countries with varying characteristics. In addition, the analyses suggest general features of national competitiveness: countries with high competitiveness are more vulnerable to wrong strategic choices; countries differ in competitive structures from others such that they need to employ either cost strategy or differentiation strategy to enhance national competitiveness. These findings also provide strategic implications for MNCs to develop their competitive advantages.

While the firms' activities closely interact with the conditions of national competitiveness, business scholars have paid much more attention to the *inside* of the firms rather than the *outside*. The location variable, however, no longer remains exogenous to firms. This is particularly true for MNCs because they can easily change locations across national boundaries. In this light, this study can provide an arena for further discussion to enhance competitiveness and sustainability of MNCs in connection with competitive advantages of nations.

REFERENCES

Cho, D. S. (1994). A dynamic approach to international competitiveness: The case of Korea. *Journal of Far Eastern Business*, 1(1): 17–36.

Cho, D. S. and Moon, H. C. (2000). *From Adam Smith to Michael Porter*, Singapore: World Scientific.

Cho, D. S., Moon, H. C. and Kim, M. Y. (2006). Competitive strategy to enhance national competitiveness. *Proceedings in Academy of International Business* 2006 *Annual Meeting*, Beijing, China, 23–26 June.

Cho, D. S., Moon, H. C. and Kim, M. Y. (2007). Beyond Porter's single diamond: A dual double diamond model approach to national competitiveness. *Proceedings of the Academy of International Business 2007 Annual Meeting*, Indianapolis, Indiana, 25–28 June.

Cho, D. S., Moon, H. C. and Kim, M. Y. (2008). Characterizing international competitiveness in international business research: A MASI approach to national competitiveness. *Research in International Business and Finance*, 22(2): 175–192.

Dunning, J. H. (2003). The role of foreign direct investment in upgrading China's competitiveness. *Journal of International Business and Economy*, 4(1): 1–13.

Hair, J. F., Anderson, R. E., Tatham, R. L. and Black, W. C. (1998). *Multivariate Data Analysis*, 5th Edn., Upper Saddle River, N. J.: Prentice Hall.

IPS (2005). *IPS National Competitiveness Research 2005 Report*, Seoul: IPS and IPS-NaC.

Moon, H. C., Rugman, A. M. and Verbeke, A. (1998). A generalized double diamond approach to the global competitiveness of Korea and Singapore. *International Business Review*, 7: 135–150.

Porter, M. E. (1980). *Competitive Strategy: Techniques for Analyzing Industries and Companies*, New York: Free Press.

Porter, M. E. (1990). *The Competitive Advantage of Nations*, New York: Free Press.

Porter, M. E. (1996). What is strategy? *Harvard Business Review*, 74(6): 61–78.

Porter, M. E. (1998). Clusters and the new economics of competition. *Harvard Business Review*, 76(6): 77–90.

Porter, M. E. (2003). *Malaysia's Competitiveness: Moving to the Next Stage*, Kuala Lumpur, Malaysia (Presentation slides).

Porter, M. E., Takeuchi, H. and Sakakibara, M. (2000). *Can Japan Compete?* Cambridge, MA: Perseus Publishing.

Rugman, A. M. (1991). Diamond in the rough. *Business Quarterly*, 55(3): 61–64.

Rugman, A. M. and D'Cruz, J. R. (1993). The double diamond model of international competitiveness: The Canadian experience. *Management International Review*, 33(2): 17–39.

Ryan, R. (1990). A grand disunity. *National Review*, 42(13): 46–47.

Saaty, T. L. (1980). *The Analytic Hierarchy Process*, New York: McGraw-Hill.

Smith, A. (1937) (orig. pub. 1776). An inquiry into the nature and causes of the wealth of nations, in Eliot, C. W. (ed.), *The Harvard Classics*, New York: P. F. Collier & Son Corporation.

Sureshchandar, G. S. and Leisten, R. (2006). A framework for evaluating the criticality of software metrics: An analytic hierarchy process (AHP) approach. *Measuring Business Excellence*, 10(4): 22–33.

Thain, D. H. (1990). The war without bullets. *Business Quarterly*, 55(1): 13–19.

Part III

MICHAEL PORTER AND PRACTICAL
EXTENSIONS

9

APPLICATION: FIRM LEVEL

SUMMARY AND KEY POINTS

So far, we have discussed what determines a nation's competitiveness and which model is more appropriate to define the determinants and more accurately measure the competitiveness. From this chapter to the last of this book, we will discuss the applications of these analytical frameworks to the real world and at different levels — firm, industry, nation, and international cluster — of analysis. First, this chapter deals with the firm-level analysis.

In the literature of competitiveness, to the extent that Porter's model brings together firm-specific linkages between the determinants, his model is useful and potentially predictive for firm level as well as industrial and national level studies (Bark and Moon, 2002). Likewise, its extended models which have determinants related to international environments and human factors can be used to explain individual firm's competitiveness more comprehensively. In this chapter, Moon and Lee suggest that the diamond model of Porter (1990) may do a job, but the GDD model (Moon *et al.*, 1995, 1998) will do a job better.

Source:
Moon, H. C., and Lee, D. H. (2004). The competitiveness of multinational firms: A case of study of Samsung Electronics and Sony. *Journal of International and Area Studies*, 11(1): 1–21.

In this article, they utilize the GDD model to compare the competitiveness of Samsung Electronics Co., Ltd. (SEC) and Sony. Since both SEC and Sony are multinational companies and their operations are much internationalized, the GDD model which has international variables is appropriate to measure their competitiveness. This study suggests that most of the other reports and studies comparing the competitiveness of SEC and Sony have not shown the whole picture, meaning that there are more comprehensive determinants to evaluate the competitiveness of these firms. Although the data of this study are old, the methodology is still quite valid. The researchers can use a similar methodology with updated data to analyze a more recent status of these firms and other competitors.

In this Part III (from Chapters 9 to 12), since each chapter was individually published, there are overlaps in the literature review between articles. Therefore, the readers can selectively read the literature part of Chapter 9 through Chapter 12, if they are now familiar with the related theories. They can then pay more attention to the analytical techniques and practical implications.

INTRODUCTION

Samsung Electronics Co., Ltd. (SEC) started out as a producer of cheap 12-inch, black and white televisions under the Sanyo label in 1971. After 30 years, SEC is now entering the top tier of the world's technology companies. Not only Korean newspapers but also renowned international magazines such as *Forbes* (2001), *Newsweek* (2002), *Fortune* (2002), *Time* (2002), and *Business Week* (2003) have been comparing SEC and Sony in terms of competitiveness, especially since early 2002. According to Daewoo Securities, on April 1, 2002, SEC's market value (market capitalization) reached $46.46 billion, surpassing Sony's $46.24 billion. At the start of 2001, the market capitalization of Samsung Electronics was equal to 35.38 percent of Sony and it increased to 81.78 percent at the beginning of 2002. Does this mean that SEC is now more competitive than Sony? In this research, we focus on the competitiveness of SEC compared to that of Sony in order to shed light on its true character. This chapter concludes that most of the reports comparing the competitiveness of SEC and Sony have not "drawn the whole picture," meaning that there are other determinants to consider when assessing the competitiveness of a firm.

Company Profile

Samsung Electronics Co., Ltd. SEC was founded in 1969 and sold its first product (a black and white television) in 1971. It is one of the world's largest chipmakers and also South Korea's top electronics company. SEC produces various consumer devices, including DVD players, TVs, and digital cameras; computers, color monitors, LCD panels, and printers; semiconductors such as DRAM, SRAM, and flash memory; and communications devices ranging from cellular phones to networking switches. SEC intends to maintain its leadership stance in high value-added memory by being the first to market with leading- edge technologies in a wide range of configurations and densities. The company is also looking forward to greatly accelerated sales of its RDRAM (Rambus Dynamic Random Access Memory) Modules as new, inherently low cost versions of RDRAM become available. These modifications are projected to lower overall production costs. SEC is currently organized into four main areas of operation: Digital Media, Digital Appliance, Device Solution and Telecommunication.

Sony. Established in 1946, Sony Corporation is engaged in the development, design, manufacturing, and sales of various kinds of electronic equipment, instruments and devices for consumer and industrial markets. The company develops, produces, manufactures and markets home-use game consoles and software. It is engaged in recorded music in all commercial formats and musical genres; businesses including insurance operations through a Japanese life insurance subsidiary and non-life insurance subsidiaries; banking operations through a Japanese Internet-based banking subsidiary; leasing and credit financing operations. Sony's strategies are making great strides in a knowledge society, vertical integration and "Soft Alliances," and speedy and unique management. Table 9-1 shows a comparison of the two companies in numbers.

Importance of Research and Conceptual Framework

So far, various reports have claimed that SEC has increased its competitiveness and is now taking the role of the world leader in several areas such as high-end cell phones, DVD players, plasma TVs, and a wide range of other consumer products. Also, these reports are saying that compared to Sony, SEC is exceeding in brand recognition in consumer-electronics, revenue growth (*Time*, 2002), market capitalization (*BusinessWeek*, 2003), etc. Other criteria of comparison are brand value, profits, sales and market share. However, if a report is not balanced and is focused on only one or two criteria, there is a possibility

Table 9-1 Comparison of SEC and Sony in Numbers

	SEC	Sony
Rank in the Electronics, Electrical Equipment Industry	5	3
Global 500 Rank by Revenues	59	32
Revenues	$47.6 billion	$61.3 billion
Profits	$5.6 billion	$948 million
Number of Employees	80,000	161,100
Market Value (April 2, 2002)	$49 billion	$48 billion

Sources:
Fortune Global 500 (2003). http://www.fortune.com;
Samsung Electronics (2003);
Sony (2003);
Daewoo Securities (2002).

that the evaluation may be biased or overestimating the competitiveness of a firm. This is why we need a more comprehensive and balanced framework.

Among the previous reports, Fortune Global 500 is considered the most reliable framework, ranking 500 global enterprises using diverse variables. SEC and Sony were also ranked in the electronics, electrical equipment industry as shown in Table 9-1. However, we believe that this framework is biased towards a few determinants, not showing the whole picture of competitiveness. To the extent that Porter (1990) brings together firm-specific linkages between the determinants, his model is useful and potentially predictive for firm level as well as industrial and national level studies (Bark and Moon, 2002). This chapter suggests that the diamond model of Porter (1990) may do a job, but the generalized double diamond model (Moon *et al.*, 1995, 1998) will do a job better, as shown in Figure 9-1.

Especially, since both SEC and Sony are multinational companies and much of their operations are internationalized, it is necessary to discern domestic and international determinants. Porter's diamond is somewhat ambiguous in explaining the utilization of multinational activity of firms to enhance their competitiveness. Also, Dunning (1992, 2003) treats multinational activities as an exogenous variable that should be added to Porter's model, as shown in Figure 9-2.

However, in today's global business, multinational activities represent much more than just an exogenous variable (Cho and Moon, 2000). Therefore,

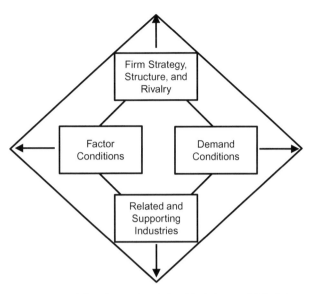

Fig. 9-1 The Generalized Double Diamond Model
Source:
Moon *et al.* (1995, 1998).

Porter's single diamond model and Dunning's model have been extended to the generalized double diamond model (Moon *et al.*, 1995, 1998), including multinational activity as an indigenous variable rather than an exogenous variable, making it a more comprehensive framework. Following is a comparison of the determinants on the previous reports including Fortune Global 500 and the generalized double diamond model (see Table 9-2). It is notable that these existing studies are either lacking a number of determinants according to the generalized double diamond model or biased towards *factor conditions* and do not provide a satisfactory framework of analysis.

DIAMOND VARIABLES AND DESCRIPTIVE DATA

In this chapter, we selected several variables for the determinants of the generalized double diamond model to compare the competitiveness of SEC and Sony. According to the model, the four determinants are factor conditions; demand conditions; related and supporting industries; and firm strategy, structure, and rivalry, which are based on Porter's diamond model. Each determinant is divided into domestic and international variables. Proxy variables are then distinguished and weighted to represent the concept of each variable.

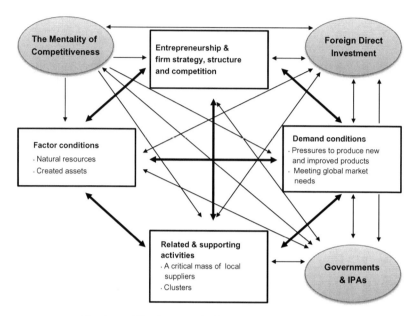

Fig. 9-2 The Diamond of Competitive Advantage

Source:
Dunning (2003).

Factor Conditions

Domestic factor conditions

Porter (1990) distinguishes between basic factors and advanced factors. His basic factors include natural resources, climate, location, unskilled and semiskilled labor, and debt capital. In this study, we choose firm size and productivity for the domestic basic factor conditions. Firm size is represented by the number of employees, total sales, and total assets of the fiscal year 2002. Productivity is represented by profitability, which is composed of both return on equity (ROE) and return on investment (ROI).

According to Porter (1990), advanced factors include modern communications infrastructure and highly educated personnel such as engineers and scientists. For the advanced domestic factor conditions, we chose R&D investment and research facility. R&D investment is represented by the five-year average (1998–2002) of R&D expenses over total sales. The number of research centers represents the research facility variable.

Table 9-2 Comparison of Reports and the Generalized Double Diamond Model

Generalized Double Diamond Model (1995, 1998)			Forbes (2001)	Newsweek (2002)	Fortune (2002)	Time (2002)	Business Week (2003)
Factor Conditions	Domestic	Basic	V		VVVV	VVV	VVV
		Advanced			VVV		VVV
	International	Basic	VVVV	VVV	VVV	VVVV	VV
		Advanced	VVV	VVV		VV	
Demand Conditions	Domestic	Size					
		Quality	V		V	V	V
	International	Size	V				
		Quality	V	V			V
Related and Supporting Sectors	Domestic		V				V
	International		V			V	
Firm Strategy, Structure and Rivalry	Domestic	Strategy	V	V	V		VVV
		Structure			V		V
		Rivalry	V				
	International	Strategy	VV	V	V		VV
		Structure				V	V
		Rivalry	V				V

International factor conditions

For the international basic factor conditions, the variables are international sales and overseas factories. The proxies for international sales are the three-year average (2000–2002) of international sales and the three-year average (2000–2002) of the international sales ratio (international sales over total sales). Also, the proxies for overseas factories are the number of overseas factories in the year 2002. For the international advanced factor conditions, patents and research facilities are chosen as variables. Also, the five-year sum (1998–2002) of patents registered in the U.S. and the number of overseas laboratories of each firm are used as proxies, respectively. Table 9-3 shows the descriptive data of the variables for the domestic and international factor conditions.

Table 9-3 Descriptive Data for Factor Conditions

Variable	Proxy	SEC	Sony
	Domestic		
Firm Size	Number of employees	80,000	161,100
	Total assets ($, mil.)	54,766	70,590
	Total sales ($, mil.)	49,640	62,280
Productivity	Profitability (ROE, %)	25	5
	Profitability' (ROI, %)	10.7	1.4
R&D Investment	Five-year average of R&D expenses over total sales	5.58%	5.64%
Research Facility	Number of research centers	9	15
	International		
International Sales	Three-year average of international sales	27,374	43,464
	Three-year average international sales ratio	0.69	0.71
Overseas Factories	Number of overseas factories	21	33
Patents	Five-year sum of patents in U.S.	7,069	6,930
Research Facility	Number of overseas research centers	6	8

Sources:
Fortune Global 500 (2003). http://www.fortune.com;
Samsung Electronics (2003);
Sony (2003).

Demand Conditions

Domestic demand conditions

Porter distinguishes the size of demand and the sophistication of demand. The growth rate of home demand can be more important to competitive advantage than its absolute size. Rapid domestic growth leads a nation's companies to adopt new technologies quicker, with less fear that such technologies would make existing investments redundant, and to build large, efficient facilities with the confidence that they will be utilized (Porter, 1990). Meanwhile, companies gain competitive advantage where home demand gives them a clearer or timelier picture of emerging buyer needs, and wherein demanding consumers give pressure on companies to innovate faster and achieve more sophisticated competitive advantages. They pressure them to meet high standards and prod them to improve, innovate and move up into more advanced segments (Bark and Moon, 2002).

In this chapter, the market size variable represents the size of domestic demand. Market size is divided into three proxies. The first is the population of the age group of 15 to 64, regarded as the main consumers of electronics in each country of Korea and Japan. The second proxy is the three-year (2000–2002) average of GDP in each country and the third proxy is the four-year (1998–2001) average of real GDP growth rates of each country. The variables for the sophistication of demand are consumer sophistication and customer satisfaction. Consumer sophistication is expressed through the 2002 Education Index announced by the United Nations Development Programme and the three-year average of GDP per capita of each country. According to Cho and Moon (2000), it can be hypothesized that a higher level of education of the consumers leads to higher demand sophistication. Thus, this chapter also uses this index. It can also be hypothesized that a higher level of GDP per capita, which implies a high standard of living, leads to higher demand sophistication. The proxy for customer satisfaction was the rank of each firm from its domestic customer satisfaction index.

International demand conditions

Multinational companies may need to expand their markets internationally to achieve economies of scale and economies of scope. Especially, innovative firms such as SEC and Sony are constantly on the lookout for new markets. When the domestic market reaches saturation, firms have to turn to international markets and they often introduce new products simultaneously into the global market

(Bark and Moon, 2002). Thus, there is a need to consider the international demand as a determinant of a firm's competitiveness.

For the international size of demand, we use market size as a variable. It is represented by two proxies: (1) the number of main areas of each firm multiplied by the number of countries where the products are sold; (2) the three-year (2000–2002) average of exports as a percentage of total sales. SEC focuses on home appliances, computer and related products, mobile phone, memory, and TFT-LCD (Thin Film Transistor-Liquid Crystal Display) and sells its products in 43 different countries. Sony focuses on home appliances, computer and related products, non-memory, music, movies, and video games and sells its products in 54 different countries. Meanwhile, the international sophistication of demand is composed of two variables: customer satisfaction and the diversification of markets. Customer satisfaction is represented by the brand value of each firm and the rank from *Financial Times*/PricewaterhouseCoopers' "The World's Most Respected Companies," 2002. The diversification of markets is represented by the ratio of the number of countries of sales over the three-year (2000–2002) average of total export amount. It can be hypothesized that a high ratio of the diversification of markets indicates a highly sophisticated international market. The descriptive data for the domestic and international demand conditions are summarized in Table 9-4.

Related and Supporting Industries

Domestic related and supporting industries

Related and supporting industries are those whereby firms coordinate or share activities in the value chain or those that involve products that are complementary to the firms of a given nation (Porter, 1990). Also, firms can improve their competitiveness through easy access to components from suppliers and there may be both forward and backward linkages between the firm and suppliers. Furthermore, end-users and suppliers can share information to improve the process of innovation and upgrading.

For determinants, we chose infrastructure and the competitiveness of the domestic academy as variables. It is possible that domestic infrastructure can be regarded as an advanced factor. However, since the proxies are focused on technology synergy and diffusion, we believe that it is better to incorporate infrastructure in the category of related and supporting industries. The first proxy for infrastructure is the three-year average (1999–2001) of

Table 9-4   Descriptive Data for Demand Conditions

Variable	Proxy	SEC	Sony
	Domestic		
Market Size	Population of the age group of 15 to 64	32,972,859	85,706,000
	Three-year average of GDP ($, bil.)	455.3	4,295
	Four-year average of real GDP growth rates	3.3	−0.3
Consumer Sophistication	Education index	0.96	0.94
	Three-year average of GDP per capita ($)	9,540	34,195
Customer Satisfaction	Rank percentage of each firm from its domestic customer satisfaction index (from under)	80%	78%
	International		
Market Size	Number of main areas of each firm multiplied by the number of countries where the products are sold	215	324
	Three-year average of export as a percentage of total sales	68.7%	70.8%
Customer Satisfaction	Brand value of firm ($, bil., 2003)	10.85	13.15
	Financial Times/PricewaterhouseCoopers: 'The World's Most Respected Companies'. 2002 rank	42 (in 84%)	6 (in 12%)
Diversification of Markets	Ratio of number of countries of sales over the three-year average of total export amount	0.0062	0.0072

Sources:
Fortune Global 500 (2003). http://www.fortune.com;
OECD Main Economic Indicators (2002);
Ministry of Commerce, Industry, Energy (http://www.mocie.go.kr);
United Nations Development Programme Education Index, 2002;
National Consumer Satisfaction Index (http://www.ncsi.or.kr);
Interbrand (http://www.interbrand.com).

the National Informatization Index announced by the Ministry of Commerce, Industry and Energy of Korea. The index consists of the condition of broadcasting; the state of communication; and the spread rate of personal computers, televisions, internet users, telephones, and cellular phones. Thus, a high score based on the index indicates a good infrastructure for electronic businesses. The second proxy for infrastructure is the ICT (Information and Communication Technologies) Development Index. This index measures the technology development environment level of a country. Some of the indicators are R&D expenditure, average incoming/outgoing telecom traffic and the number of internet hosts. The proxy for the competitiveness of academy is the number of schools per 10 million persons of each country in "The World Best Science and Technology Universities" ranking list announced by *Asiaweek* (2000). This proxy represents the cooperation between academia and business.

International Related and Supporting Industries

When multinational firms coordinate or share activities in the value chain within a geographic vicinity such as the clusters of Silicon Valley in the U.S. and Bangalore in India, they bring in new technologies and also benefit from acquiring related and supporting technologies (Bark and Moon, 2002). In order to do so, these firms need a constant flow of financing, which itself requires a sound credit status and also that of the country where the firm is based.

Here, we have chosen three variables for determinants — credit, international competitiveness of academy, and cooperation. Credit comprises the Moody's Credit Ranking of SEC and Sony in 2003 and the Moody's Credit Ranking of Korea and Japan in 2002. Credit ranking can be considered as a sign of the competitiveness to raise international funding and stimulate international strategic alliances. Funding entities and strategic alliance partners will have considered a firm's credit ranking before any actions are made. The number of international academic publications per ten thousand persons represents international competitiveness of academy, which shows the academic infrastructure. The number of overseas component complexes represents cooperation. The descriptive data for domestic and internationally related and supporting industries are summarized in Table 9-5.

Table 9-5 Descriptive Data for Related and Supporting Industries

Variable	Proxy	SEC	Sony
	Domestic		
Infrastructure	Three-year average National Informatization Index	80	74.3
	ICT Development Index (2000)	0.5104	0.6090
Competitiveness of Academy	Number of schools in "The World Best Science and Technology Universities" list per 10 million persons	0.63	0.58
	International		
Credit	Moody's Credit Ranking of Company (2003)	A3	A1
	Moody's Credit Ranking of Country (2002)	A3	A2
International Competitiveness of Academy	Number of international academic publications per 10 thousand persons	10.85	13.15
Cooperation	Number of overseas component complexes	6	10

Sources:
Ministry of Commerce, Industry and Energy, Korea (http://www.mocie.go.kr);
UNCTAD Statistics for ICT Index (2000, http://www.unctad.org);
Asiaweek, "Asia's Best Universities" (2000, http://www.asiaweek.com);
Moody's Investors Service (http://www.moodys.com);
Analysis Report for SCI Publications of Korean Universities (2001);
Ministry of Education and Human Resources Development (http://www.moe.go.kr);
Samsung Group homepage (http://www.samsung.com);
Sony Corporation homepage (http://www.sony.net).

Firm Strategy, Structure, and Rivalry

Domestic firm strategy, structure, and rivalry

This determinant reflects the context in which firms are created, organized and managed. However, Porter (1990) finds that no one managerial system is universally appropriate. Instead, he expresses a strong preference in favor of vigorous domestic rivalry for creating and sustaining competitive advantage. In this study, we have incorporated the results of a survey conducted in a previous study evaluating the strategy and structure of the two firms.

Table 9-6   Main Competitors of SEC and Sony

Firm	Main Product	Domestic Competitors	International Competitors
SEC	Semiconductor	Hynix	Elpida, Hynix, Infenion, Micron
	Telecom	LG	Ericsson, Motorola, Nokia, Siemens
	Television	LG, Panasonic, Sony	LG, Panasonic, Philips, Sony
	Computer and Related	HP Compaq, LG, Philips, LG IBM, Fujitsu, Sony, Toshiba, TriGem	Dell, Fujitsu, HP Compaq, LG, Philips, LG IBM, Sony, Toshiba
Sony	Television	Panasonic, Samsung	LG, Philips, Panasonic, Samsung
	Games	Microsoft	Microsoft
	Music	Avex, B-Gram, Trax, Toshiba EMI	BMG, EMI, Universal Music
	Movie Pictures	Doho, Toei, Shochiku	Disney, DreamWorks, Universal, 20th Century Fox
	Computer and Related	HP Compaq, IBM, Fujitsu, Toshiba	Dell, HP Compaq, IBM, Fujitsu, Toshiba

The variables for domestic firm strategy and structure are strategy efficiency and management efficiency, respectively. The proxy representing the firm strategy determinant is company strategy, while efficiency of organization, flexibility of organization and leadership of CEO represent the domestic firm structure determinant. The variable for the rivalry determinant is market competition and for this we chose the number of the main competitors of SEC and Sony in each domestic market (see Table 9-6).

International firm strategy, structure and rivalry

Porter (1990) argues that domestic rivalry is superior to rivalry with foreign competitors. This argument may be true in large economies such as the United States, but not in small economies such as Canada (Rugman and D'Cruz 1993), Korea and Singapore (Cho and Moon, 2000). The successful firms in these economies are more concerned about international rivalry than about domestic rivalry. What is more, multinational firms such as SEC and Sony are destined to constantly consider international rivalry since the operations of these firms are spread across the globe and much of the sales and profit are generated in foreign markets. In fact, Porter recognized the importance of international or global variables but his single diamond did not explicitly include these variables (Bark and Moon, 2002).

In this chapter, we incorporated the results evaluating the international firm strategy and structure determinants from the above survey. The variables used in the survey were global strategy and global business structure. The proxies for global business structure are global infrastructure, acceptance to global business environment and leadership of CEO in global business. The variable for the rivalry determinant is market competition and we chose the number of the main competitors of SEC and Sony in the international market (see Table 9-6). The descriptive data for the domestic and international firm strategy, structure and rivalry are summarized in Table 9-7.

Table 9-7   Descriptive Data for Firm Strategy, Structure, and Rivalry

Variable	Proxy	SEC	Sony
Domestic			
Strategy Efficiency	Company strategy	Questionnaire results	Questionnaire results
Management Efficiency	Efficiency of organization Flexibility of organization Leadership of CEO	Questionnaire results	Questionnaire results
Market Competition	Number of main competitors	12	14
International			
Global Strategy	Global strategy	Questionnaire results	Questionnaire results
Global Business Structure	Global infrastructure Acceptance to global business environment Leadership of CEO in global business	Questionnaire results	Questionnaire results
Market Competition	Number of main competitors	19	17

Source:
Han *et al.* (2003).

EMPIRICAL RESULTS OF THE DIAMOND TESTS

Calculating Scores and Drawing the Diamond

The descriptive data for each determinant of the generalized double diamond model are translated into scores to quantify the competitiveness of SEC and Sony in terms of the domestic diamond and the international diamond. Each category of proxies that composes the variables is distributed with scores according to the weight of each proxy. Then, between the proxies of SEC and Sony, the proxy that has a higher amount according to the descriptive data is given a full score and the other proxy is given a lower score in proportion. An example is given below (see Table 9-8).

Each proxy has a distributed weight and for the purpose of making a score scale from zero to ten, we have multiplied a value of ten to each weight. For example, since Sony has more employees than SEC, we gave Sony a full score of 0.6 (10×0.06). Then, we calculated SEC's score in proportion to the ratio of the number of employees from each company, which is 0.3 ($10 \times 0.06 \times 80,000 \div 161,100$).

Currently, it is hard to draw a fine line between what activities of multinational companies are purely domestic and what are foreign. One of the reasons for this is because domestic and international operations of firms are closely linked together. Namely, multinational companies such as SEC and Sony have to consider domestic and international operations simultaneously rather than separately. Therefore after drawing separate diamonds, we merged the two diamonds to explain the competitiveness of the two companies in a truly global sense. Here we name the synthesized diamond as "the global

Table 9-8   Example of Score Calculation

Variables	Proxies	SEC	Sony
Firm Size	Number of Employees	80,000	161,100

Variables	Proxies	Weight	Score	
Basic			SEC	Sony
Firm Size	Number of Employees	0.06	0.3	0.6

Table 9-9 Scores for the Domestic, International, and Global Diamonds

Diamond	Domestic		International		Global	
Company	SEC	Sony	SEC	Sony	SEC	Sony
Factor Conditions	8.17	8.33	8.12	9.94	8.15	9.14
Demand Conditions	6.43	8.82	7.67	10.00	7.05	9.41
Related and Supporting Industries	9.35	9.56	8.21	10.00	8.78	9.78
Firm Strategy, Structure, and Rivalry	9.57	9.82	10.00	9.48	9.79	9.65
Total Area of Diamond	138.10	166.20	143.80	194.20	141.00	180.20

diamond." The scores for each determinant of the three diamonds (domestic, international, global) are summarized in Table 9-9.

The Domestic Diamond

Following is the domestic diamond (see Figure 9-3) and the scores for its proxies (see Tables 9-10 and 9-11).

As shown above, the diamonds of SEC and Sony appear to be almost identical except for demand conditions. This implies that except for demand conditions, SEC is almost as competitive in Korea as Sony is in Japan. Some interesting points can be found. First, SEC is making efforts to utilize production factors as much as Sony does. In fact, while the firm size of Sony is much larger than that of SEC, SEC exceeds in profitability even when the level of R&D investment is about the same level.

Second, SEC and Sony are at a similar level of business contexts (firm strategy, structure and rivalry) in similar business environments (related and supporting industries). According to Table 9-11, the infrastructure and human resources related with the electronics business in Korea and Japan do not show much difference. Namely, when regarding the domestic situation only, SEC and Sony are competing on similar grounds and are following similar patterns to make use of their resources.

Third, the difference in the competitiveness of demand conditions of SEC and Sony confirms that the reasons not only come from the size of demand, but the sophistication of demand as well. In fact, Hofstede (1983, 1997) and Moon and Choi (2001) have confirmed that Japan has a higher level of uncertainty

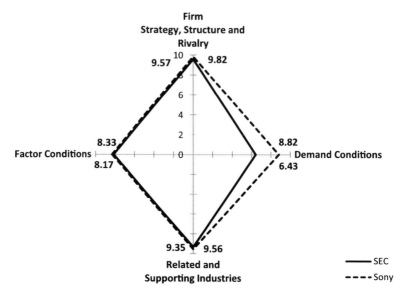

Fig. 9-3   The Domestic Diamonds of SEC and Sony

avoidance than Korea. That is, Japanese consumers tend to be relatively highly sophisticated and picky. Sony has to meet the Japanese high expectations such as quality and consumer relations. Porter (1990) also pointed out this regard from the example of picky Italian female consumers stimulating the Italian shoe industry.

The International Diamond

Following is the international diamond (see Figure 9-4) and the scores for its proxies (see Tables 9-12 and 9-13).

Considering the shape of the international diamond, Sony has a more balanced competitiveness than SEC. This may indicate that Sony has evolved into a successful international player through its long experience of international operations. When considering that the domestic diamond of Sony is relatively insufficient in factor conditions and demand conditions compared to the other two determinants, Sony has been successful in supplementing its competitiveness through multinational activities. Because Japan's economic indicators such as growth rate and productivity have been staggering recently, Sony has sought compensations through foreign resources and demand.

Table 9-10 Scores for Domestic Factor Conditions & Domestic Demand
Conditions

Variables	Proxies	Weight	Score	
Domestic Factor Conditions				
Basic			*SEC*	*Sony*
Firm Size	Number of employees	0.06	0.3	0.6
	Total assets ($, mil.)	0.07	0.54	0.7
	Total sales ($, mil.)	0.07	0.56	0.7
Productivity	Profitability (ROE, %)	0.1	1.0	0.2
	Profitability (ROI, %)	0.1	1.0	0.13
Advanced				
R&D Investment	Five-year average of R&D expenses over total sales	0.3	2.97	3.0
Research Facility	Number of research centers	0.3	1.8	3.0
Total		1.0	8.17	8.33
Domestic Demand Conditions				
Size				
Market Size	Population of the age group of 15 to 64	0.2	0.77	2.00
	Three-year average of GDP	0.1	0.11	1.00
	Four-year average of real GDP growth rates	0.1	1.0	−0.09
Sophistication				
Consumer Sophistication	Education index	0.2	2.0	1.96
	Three-year average of GDP per capita	0.2	0.56	2.0
Customer Satisfaction	Rank of each firm from its domestic customer satisfaction index	0.2	2.0	1.95
Total		1.0	6.43	8.82

Regarding size, SEC's international diamond is 74 percent of Sony's
international diamond while SEC's domestic diamond is 83 percent of Sony's
domestic diamond. Sony has an absolute advantage in terms of domestic
and international competitiveness and also a comparative advantage in terms

Table 9-11   Scores for Domestic Related and Supporting Industries & Domestic Firm Strategy, Structure, and Rivalry

Variables	Proxies	Weight	Score	
			SEC	Sony
Domestic Related and Supporting Industries				
Infrastructure	Three-year average of the National Informatization Index	0.4	4.0	3.72
	ICT Development Index (2000)	0.4	3.35	4.0
Competitiveness of Academy	Number of schools in 'The World Best Science and Technology Universities' list per 10 million persons	0.2	2.0	1.84
Total		1.0	9.35	9.56
Domestic Firm Strategy, Structure and Rivalry				
Strategy Efficiency	Company strategy	0.4	4.0	3.87
Management Efficiency	Efficiency of organization	0.1	1.0	0.98
	Flexibility of organization	0.1	1.0	0.98
	Leadership of CEO	0.1	1.0	0.98
Market Competition	Number of main competitors	0.3	2.57	3.0
Total		1.0	9.57	9.82

of international competitiveness against SEC. While SEC has a strong competitiveness in international firm strategy, structure, and rivalry compared to the other determinants of the diamond, it may not have fully utilized international resources such as foreign human resources and international technology. SEC's thrive for efficiency through an orientation to make almost everything by itself; namely, the "Samsung Way" (*BusinessWeek*, 2003) may actually be an inertia for internationalization. Therefore, when assessing the international competitiveness of SEC and Sony, we should not only consider international factor conditions but also the other three determinants as well.

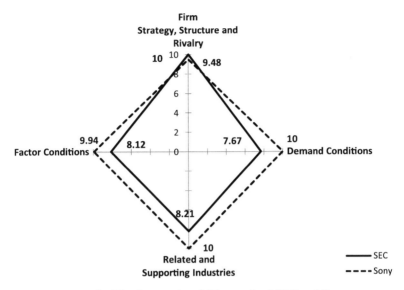

Fig. 9-4   The International Diamonds of SEC and Sony

The Global Diamond

Following is the global diamond (see Figure 9-5). All scores for the global diamond are calculated as the average sum of the scores from the domestic and international diamonds. Refer to Table 9-9 for the summary of the scores for each determinant.

Looking into the domestic and international diamonds separately and regarding the determinants of each firm's competitiveness, we can now have a clearer picture through the global diamond, which synthesizes the domestic and international diamonds. First, considering the shape of the diamond, Sony is more balanced than SEC and it has a competitive advantage in all determinants except in firm strategy, structure, and rivalry. However, Sony is not lagging behind SEC by this determinant, either. Therefore it is hard to agree with the recent headlines in the media that SEC is as competitive as Sony only because its market value has surpassed that of Sony's.

Meanwhile, SEC has recently been successful in envisioning being the world leader in its business areas and setting up strategies to catch up with the current leaders by means of aggressive rivalry. Namely, it has been successful in increasing its competitiveness of firm strategy, structure, and rivalry. However,

Table 9-12 Scores for International Factor Conditions and International Demand Conditions

Variables	Proxies	Weight	Score	
International Factor Conditions				
Basic			SEC	Sony
International Sales	Three-year average of international sales	0.1	0.63	1.0
	Three-year average international sales ratio	0.1	0.97	1.0
Overseas Factories	Number of overseas factories	0.2	1.27	2.0
Advanced				
Patents	Five-year sum of patents in U.S.	0.3	3.0	2.94
Research Facility	Number of overseas research centers	0.3	2.25	3.0
Total		1.0	8.12	9.94
International Demand Conditions				
Size				
Market Size	Number of main areas of each firm multiplied by the number of countries where the products are sold	0.2	1.33	2.0
	Three-year average of export as a percentage of total sales	0.2	1.94	2.0
Sophistication				
Customer Satisfaction	Brand value of firm (US$, bil., 2003)	0.25	2.06	2.5
	Financial Times/ PricewaterhouseCoopers' 'The World's Most Respected Companies', 2002 rank	0.1	0.18	1.0
Diversification of Markets	Ratio of number of countries of sales over three-year average of total export amount	0.25	2.15	2.5
Total		1.0	7.67	10.0

Table 9-13 Scores for International Related and Supporting Industries and International Firm Strategy, Structure, and Rivalry

Variables	Proxies	Weight	Score	
International Related and Supporting Industries				
			SEC	*Sony*
Credit	Moody's Credit Ranking of Company (2003)	0.25	2.34	2.5
	Moody's Credit Ranking of Country (2002)	0.25	2.42	2.5
International Competitiveness of Academy	Number of SCI publications per 10 thousand persons	0.2	1.65	2.0
Cooperation	Number of component complexes	0.3	1.8	3.0
Total		1.0	8.21	10.0
International Firm Strategy, Structure, and Rivalry				
Global Strategy	Global strategy	0.4	4.0	3.91
Global Business Structure	Global, infrastructure	0.1	1.0	0.96
	Acceptance to global business environment	0.1	1.0	0.96
	Leadership of CEO in global business	0.1	1.0	0.96
Market Competition	Number of main competitors	0.3	3.0	2.68
Total		1.0	10.0	9.48

to become a world leader, SEC will have to figure out how to mobilize and harmonize the other determinants of the diamond. For example, while SEC surpasses Sony in basic factor conditions such as ROE and ROI, it lags behind Sony in advanced factor conditions such as R&D investment and research facilities (see Table 9-10), which may be critical factors in the electronics business.

Second, regarding the size of the diamond, SEC has room for further improvement through internationalization. This indicates that even though a firm may be competitive in its domestic market, it may not be as successful as anticipated if it neglects international variables. On the other hand, even if

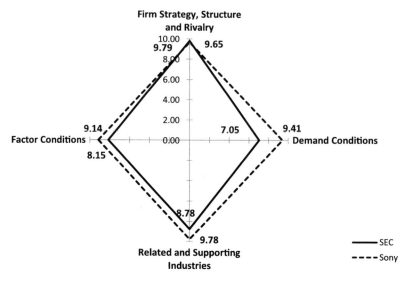

Fig. 9-5   The Global Diamonds of SEC and Sony

a firm may *lack* competitiveness in its domestic market, it can supplement its weaknesses through appropriate multinational activities.

CONCLUSION

Implications

There is much to consider when evaluating a firm's competitiveness, especially when the firm is a multinational firm that has a wide spread of activities across national borders. Internationalization makes things more complex and certainly a firm cannot be evaluated just by its market value. Porter's diamond is a good paradigm to start with for analyzing a firm's "global" competitiveness. However, Porter's original diamond model is incomplete, mainly because he does not adequately incorporate multinational activities. The paradigm of the generalized double diamond model, which extends the single diamond model, offers us a more comprehensive framework because it explicitly incorporates multinational activities. Since the global diamond model in this chapter allows us to distinguish, with relative ease, the competitiveness of SEC and Sony through the comparison based on the size and shapes of the domestic and international diamonds, major strategic differences between the two companies can be revealed. From our analysis, it is evident that Sony is more advanced than SEC in internationalization with a better balance.

Limitations of the Study and Suggestions for Further Studies

While our methodology is comprehensive in a sense that a number of proxies were used to measure the competitiveness of SEC and Sony, it can be further improved. First, it can be emphasized that a more rigorous statistical justification on proxy selection and quantitative data should be made. Therefore, our study is adequate for a relative comparison only. Absolute measurements using statistically significant data can improve the content of this chapter. Second, while this chapter has focused on competitiveness at the firm level, a further study on the aggregate competitiveness of electronic related firms at the industrial level may shed light on the relationship between a firm's competitiveness and the industry's competitiveness. It will be interesting to study how the diamonds of firms and industries interact with each other.

REFERENCES

Asiaweek (2000). Asia's Best Universities 2000. Available at: http://edition.cnn.com/ASIANOW/asiaweek/features/universities2000/scitech/sci.overall.html. Accessed October 2003.

Bark, T. and Moon, H. C. (2002). Globalization of technologies: The role of foreign direct investment. *Tech Monitor*, **19**(1): 20–25.

Business Week (2003). The Samsung way, 16 June.

Cho, D. S. and Moon, H. C. (2000). *From Adam Smith to Michael Porter*, Singapore: World Scientific.

Daewoo Securities. Available at: http://www.dwe.co.kr. Accessed September 2003.

Dunning, J. H. (1992). The competitive advantage of countries and the activities of transnational corporations. *Transnational Corporations*, **1**(1): 135–168.

Dunning, J. H. (2003). The role of foreign direct investment in upgrading China's competitiveness. *Journal of International Business and Economy*, **4**(1): 1–13.

Forbes (2001). Look out, Sony, 16 April.

Fortune (2002). Samsung's golden touch, 17 March.

Fortune Global 500. Available at: http://www.fortune.com. Accessed September 2003.

Han, D. H. *et al.* (2003). Competitiveness of Samsung Electronics versus SONY, in Moon, H. C. (ed.), *Managing Competitiveness*, Seoul: The Institute for Industrial Policy Studies (IPS).

Hofstede, G. (1983). The cultural relativity of organizational practices and theories. *Journal of International Business Studies*, **Fall**: 75–89.

Hofstede, G. (1997). *Cultures and Organizations: Software of the Mind*, New York: McGraw-Hill.

Moon, H. C., Rugman, A. M. and Verbeke, A. (1995). The generalized double diamond approach to international competitiveness, in Rugman, A. M., den Broeck, J. V. and Verbeke, A. (eds.), *Research in Global Strategic Management, Vol. 5: Beyond the Diamond*, Greenwich, CT: JAI Press, pp. 97–114.

Moon, H. C., Rugman, A. M. and Verbeke, A. (1998). A generalized double diamond approach to the global competitiveness of Korea and Singapore. *International Business Review*, 7: 135–150.

Moon, H. C. and Choi, E. K. (2001). Cultural impact on national competitiveness. *Journal of International and Area Studies*, 8(2): 21–36.

Newsweek (2002). Samsung in the bloom, 15 July, pp. 32–33.

Porter, M. E. (1990). *The Competitive Advantage of Nations*, New York: Free Press.

Rugman, A. M. and D'Cruz, J. R. (1993). The double diamond model of international competitiveness: The Canadian experience. *Management International Review*, 33(2): 17–39.

Samsung Electronics (2003). Annual Report 2002.

Sony (2003). Annual Report 2002.

Time (2002). Samsung moves upmarket, April, pp. 31–33.

10

APPLICATION:
INDUSTRY LEVEL

~

SUMMARY AND KEY POINTS

This chapter illustrates a study of the Korean textiles and apparel at
the industry level. Beginning with Porter's four determinants (factor
conditions, demand conditions, related and supporting industries,
and firm strategy, structure, and rivalry), new sources of competitive
advantage factors are identified for the evolving industry. The generalized double diamond model incorporates international activities,
which may occur either within or outside a country. Utilizing this
analytical framework, the future directions and solutions for the
industry with the identified new competitive factors are suggested.

In addition to the theoretical analysis, Jin and Moon (2006)
employs extensive literature reviews, examples of successful firms,
and four interviews with field practitioners in the industry. After
the Korean apparel industry, which is losing its competitiveness due
mainly to labor costs, is reviewed, recommendations are made for

Source:
Jin, B. H. and Moon, H. C. (2006). The diamond approach to the competitiveness of Korea's
apparel industry: Michael Porter and beyond. *Journal of Fashion Marketing and Management*,
10(2): 195–208.

its continued growth in the global marketplace. And implications pertaining to the creation of a dynamic self-reinforcing diamond system are suggested.

INTRODUCTION

The textiles and apparel-related industry has played a major role in the development and economic success of South Korea (Korea, hereinafter.). This important industry cluster in Korea has accounted for 41 percent of its total exports during 1970 and nearly 30 percent during the 1980 (Dickerson, 1999; Porter, 1990). Korea represents the fifth largest exporter of textile and apparel-related goods in the world, followed by China, Italy, the U.S., and Germany (Korea Federation of Textile Industries, 2002). However, its contribution to both the Korean and international competitiveness is decreasing due to an increase in labor costs. During 2002, while it still maintained major trade surplus and remained as the country's largest employer, it only accounted for 10.1 percent of the exports, as compared to 41 percent during 1970 (Korea Federation of Textile Industries, 2002). In 2000, the hourly wage of Korea was $5.73, as compared to $0.41 in China, nearly 14 times higher than that of China. Due to high labor costs, more clothing companies have sourced clothing for domestic consumption from lower wage countries (Korea Federation of Textile Industries, 2005).

Cheap labor serves as a developing country's competitive tool in global markets. However, as in the Korean case, cheap labor lasts for only a short time. As with the country's economic development, new sources of competitive factors need to be strategically developed and cultivated. Therefore, knowing what constitutes new sources of competitive advantage is critically important to set a future direction. The purpose of this study is to explore what constitutes a country's competitiveness in the global apparel market after losing its labor competitiveness and how a country effectively achieves it. Diversity between nations typically reflects different environmental conditions, which in turn affects the strategies, directions, and challenges of a specific industry. Therefore, it is essential to understand competitive factors within a specific country. This study chose the Korean apparel industry as it has passed the first phase and is actively seeking global competitiveness. This study employs two competitiveness models, Porter's diamond model (Porter, 1998) and a generalized double diamond model (Moon et al., 1995, 1998), as a theoretical framework. Along with two theoretical models, this study employs extensive literature reviews, examples of successful firms, and four interviews with field practitioners in the Korean apparel industry. The four interviewees were selected from leading Korean apparel and retail companies and all were at the rank of director or higher. The interviews were conducted from August 2000 to August 2001, in Seoul, Korea. Interview questions included general firm information, the firm's challenges/successes, and future goals. Each interview was one hour in length and taped, with the interviewee's permission, for further analysis.

This study consists of three parts. Beginning with Porter (1998) diamond model, new sources of competitive advantage factors are suggested for the evolving industry. The second part of this chapter introduces the generalized double diamond model (Moon *et al.*, 1995, 1998) to provide future directions and solutions for the industry with the identified new competitive factors. The last section concludes how a dynamic self-reinforcing diamond can be created, and suggests future studies. The unit of analysis for this study lies in the Korean apparel industry as a whole, not individual Korean apparel firms, following Porter's (1998) example. That is, the purpose of this study does not lie in generalizing strategies for every Korean apparel firm.

PORTER'S FOUR DETERMINANTS AND NEW COMPETITIVE ADVANTAGES

To investigate why nations gain the competitive advantage in particular industries, Porter (1998) conducted a four-year study of ten important trading nations and suggested "the diamond model." Porter concluded that a nation succeeds in a particular industry if it possesses a competitive advantage relative to the best worldwide competitors. His model consists of four determinants: factor conditions; demand conditions; related and supporting industries; and firm strategy, structure, and rivalry. As this study looks into an apparel industry it is essential to interpret competitive factors within this industry and to examine what constitutes new competitive factors as the industry evolves. Porter (1998) competitive advantage factors are summarized, and new sources of competitive advantages are suggested.

Factor Conditions

According to Porter (1998), factor conditions refer to the factors of production that are necessary to compete in a given industry. He grouped the factor endowment into a number of broad categories, such as human resources, physical resources, knowledge resources, capital resources, and infrastructure. He further discriminated among these factors: basic factors versus advanced factors, and generalized factors versus specialized factors. A basic factor is passively inherited, such as climate, unskilled and semiskilled labor, while advanced factors include conditions a nation creates, such as highly educated personnel. He suggested that competitive advantage based on basic or generalized factors is unsophisticated and often fleeting, contending that advanced or specialized factors are necessary for more sophisticated forms of competitive advantages. The advanced or specialized factors can be created through factor-creating mechanisms such as public and private educational institutions. Nations succeed in industries where they are particularly good at creating and upgrading the needed factors. Porter (1998) also argued that the standard for what constitutes an advanced or specialized factor tends to rise continuously as the states of knowledge, science, and practice improve.

Thus, we suggest that new competitive factor conditions in apparel industry lie in advanced or specialized factors. Basic factors such as cheap labor for production are no longer viable in achieving competitive advantages since those factors can be successfully secured through global sourcing. Global sourcing has been considered a critical component in achieving competitive advantages (Frear et al., 1992). Numerous apparel firms in countries where the apparel industry is advanced, such as Gap, Liz Claiborne, Nike, and The Limited, source labor as well as raw materials globally without owning any production facilities. Then, the most necessary new factor conditions to compete should be sought in advanced or specialized factors, such as skilled human resources (e.g., creative designers), and production and process technology that are specific to global sourcing and management (e.g., EDI, information technology). These new sources of competitive factors can be easily observed in the most advanced fashion countries. France and Italy boast about their creative designers, and the U.S. is active in developing production and process technologies such as quick response technologies and, currently, the Demand-Activated Manufacturing Architecture (DAMA) project (Techexchange, 2005).

Demand Conditions

This determinant refers to the nature of home-market demand for an industry's product or service. Porter (1998) views demand conditions in terms of the size of the home market and sophisticated and demanding buyers. That is, if the size of home demand is large, firms will invest to reap economies of scale. In countries where the domestic buyers (either industrial buyers or consumers) are the world's most sophisticated and demanding, companies are forced to meet high standards, to upgrade, and to respond to tough challenges. Porter (1998) sees a wide variety of reasons for unusually demanding needs: social norms, distribution channels, and national passions. For example, the distribution channels of Italy contribute to the higher levels of consumer sophistication (Porter, 1998). That is, in Italy, shoes, clothing, furniture, and lighting are sold in greater proportion through specialty stores than in other nations. These sophisticated retailer's pressure Italian manufacturers to constantly introduce new models and reduce prices. Italians are also known for their sophistication about clothes, food, and fast cars, the areas in which Italy had international success. The French have a national passion for the fashion industry, and it is no surprise that this country keeps its globally competitive position.

Porter (1998) acknowledges that the size of domestic demand in a particular industry may be important to national advantage where there are significant economics of scale or learning, but he considered the presence of sophisticated and demanding buyers more important. As an industry evolves, domestic consumers demand diverse and higher levels of needs, such as creative designs, services, or brands along with competitive prices. In countries where the apparel industry is less developed, functionality, and availability of apparel items may be enough to satisfy consumer needs. As the industry advances, domestic buyers demand a higher level of design to suit their taste as well as various items that are needed in their diverse lifestyles (e.g., time, place, occasions).

These higher levels of needs can be epitomized in a brand since it encompasses creative design, service, as well as the diverse needs of different target markets. Branding in the apparel industry is even more critical since differentiation and evaluation among items often depend on the brand of the items. Brand here does not mean just trademark. Rather, it broadly covers what branded apparel conveys: a symbolic meaning or a unique design. In the countries where the industry is globally competitive, many brands are globally recognized. For example, France possesses the LVMH group, a giant fashion group that has 60 prestigious brands including Louis Vuitton, Fendi, and Celine; Italy owns famous global brands such as Prada, Versace, Giorgio Armani, Missoni, and Benetton; England, Burberry and Hermes; Germany,

Jill Sander, Hugo Boss, Escada, and Adidas; and the U.S., the Gap, Calvin Klein, Donna Karen and Polo Ralph Lauren.

Related and Supporting Industries

Porter (1998) asserted that the presence of supplier and related industries within a nation that are internationally competitive provides benefits such as innovation, upgrading, information flow, and shared technology development which create advantages in downstream industries. Therefore, national success in an industry is particularly likely if the nation has a competitive advantage in a number of related industries. One of Porter's examples for this factor is the Italian ski boot industry and its close relationship with the leather industry. Because of the high quality of its leather, Italy can succeed in producing world-class ski boots.

However, in today's global apparel environments, raw materials are largely sourced globally, so having competitive supplier industries within a nation may not be as important as Porter (1998) suggests. Instead, related and supporting industries at the front-end, such as buying office, advertising, and information technology that support coordination of global sourcing or efficient management of the global supply chain, may be more important. For example, Liz Claiborne, Inc., sources from as many as 31 different countries using 240 factories. Therefore, coordinating the production and efficient communications with suppliers becomes critical. For this reason, most U.S. apparel companies own buying offices overseas, which assist and coordinate global production and management. Hong Kong keeps its competitive position not because of factor or demand conditions but because of efficient coordination of apparel manufacturing. Hong Kong serves as a business-networking center for apparel manufacturing (Lui and Chiu, 2001) with the production headquarters of large retailers like Gap. Hong Kong's first and largest buying office, Li & Fung, was founded in 1906 and provides integrated service in what they call "a virtual factory" or "a private label manufacturing program." This service includes assistance in product design through materials sourcing for its manufacture to the handling of logistics for delivery to the customer (George, 1998; Magretta, 2000).

Firm Strategy, Structure, and Rivalry

The last determinant is firm strategy, structure, and rivalry, referring to "the conditions in the nation governing how companies are created, organized, and managed, as well as the nature of domestic rivalry" (Porter, 1998, p. 107). Porter contended that nations tend to succeed in industries where the management practices and modes of organization favored by the nation are well suited to the industries' sources of competitive advantage. For example, many Italian firms are relatively small- or medium-sized firms that are privately owned and operated like extended families. Italian firms usually employ focus strategies, avoiding standardized products and operating in small niches. Consequently, Italy is an international leader in footwear and wool fabrics in which economies of scale are either modest or can be overcome through cooperation among loosely affiliated companies. Domestic rivalry is, arguably, the most important because of its powerful effect on all the other determinants. Porter took note of geographic concentration, which magnifies the power of domestic rivalry: the more localized the rivalry, the more intense the competition.

One important source of competitive advantages in the apparel industry has been high quality design. Italy, France, and the U.S. have succeeded because of their innovative designs. However, a new and different source of competitive advantage in the apparel industry, agility, should be added along with high-quality design. The apparel industry has been characterized by extensive and diverse sources of uncertainty due to fluctuating demands from fashion, and seasonal change and varying in style preferences. In response to market instability, apparel firms should react rapidly, thus "agility" becomes a means of achieving competitive advantage. Agility in the fashion business means more than just speed. Agility also means a firm can respond quickly, canceling lines that do not sell, avoiding clearance sales, and operating with small stockrooms and lower inventory holding costs (McGuire, 2001; Vitzthum, 2001).

Agility is the competitive weapon that Zara uses to achieve its success: it takes less than two weeks for a skirt to get from Zara's design team to a store in Paris or Tokyo. Design-to-delivery is as much as 12 times faster for Zara than for its competitors. With shorter lead times, Zara can ship a greater variety of goods more frequently (twice a week compared with once every 12 weeks) than many of its competitors. Thus, those countries where their strategy, management style, and domestic rivalry accommodate "high quality design with agility" will gain new international competitiveness and sustain their current positions. Table 10-1 summaries traditional and new sources of competitive advantage factors.

In addition to these four determinants, Porter (1998) suggested two external determinants: chance and government. Chance events just happen;

Table 10-1 Traditional Versus New Competitive Advantage Factors Using Porter's Diamond Model (1998)

Porter (1998) Determinants	Traditional Competitive Advantage Factors	New Competitive Advantage Factors
Factors Conditions	Basic factors: such as unskilled labor and raw materials	Advanced factors: skilled human resources such as creative designers. Specialized factors such as production and process technologies that are specific to handling global sourcing and management (e.g., EDI)
Demand Conditions	Demanding functionality and availability of apparel items	Demanding higher levels of needs such as brand name and service
Related and Supporting Industries	Presence of internationality competitive back-end supplier industries (e.g., raw materials producers)	Demanding higher levels of needs such as brand name and service presence of internationally competitive front-end industries that efficiently coordinate global supply chain management (e.g., buying office, advertising, information technology)
Firm Strategy, Structure, and Rivalry	Organization and strategy of most apparel firms are suited to industries' source of competitive advantage: high quality design	Organization and strategy of most apparel firms are suited to industries' source of competitive advantage: high quality design plus agility

however, the nation with the most favorable "diamond" will most likely convert chance events into competitive advantage (Porter, 1998). Government can influence each of the four determinants either positively or negatively. The complete diamond system is presented in Figure 10-1.

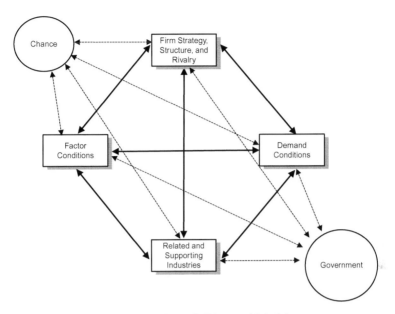

Fig. 10-1   Porter's Diamond Model

Source:
Porter (1990).

EXTENDING PORTER'S DETERMINANTS THROUGH INTERNATIONALIZATION

As internationalization often explains national competitiveness in small countries like Korea, most of the new competitive factors can be maximized through "internationalization." Therefore, the Korean apparel industry is further analyzed using Moon *et al.*'s (1995, 1998) generalized double diamond model. Moon *et al.* (1998) argue that sustainable value added in a specific country may result from both domestically owned and foreign owned firms. In addition, they contend that as today's sustainability often comes from geographic configuration spanning many countries, firm-specific and location advantages present in several nations can contribute to a nation's competitiveness. Therefore, these international activities, which may occur either within a country or outside, a country need to be incorporated in the explanation of national competitiveness. Figure 10-2 presents the generalized double diamond model, where the inside diamond represents the domestic situation and the dotted line denotes the international dimension. The difference between the international diamond and the domestic diamond

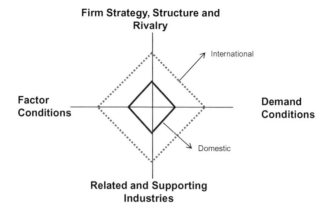

Fig. 10-2   The Generalized Double Diamond Model

Source:
Moon *et al.* (1998). Modified by author.

represents international or multinational activities (Moon *et al.*, 1998). Unlike Porter, if we double the diamond using domestic plus international activities, the above identified new sources of competitive factors can be maximized through "internationalization." Below we further analyze the Korean apparel industry with the aid of the generalized double diamond model.

Korean Factor Conditions

The competitive advantage factor of the Korean apparel industry has mainly been cheap labor. However, as wage costs rose, the country began to outsource labor and raw materials globally. Acknowledging that unskilled labor is no longer a viable factor, Korean companies all alike are eager to create change. Education is the top priority of all Korean parents and a proven proactive factor for the development of the Korean economy (Chung *et al.*, 1997; Porter, 1998). At the prestigious Fashion Institute of Technology in New York, Koreans represent a significant portion of foreign students.

The training of creative designers would be a new competitive advantage. This new factor can be achieved through internal development or internationalization. For example, the Korean apparel industry can:

- Work toward higher international recognition of its designers.
- Hire foreign creative designers to work for them.
- Co-develop designs with foreign creative designers.

Korean designers are starting to gain some recognition. Hanii Yoon and Gene Kang of Y & Kei, received a rising star award in the women's apparel category during 2002. The award is annually, given to eight brilliant, creative, and promising designers, by the Fashion Group International of the U.S. (Winters, 2003). To gain international recognition, more Korean fashion designers present their design lines in Paris and Tokyo collections. Younghee Lee has presented her line in the Paris Prêt-à-Porter collection more than 20 times for 11 years. Icinoo was invited to the Tokyo collection during 1990, and she also has presented her lines in Paris since 1993. Judging from the national zeal for education and fashion, Korea is likely to be in a favorable position to produce creative fashion designers.

Another new competitive factor for this dimension is production and process technology. Generally the Korean technology infrastructure matches that of most advanced nations (Porter, 1998). Especially in the internet industry, Korea ranks the third in the world in internet, just after the U.S. and Canada (Ipsos reid, 2002). In terms of broadband access such as cable modem, DSL, and other broadband technologies, Korea ranks first as of September of 2002; whereas, the U.S. ranks sixth, Japan ninth, Germany twelfth, France sixteenth, and Italy twentieth. More than 20 out of 100 Koreans have broadband internet access at home (OECD, 2002). However, for specialized production and process technologies that are specific to global sourcing and management such as EDI, the Korean apparel industry has invested less at the industrial and national levels for two reasons. First, the size of the Korean apparel industry is relatively small: only $11 billion compared to $200 billion, or approximately one twentieth of the U.S. market. The benefits obtained through such investments may not be significant in the smaller market. Second, the land size of South Korea is half that of the Florida peninsula. Therefore, the benefits of having process technology are significantly less than a country with a large land size. Once the Korean apparel industry has bigger markets by expanding internationally, companies may recognize the importance of production and process technologies to handle large volume orders more efficiently.

Korean Demand Conditions

Korean consumers are notorious for being demanding. As one manager of a multinational company operating in Korea once confessed, "once we can satisfy Korean consumers, then we are sure of our success in other countries, too" (Kim, personal communication, August 13, 2000). Korean fashion consumers are also extremely demanding. Due to their Confucian heritage, they are sensitive about their appearance. They believe they lose face if they are not properly dressed in a public setting. This belief can explain their higher tendency toward fashion consciousness and brand loyalty (Jin and Koh, 1999). In addition, the high import rates of prestigious global fashion brands (The U.S. Commercial Service, 2001) and increasing rates of overseas travel force domestic apparel firms to rise to the challenge of continually changing customer needs.

As of 2000, 1638 domestic brands and 565 foreign brands were competing with each other for the $11 billion Korean fashion market. During 2000, approximately 150 domestic brands were launched (Fashion View, 2001). Increasing rates of imports from lower labor cost countries make the competition even more intense. This severe domestic competition in Korea's apparel market can enhance its competitiveness through internationalization. Acknowledging home market saturation and strong domestic rivalry, Korean apparel firms have started to internationalize their own brands to some Asian markets, such as Vietnam, China, and Taiwan, and the U.S. One of the successful Korean brands in China is Deco, which initially set up manufacturing firms in Tianjin and Beijing and started to sell its own designs in 13 stores in Beijing and Shanghai. The brand is perceived in China as prestigious, and a Chinese woman is willing to spend a two to three months salary for one suit. Deco also has stores in Japan and Hong Kong (*Financial News*, 2001; Chang, personal communication, June 30, 2001). Korean apparel brands are also starting to gain visibility in the U.S. market. E-land Kids has been marketed in the U.S. since 1999 through 500 retail stores including high-end department stores (Sak's Fifth Avenue) as well as fashion-conscious trading areas (Beverly Hills, California, and New York City). The brand marked a $7 million sales record during 2002 in the U.S. market (Han, 2003).

While the above examples are an encouraging start, there are still challenges for the Korean apparel industry:

- It needs to diversify beyond selected Asian countries and the U.S. Often high design quality includes the tastes of the consumers. Once the industry expands to more diverse markets, it will strive to reflect the tastes of diverse international consumers when developing new products.
- To establish strong brands and effectively expand, along with the internationalization of domestic brands, the industry can also utilize inbound and outbound foreign direct investment.

For example, firms can purchase foreign brands and hire foreign experts in marketing and promoting the brand image.

Korean Related and Supporting Industries

Rather than back-end raw material industries, front-end industries, such as buying offices, advertising, and information technology centers, that assist the coordination of global sourcing or global supply chain management, would be a new source of competitive advantage. While Korea may have a lower capacity to create internationally competitive advertising, it can always outsource. There is already a precedent set for using multinational advertising companies by such well-known Korean brands as Samsung, LG, and Hyundai.

Korea has already experienced triangle manufacturing (buying office function), another new source of competitive factors. Triangle manufacturing allows Korea to move beyond OEM (Original Equipment Manufacturing) production and into a facilitator role in organizing global production. Under this arrangement, U.S. buyers place their orders with Korean manufacturers that they have sourced from in the past. These manufacturers, in turn, sub-contract some or all of the requested production to factories, in lower wage locations, such as: China, Sri Lanka, Thailand, and Indonesia to reduce production costs (Bonacich and Appelbaum, 2000; Christerson and Appelbaum, 1995; Gereffi, 1999). Korea, then serves as a logistical center by supplying fabric and other intermediate materials made in other Asian countries and by coordinating a variety of needed services, such as quality control inspections, shipping, and the transfer of funds for letters of credit (Gereffi, 1999). These functions are the essence of what Gereffi (1994) claimed. He maintained that the main job of apparel firms doing business globally is to manage production and trade networks and to make sure all the pieces of the business come together as an integrated whole. Korea's capabilities and expertise in triangle manufacturing will further assist them to perform better when competing in global marketplace.

Korean Firm Strategy, Structure, and Rivalry

International competitiveness can only improve when most of the leading firms' strategies, structures, and rivalries are well suited to "high quality design and agility." For example, the Dong Dae Mun market, Seoul, Korea, is one example of how the Korean apparel industry is clustered in a specific area and of how that geographic concentration caters to agility. Dong Dae Mun has had a long history as a traditional wholesale market complex since 1905.

The Dong Dae Mun General Shopping Center consists of 26 markets and 26,000 shop stands. One of these markets is the newly built modern apparel shopping mall called Miliore, which was opened in 1998. This apparel market complex is gaining fame in neighboring countries and has even become a tourist attraction. Individual stores within Miliore produce small-customized batch orders from Japanese retailers and export them. This success can be explained in two ways. One is the geographic concentration of related suppliers and vendors: fabric, trims, sewing facilities, retail, and related industries, which are clustered in that area. The other is agility: the manufacturers can produce a small batch of an apparel item within 48 hours from design to rack (Suh et al., 2002).

Note here how this extreme agility is possible. Unlike more fashion-advanced countries, Korea achieves agility using personal networks, rather than employing technology. One director at a leading Korean apparel company confessed that he received repeat orders for long sleeve knit shirts from several major Korean retailers. Knowing that long sleeve shirts should be sold within one month otherwise the stocks would be useless, he had to push one manager. The manager then contacted a former boss and begged for special yarn production for the knit, and then desperately searched for knit production facility, again using his personal network. He managed to produce the orders within two weeks, from yarn to retail stores, which normally takes at least two months. He believes agility in Korea cannot be completed without personal networks (Kim, personal communication, April 3, 2001).

This speedy production in Dong Dae Mun was possible because the production volume was small. The degree of agility to market is a trade-off between cost efficiency and the benefits of agility on a global scale. If the Korean apparel industry expands internationally, personal and business networking alone cannot secure agility. To meet large volumes cost efficiently, it needs to have a solid system that supports the whole supply chain. Therefore, a firm needs to carefully consider global sourcing and upgrading production and process technologies.

While the above analyses of the Korean apparel industry show a generally favorable environment in which the industry can move forward to gain a competitive advantage in global apparel markets, there are some challenges that should be addressed. These challenges can be mostly solved through internationalization. Table 10-2 summarizes current status of the Korean apparel industry and solutions through internationalization.

Table 10-2 Current Status of the Korean Apparel Industry and Solutions Through Internationalization Using the Generalized Double Diamond Model

Porter (1998) Determinants	New Competitive Advantage Factors	Current Status	Solutions Through Internationalization
Factor Conditions	Advanced factors: skilled human resources such as creative designers. Specialized factors such as production and process technologies that are specific in handling global sourcing and management (e.g., EDI).	Factors creating zeal (e.g., eagerness to learn contributors in creating abundant educated human resources). Fashion designers start to gain international recognition.	Factors can be created by hiring foreign expert designers and co-development of designs. While level of general technology infrastructure is the match of most advanced nations, specialized production and process technology remains a challenge.
Demand Conditions	Demanding higher levels of needs such as brand name and service.	Fashion consumer are extremely demanding and sophisticated. Some Korean brands have a presence in some Asian countries as well as in the U.S.	The firm needs to diversify its international markets. The firm should utilize inbound and outbound FDI effectively to create global brands. Understanding demand of global consumers is challenging.

(*Continued*)

Table 10-2 (*Continued*)

Porter (1998) Determinants	New Competitive Advantage Factors	Current Status	Solutions Through Internationalization
Related and Supporting Industries	Presence of internationally competitive front-end industries that efficiently coordinate global supply chain management (e.g., buying office, advertising, information technology).	Ample experience of triangle manufacturing in which Korea learns how to organize global production and trade networks.	However, Korea has not owned an internationally competitive advertising industry and IT industries. These can be achieved using an international workforce.
Firm Strategy, Structure, and Rivalry	Organization and strategy of most apparel firms are suited to industries' source of competitive advantage: high quality design plus agility.	Geographic concentration, domestic rivalry and personal networks facilitate agile reaction to the market.	For agility to global markets, a solid system is needed greater than personal networking. However, high quality design with agility remains a challenge.

Source:
Moon *et al.* (1995, 1998).

CONCLUSION

This study is designed to suggest how the Korean apparel industry can achieve competitive advantage in a global market. We believe this study is the first attempt in explaining the competitive advantage of an apparel industry within a specific country using Porter (1998) diamond model. As he indicated, in most countries, a nation succeeds because it combines some broadly applicable advantage with advantages that are specific to a particular industry or small groups of industries (Porter, 1998, p. 147). In this sense, we hope this study provides a benchmark for how an apparel industry in one nation can be analyzed. This study further contributes to analysis of the industry by extending Porter's diamond model and using the generalized double diamond model (Moon *et al.*, 1995, 1998) that appropriately explains the international perspectives of competitiveness.

This study indicates new competitive advantages and solutions for the industry in each of the four competitive determinants. However, it is not always necessary to have every determinant at an optimum level because one sufficient determinant could assist and strengthen an insufficient one. Therefore, instead of having four perfect individual determinants it can be equally as important to establish a self-reinforcing system using a range of robust competitive advantages. A well-functioning system blends each determinant so competitors cannot easily copy the entire system.

For the establishment of a self-reinforcing diamondm, we suggest that internationalization should come first. Once an industry secures a larger market (that is, a global market), the factors of the diamond will create dynamics, where many of the challenges can be solved. For example, once the industry has bigger markets by expanding internationally, it will capture the needs to invest in upgrading its production and process technologies to handle large volume orders quickly and efficiently (factor, related and supporting industries, and firm strategy, structure, and rivalry). In addition, the industry will strive to reflect tastes of diverse international consumers when developing its products (demand conditions). Internationalization of the Korean apparel industry will make each competitive determinant more active and will contribute to creating a self-reinforcing cohesive system. The diamond is dynamic and self-reinforcing. If the industry continuously challenges itself then the dynamics of the determinants of competitive advantage will create a unique system in which national advantage arises.

While this study does not examine effects of two external determinants, chance and government, on the four determinants, the following recent changes in the global apparel industry will likely influence the Korean apparel industry:

- Final phase-out of quota by the year of 2005.
- China's admission to membership in the WTO in 2001.
- Passage of the Trade and Development Act of 2000 (TDA), which, extended NAFTA-like privileges to the Caribbean Basin Initiative (CBI) countries, making the CBI region a more threatening competitor.
- Passage of the African Growth and Opportunity Act of 2000 (AGOA), which, expanded production opportunities in Africa.
- The decline of finished apparel exports from developed countries in Eastern Asia due to financial concerns (paying in advance by letter of credit) and the need for a quick response (Gereffi, 1999; Speer, 2001).

For these future studies, the framework suggested in this study will be useful to investigate how the Korean diamond system can take advantage of these chances, overcome unfavorable environments, and convert them to competitive advantages for its continued growth.

REFERENCES

Bonacich, E. and Appelbaum, P. P. (2000). *Behind the Label: Inequality in the Los Angeles Apparel Industry*, Berkeley, CA: University of California Press.

Christerson, B. and Appelbaum, R. P. (1995). Global and local subcontracting: Space, ethnicity, and the organization of apparel production. *World Development*, 23(8): 1363–1374.

Chung, H. K., Yi, H-C., Jung, K. H. and Lee, H. C. (1997). *Korean Management: Global Strategy and Cultural Transformation*, New York: Walter de Gruyter, Inc.

Dickerson, K. (1999). *Textiles and Apparel in the Global Economy*, 3rd Edn, New York: Prentice-Hall.

Fashion View (2001). Big changes in apparel market, *Fashion View*, 1(6): 1–6 (In Korean).

Financial News (2001). Apparel industry expanding to Chinese market, 27 November (In Korean). Available at: http://www.fnnews.com/html/fnview/2001/1127/09185024911511100.html. Accessed 6 February 2002.

Frear, C. R., Metcalf, L. E. and Alguire, M. S. (1992). Offshore sourcing: Its nature and scope. *International Journal of Purchasing and Materials Management*, 28(3): 2–11.

Gereffi, G. (1994). The organization of buyer-driven global commodity chains: How U.S. retailers shape global production networks, in Gereffi, G. and

Korzeniewicz, M. (eds.), *Commodity Chains and Global Capitalism*, Westport, CT: Greenwood Press, pp. 95–122.

Gereffi, G. (1999). International trade and industrial upgrading in the apparel commodity chain. *Journal of International Economics*, **48**, 37–70.

George, A. (1998). Li & Fung: Beyond 'filling in the mosaic', 1995–1998. *Manuscript no. 9-398-092*, Boston, MA: Harvard Business School Press.

Han, S. (2003). The Korea textile news, 6 March (In Korean). Available at: www.ktnews.com. Accessed 19 May 2003.

Ipsos reid (2002). Internet use continues to climb in most markets, 10 December. Available at: www.ipsos-reid.com. Accessed 22 March 2003.

Jin, B. and Koh, A. (1999). Differences between South Korean male and female consumer in the clothing brand loyalty formation process: model testing. *Clothing and Textiles Research Journal*, **17**(3): 117–127.

Korea Federation of Textile Industries. Available at: www.kofoti.org/textile/introduction/introduction_main.htm (In Korean). Accessed 19 May 2002.

Korea Federation of Textile Industries (2005). Available at: www.kofoti.or.kr/info/index03.php (In Korean). Accessed 25 July 2005.

Lui, T. L. and Chiu, S. W. K. (2001). Flexibility under unorganized industrialism? The experience of industrial restructuring in Hong Kong, in Deyo, F. C., Doner, R. F. and Hershberg, E. (eds.), *Economic Governance and the Challenge of Flexibility in East Asia*, New York: Rowan and Littlefield, pp. 55–77.

McGuire, S. (2001). Fast fashion: how a secretive Spanish tycoon has defied the post war tide of globalization, bringing factory jobs from Latin American and Asia back to Continental Europe. *Newsweek International*, 17 September, p. 36.

Magretta, J. (2000). Fast, global, and entrepreneurial: Supply chain management, Hong Kong style: An interview with Victor Fung, in Clark, K. B., Magretta, J., Dyer, J. H., Fisher, M., Fites, D. V. and Baldwin, C. Y. (eds.), *Harvard Business Review on Managing the Value Chain*, Boston, MA: Harvard Business School Press.

Moon, H. C., Rugman, A. M. and Verbeke, A. (1995). The generalized double diamond approach to international competitiveness, in Rugman, A. M., den Broeck, J. V. and Verbeke, A. (eds.), *Research in Global Strategic Management, Vol. 5: Beyond the Diamond*, Greenwich, CT: JAI Press, pp. 97–114.

Moon, H. C., Rugman, A. M. and Verbeke, A. (1998). A generalized double diamond approach to the global competitiveness of Korea and Singapore. *International Business Review*, 7(2): 135–150.

OECD (2002). Broadband access in OECD countries per 100 inhabitants, OECD, September. Available at: www.oecd.org/EN/document/0,EN-document-29-nodirectorate-no-1-39262-29,00.html. Accessed 24 March 2003.

Porter, M. E. (1998). *The Competitive Advantage of Nations*, New York: Free Press.

Speer, J. K. (2001). Mexico: Mapping out a course of action. *Bobbin*, **January**: pp. 16–22.

Suh, S. M., Hong, B. S. and Jin, B. (2002). *Fashion Business*, Seoul: Hyung-Sul Publication Co. (In Korean).

Techexchange (2005). An introduction to the DAMA project. Available at: www.dama.tc2.com. Accessed 23 July 2005.

(The) US Commercial Service (2001). Overview of the apparel market, 14 April. Available at: www.usatrade.gov/website/mrd.nsf/MRDurl/ISA_KOREA_APP_OVERVIEW-OF-THE-APPA_001A8052. Accessed 26 September 2003.

Vitzthum, C. (2001). Just-in-time fashion: Spanish retailer Zara makes low-cost lines in weeks by running its own show. *Wall Street Journal* (Eastern Edition), 18 May, p. B1.

Winters, W. (2003). 6th annual rising star awards. Available at: www.fgi.org. Accessed 19 May 2003.

11

APPLICATION: NATIONAL LEVEL

SUMMARY AND KEY POINTS

By utilizing the frameworks of analyzing national competitiveness introduced in Chapters 7 and 8, this chapter introduces three ways of enhancing national competitiveness. First, we apply the MASI framework to the Korean case and propose specific strategies which Korea can adopt to improve its current competitiveness. Compared to the MASI methodology introduced in Chapter 8, this chapter introduces one more analytical framework, called Term-Priority Matrix, in the Implementation section of MASI methodology.

There are two strategies for enhancing national competitiveness. One is to benchmark the country's competitors, in particular, countries in the same group of 3×3 matrix explained in Chapter 8 and the other is to enhance its competitiveness through cooperation with other countries, in particular, countries in the different group. This chapter highlights how a country can enhance its competitiveness not by competing but by cooperating with other countries. A case

Source:
This chapter is abstracted and modified from IPS National Competitiveness Research 2011–2012, pp. 41–70.

study of Korea and China is conducted to show the areas of potential cooperation between the two countries through investigating their competitiveness structure.

Finally, this chapter empirically proves the importance of created advantage for a country's prosperity. Based on the framework of double-diamond-based nine-factor model, this article conceptualizes and operationalizes the inherited and created advantages. In order to investigate the varying characteristics of inherited and created advantages across different groups, we classify countries into four groups in terms of differing degrees of inherited and created advantages and derive some important implications.

APPLICATION OF MASI: THE KOREA CASE
MASI Methodology

As explained in Chapter 8, MASI (Measure-Analyze-Simulate-Implement) is structured with a series of tools for analyzing and enhancing national competitiveness. The MASI approach includes (1) the double-diamond (DD) based nine-factor model for measuring national competitiveness (*Measure*); (2) the 3 × 3 framework for classifying country groups (*Analyze*); (3) an application of business strategy models (cost vs. differentiation) to the analysis of national competitiveness (*Simulate*); and (4) a list of strategies recommended for enhancing national competitiveness (*Implement*). Compared to Chapter 8, this chapter introduces one more framework, *term-priority matrix,* for the implementation of MASI methodology.

Term-Priority Matrix

The detailed methodology for term-priority matrix is as follows[1]: first, the 207 criteria are classified into strong (criteria in which Korea displays relative strengths), mediocre (criteria in which Korea ranks in moderate positions), and weak categories (criteria in which Korea shows relative weaknesses). Second, the sub-factors with weak criteria are categorized into 12 groups by terms (or time span) and priorities of policies. Terms are classified into short, mid, long,

---

[1]The term-priority matrix is quantified utilizing the data of IPS National Competitiveness Research 2011–2012. Double-diamond-based nine-factor model is the foundation of this research for assessing national competitiveness. The model is composed of 9 factors, 23 sub-factors, which are further made up of 207 criteria. For more information, please refer to IPS National Competitiveness Research 2011–2012.

and very long term depending on whether the policy is in the public or private sector. The sub-factors that are more related to private sectors are categorized under a longer term because those sectors are less controllable than those of the public sectors, and thus less likely to have immediate impact by government policy.

The level of priority (Y-axis) is determined by the correlation between sub-factors and GDP per capita over the last six years (2004–2009). The sub-factors categorized under higher priority are those that have higher correlation coefficients with GDP per capita, thereby, these are more important criteria for influencing the growth of an economy. The upper-left triangle represents the more important polices while the lower-right triangle designates the less important ones (see Figure 11-1).

In order to recommend policies to fill out in this term-priority matrix, we will apply MASI methodology to the Korean case. As the MASI methodology is already explained in detail in Chapter 8, we will focus more on how to operationalize this model to the real world. The first step of the MASI methodology is to measure Korea's competitiveness by using the IPS model. The next step is to analyze the relative position of Korea by comparing it with other countries. The third step is to simulate different strategic options in order to find the optimum strategy. Finally, specific strategic directions will be suggested for implementation.

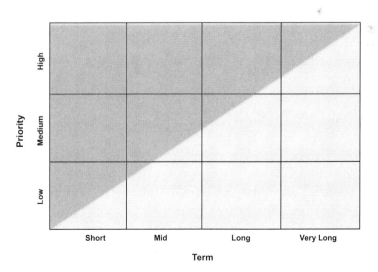

Fig. 11-1   Term-Priority Matrix

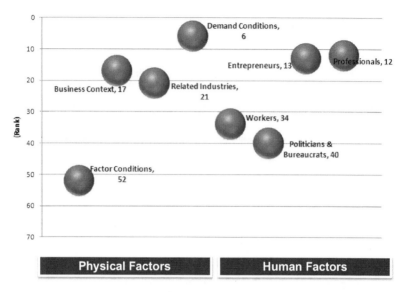

Fig. 11-2   Korea's National Competitiveness Structure (Factor Level)

Note: The number after each factor represents the ranking of each factor.

Measurement

When measured by the IPS model, Korea ranks in 19th place among 65 countries in the overall rankings.[2] Korea's competitiveness structure at specific factor-levels is shown in Figure 11-2. Factor Conditions (52nd) is ranked in the lower level, Workers (34th) and Politicians & Bureaucrats (40th) are ranked in the medium level, while Business Context (17th), Related Industries (21st), Demand Conditions (6th), Entrepreneurs (13th), and Professionals (12th) are ranked in the upper level.

Analysis

Among the nine groups classified by country size and competitiveness, Korea is categorized in the Medium-Strong Group. Korea can then be compared with other six Medium-Strong countries in order to analyze its relative strengths and weaknesses. For this purpose, we give 100 points to the base country. In order to find out the difference between Korea and the average of the other

---

[2]For a detailed information of the data, refer to IPS National Competitiveness Research 2011–2012.

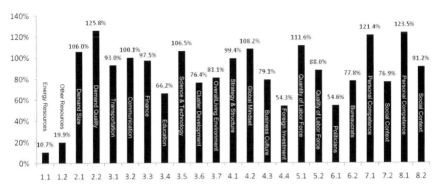

Fig. 11-3 Relative Position of Korea at Sub-Factor Level

Note: 1.1 & 1.2: Factor Conditions, 2.1 & 2.2: Demand Conditions, 3.1–3.7: Related Industries, 4.1–4.4: Business Context, 5.1 & 5.2: Workers, 6.1 & 6.2: Politicians & Bureaucrats, 7.1 & 7.2: Entrepreneurs, 8.1 & 8.2: Professionals.

Medium-Strong countries (OMSC), we calculate the Relative Index of Korea, as (I_{Korea}/I_{OMSC}) multiplied by 100, where I_{Korea} denotes the standardized competitiveness score of Korea, and I_{OMSC} denotes the standardized competitiveness score of other Medium-Strong countries in terms of a criterion, sub-factor, or factor.

Figure 11-3 shows that Korea is weaker than the Medium-Strong countries in one half of the total sub-factors, particularly in Education, Cluster Development, Overall Living Environment, Business Culture, Foreign Investment, Politicians, Bureaucrats, Social Context of Entrepreneurs, all of which are less than 85 percent of the level of the other six Medium-Strong countries. In addition, Transportation, Quality of Labor Force, and Social Context of Professionals are 85 percent–95 percent of the level of the other six Medium-Strong countries. However, with respect to Demand Size and Quality, Communication, Science & Technology, Strategy & Structure, Global Mindset, Quantity of Labor Force, Personal Competence of Entrepreneurs and Professionals, Korea has a similar or higher competitiveness than the other six Strong-Medium countries. Among the 23 sub-factors, Energy Resources and Other Resources of Factor Conditions are lower than 20 percent of the level of the other Medium-Strong countries.

Simulation

In order to find the changing landscape of competition, competitive structures of countries, and general implications of competitive strategy, we calculate and compare three different indices (Present Strategy Index, Cost Strategy Index, and Differentiation Strategy Index) by giving different weight to the factors and sub-factors. Present Strategy Index is calculated by giving an equal weight to all the factors and sub-factors while Cost Strategy Index and Differentiation Strategy Index are calculated by giving more weight to Factor Conditions and Workers (for cost strategy) and Demand Conditions and Professionals (for differentiation strategy) respectively. Korea's Present Strategy Ranking (i.e., the current ranking) is 19th. If Korea pursues cost strategy, it would go down to the 39th place. If Korea applies differentiation strategy, however, it would move up to the 10th place, which is higher than its current ranking (19th) by nine rankings. Korea has a competitive structure with relatively high scores on Demand Conditions in the physical factors and Entrepreneurs and Professionals in the human factors. Therefore, Korea should pursue differentiation strategy for further enhancement of national competitiveness.

Implementation: Optimal Strategic Mix (Macro Level)

Table 11-1 lists key strategic variables in different stages of economic development. In the farthest right column of Table 11-1, specific strategic implementations are suggested. For example, in the case of Factor Conditions, Korea's deficiency in natural resources can be overcome through internationalization such as imports of raw materials or investment in foreign extractive industries. Korea's manufacturing-based economy can be upgraded to a knowledge-based economy through creating high value-added products.

The strategic guidelines of this table are illustrated for Korea after an in-depth analysis of Korea's competitiveness. A similar illustration can be provided for other countries with their competitiveness data included in this National Competitiveness Research.

Implementation: Term-Priority Matrix (Micro Level)

Identification of weak criteria

There are two ways to enhance a nation's competitiveness. One is to further strengthen its strong points and the other is to correct its weaknesses. Both are important but correcting the weaknesses is probably more important when an economy is already developed to some extent and the economy is preparing for another takeoff. With some serious weaknesses, it would be difficult for

Table 11-1 Development Stages and Policy Implementations: The Case of Korea

Stage/Item	Developing	Transitional	Developed	Strategy for Enhancing Competitiveness
Physical Factors				
Factor Conditions	Resource-based	Manufacturing-based	Knowledge-based	• Overcome problems through internationalization • Create high value-added products by applying high technology and design to production processes
Business Context	Protectionism	Efficiency	Competition	• Enhance corporate competence, such as management techniques and labor-management relations • Attract investments and establish competition system through opening the domestic market
Related Industries	Physical Infrastructure (Roads & Ports)	Industrial Cluster	Regional Integration	• Enhance R&D competence by strengthening academic-industrial cooperation and increasing R&D expenditures • Regional integration for creating synergies of technology, human resources, and services
Demand Conditions	Quantity	Quality	Sophistication	• Enlarge the market size by exporting and investing abroad • Pay more attention to the sophistication of the market

(*Continued*)

Table 11-1 (*Continued*)

Stage/Item	Developing	Transitional	Developed	Strategy for Enhancing Competitiveness
Human Factors				
Workers	Cheap	Motivated	Skilled	• Establish the mutually beneficial labor-management relations and improve the working motivation • Improve worker's skill level by establishing a life-long education system
Politicians & Bureaucrats	Facilitation	Support & Regulation	Advice	• Enhance the stability and efficiency of the political system • Regulate as an advisor the critical issues such as environment, health, and safety; reduce other regulations and unnecessary intevention
Entrepreneurs	Risk Taking	Efficiency Developing	Value Creating	• Improve the market mechanism for enhancing entrepreneurs' creative mindset and reduce direct support for start-up firms
Professionals	Operational	Managerial	Strategic	• Improve the tertiary education system and open the skilled-labor market • Create the social context for professionals

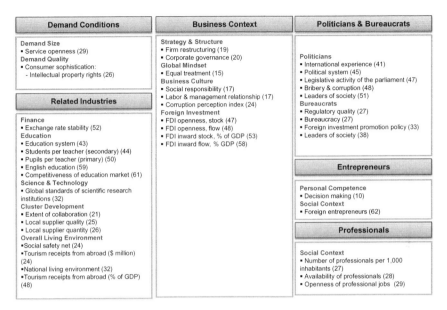

Demand Conditions	Business Context	Politicians & Bureaucrats
Demand Size • Service openness (29) **Demand Quality** • Consumer sophistication: - Intellectual property rights (26)	**Strategy & Structure** • Firm restructuring (19) • Corporate governance (20) **Global Mindset** • Equal treatment (15) **Business Culture** • Social responsibility (17) • Labor & management relationship (17) • Corruption perception index (24) **Foreign Investment** • FDI openness, stock (47) • FDI openness, flow (48) • FDI inward stock, % of GDP (53) • FDI inward flow, % GDP (58)	**Politicians** • International experience (41) • Political system (45) • Legislative activity of the parliament (47) • Bribery & corruption (48) • Leaders of society (51) **Bureaucrats** • Regulatory quality (27) • Bureaucracy (27) • Foreign investment promotion policy (33) • Leaders of society (38)

Related Industries
Finance • Exchange rate stability (52) **Education** • Education system (43) • Students per teacher (secondary) (44) • Pupils per teacher (primary) (50) • English education (59) • Competitiveness of education market (61) **Science & Technology** • Global standards of scientific research institutions (32) **Cluster Development** • Extent of collaboration (21) • Local supplier quality (25) • Local supplier quantity (26) **Overall Living Environment** •Social safety net (24) •Tourism receipts from abroad ($ million) (24) •National living environment (32) •Tourism receipts from abroad (% of GDP) (48)

Entrepreneurs
Personal Competence • Decision making (10) **Social Context** • Foreign entrepreneurs (62)

Professionals
Social Context • Number of professionals per 1,000 inhabitants (27) • Availability of professionals (28) • Openness of professional jobs (29)

Fig. 11-4 Criteria for Public Policy Formulation

Note: (1) The figures in parentheses are the rankings of each criterion. (2) Criteria which are hard to control by policy implementation are excluded.

the economy to grow further. Therefore, this study focuses on the weaknesses of the Korean economy and identified them in Figure 11-4.

Constructing term-priority matrix

The sub-factors listed in Figure 11-4 are organized into a 4 × 3 matrix for policy suggestions. First, the sub-factors are categorized into four terms according to the extent to which each sub-factor is related to the public or private sector. Next, the sub-factors of each term are subdivided into three groups of priority (high, medium, or low) utilizing the cluster analysis, according to the degree of correlation between GDP per capita and the sub-factor in terms of medium-sized countries, which are similar to Korea in size (see Table 11-2). This is based on the assumption that the sub-factors that have higher correlations with GDP per capita contribute more to the increase of GDP per capita.

Figure 11-5 shows the following: the sub-factors in the short term (Term 1) in the order of correlation are Social Context of Professionals, Politicians, Social Context of Entrepreneurs, and Bureaucrats. The sub-factors under the

Table 11-2   Correlation with GDP Per Capita (2004–2010)

Priority	Term 1		Term 2		Term 3		Term 4	
	Sub-factor	r	Sub-factor	r	Sub-factor	r	Sub-factor	r
High	Social context (P)	0.829	Global mindset	0.825	Business culture	0.885	Overall living environment	0.885
Medium	Politicians	0.791	Finance	0.703	Education	0.841	Demand quality	0.813
	Social context (E)	0.728	Foreign investment	0.670	Strategy & structure	0.830	Science & Technology	0.803
Low	Bureaucrats	0.716	Cluster development	0.592	Demand size	0.604	Personal competence (E)	0.738

Note: (1) E: Entrepreneurs, P: Professionals (2) As for the sub-factor of Demand Size, GDP per capita related criteria (i.e. GDP per capita and GDP per capita growth index) are excluded when calculating the correlation coefficient between Demand Size and GDP per capita.

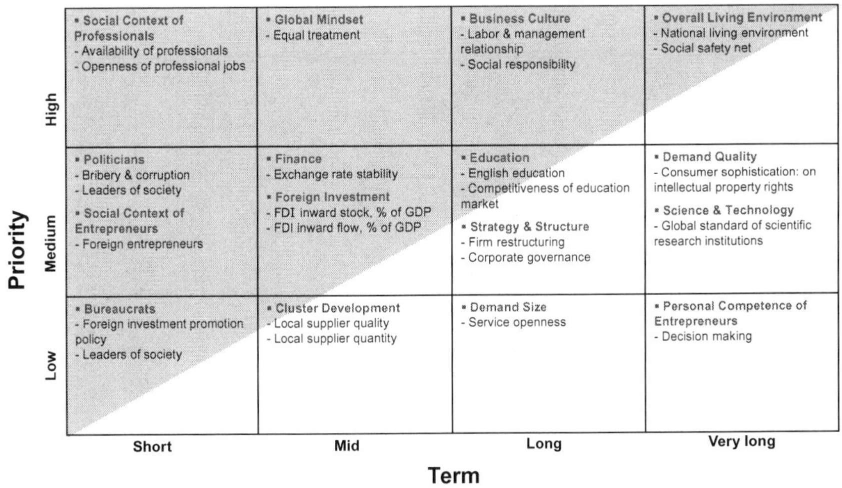

	Short	Mid	Long	Very long
High	• Social Context of Professionals - Availability of professionals - Openness of professional jobs	• Global Mindset - Equal treatment	• Business Culture - Labor & management relationship - Social responsibility	• Overall Living Environment - National living environment - Social safety net
Medium	• Politicians - Bribery & corruption - Leaders of society • Social Context of Entrepreneurs - Foreign entrepreneurs	• Finance - Exchange rate stability • Foreign Investment - FDI inward stock, % of GDP - FDI inward flow, % of GDP	• Education - English education - Competitiveness of education market • Strategy & Structure - Firm restructuring - Corporate governance	• Demand Quality - Consumer sophistication: on intellectual property rights • Science & Technology - Global standard of scientific research institutions
Low	• Bureaucrats - Foreign investment promotion policy - Leaders of society	• Cluster Development - Local supplier quality - Local supplier quantity	• Demand Size - Service openness	• Personal Competence of Entrepreneurs - Decision making

Priority (vertical axis) — **Term** (horizontal axis)

Fig. 11-5   Term-Priority Matrix

midterm (Term 2) are Global Mindset, Finance, Foreign Investment, and Cluster Development. The sub-factors in the long term (Term 3) are Business Culture, Education, Strategy & Structure, and Demand Size. The sub-factors in the very long term (Term 4) are Overall Living Environment, Demand Quality, Science & Technology, and Personal Competence of Entrepreneurs. By considering the term and priority of the matrix, we can suggest the policies illustrated in Figure 11-5. The Korean government can then pay more strategic attention to the areas in the upper-left hand corner.

COOPERATIVE STRATEGY: A CASE OF KOREA AND CHINA

Overall Ranking

We incorporate the case of Korea and China to illustrate the analytical framework. The overall ranking of China's national competitiveness has increased dramatically from 45th to 15th over the past 10 years. China surpassed Korea in 2007 and entered the top 15 group. In contrast, Korea has been stable in the same period, oscillating between 21st and 25th by 2010, and in 2011 stepped into the top 20 (see Figure 11-6). If we look at the change of the overall ranking, it can be easily concluded that the competition between Korea and China is becoming more and more severe because of the narrowing national competitiveness ranking gap between them. However, if

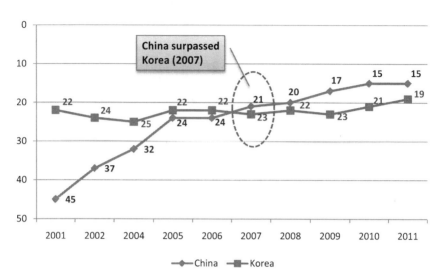

Fig. 11-6 Comparison of Competitiveness (Korea and China)

we look into the structure of the two countries, we will find that they have different competitive advantages in different areas.

Structure of National Competitiveness (Main Factor Level)

As Figure 11-7 shows, China is strong in Factor Conditions and Workers, but weak in Business Context, Entrepreneurs, and Professionals. In contrast, Korea is relatively strong in Demand Conditions, Entrepreneurs, and Professionals, but weak in Factor Conditions, Workers, and Politicians & Bureaucrats. Thus, Korea shows strong performance in the areas where China is weak, and displays weakness in the areas where China is strong. In other words, their structures of national competitiveness are more complementary than competitive.

OPERATIONALIZATION OF INHERITED AND CREATED ADVANTAGES

Theoretical Background and Conceptualization

Porter (1990) said in his book *The Competitive Advantage of Nations*, that competitiveness is no longer limited to those nations with a favorable inheritance, and argued that national prosperity is created, not inherited. On one hand, the importance of basic factors has been undermined by their diminished necessity, their widening availability, or ready access to

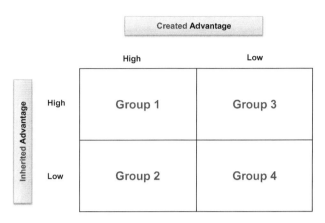

Fig. 11-7   Country Groups by Inherited and Created Advantages

them through foreign activities or sourcing on international markets. On the other hand, the factors most important to competitive advantage in most industries, especially the industries most vital to productivity growth in advanced economies, are created within a nation. Porter attested the argument by studying the competitive performance of ten countries, each involving around ten industry cases. However, Porter conducted just simple case studies to prove his model.

To improve his work, we have conducted rigorous empirical works. In order to measure and compare the relative size of inherited and created advantages, among the eight factors of the IPS model, Factor Conditions, composed of energy resources (e.g., oil, natural gas, and coal) and other resources (e.g., wood, land, freshwater, etc.), is categorized as inherited advantages, and the other seven factors (Business Context, Related Industries, Demand Conditions, Workers, Politicians & Bureaucrats, Entrepreneurs, and Professionals) are categorized as created advantages.

Empirical Test

Methodology and data

In order to suggest more practical implications, 65 countries are classified into four groups sharing similar characteristics in terms of inherited and created advantages. For inherited advantage, countries are grouped into high and low according to the index of Factor Conditions. As for created advantage, countries are similarly classified into high and low according to the average score of seven variables. Figure 11-7 shows the 2 × 2 matrix of country groups.

Cluster analysis is a statistical technique that classifies a set of observations into clusters according to the characteristics of the observations. Observations in the same cluster share significant similarities, while there are significant differences among observations in different clusters (Hair *et al.*, 1998). We employ K-means clustering techniques for country classification in terms of two variables, inherited advantage and created advantage. For the empirical analysis, data were selected from the IPS National Competitiveness Research 2011–2012.

Results

The 65 countries are classified into four country groups with the application of the cluster analysis. Table 11-3 shows the member countries of each group. Group 1 with relatively both high inherited and created advantages includes 13 countries. Group 2 which is high in created advantages but relatively weak in inherited advantages has 11 countries. In contrast to Group 2, Group 3 is high in inherited advantages but relatively weak in created advantages. The 21 countries are categorized in this group. Group 4 encompasses the remaining 20 countries, which are low in both inherited and created advantages. As a result, most advanced countries are classified in Groups 1 and 2, while most developing countries are in Groups 3 and 4.

In order to find out the characteristics or pattern of competitive advantages of countries with high or low productivity, we utilize GDP per capita of 2009 as the proxy variable of a country's productivity. We then depicted a graph, where the X-axis represents the national competitiveness index, a composite index of the eight factors of the IPS model, and the Y-axis represents GDP per capita. As Figure 11-8 shows, countries with GDP per capita of higher than $30,000 dollars are mostly countries from Groups 1 and 2. In other words, wealthy or advanced countries are mostly those that have high created advantages, while developing countries with low created advantages are mostly distributed in the area with lower GDP per capita. This result shows that a country's prosperity is not determined by inherited advantages but by created advantages.

In order to investigate the benefits of inherited advantage for different country's development stage, we compare the difference in GDP per capita between advanced (Groups 1 and 2) and developing (Groups 3 and 4) countries. As Figure 11-9 shows, the difference in the average GDP per capita between Groups 1 and 2 is $1,693 dollars, which is much smaller than that between Groups 3 and 4 ($8,403). Another important point is that

Table 11-3   Country List of Four Groups

Group 1	Group 2	Group 3	Group 4
Created Advantage (H) Inherited Advantage (H)	Created Advantage (H) Inherited Advantage (L)	Created Advantage (L) Inherited Advantage (H)	Created Advantage (L) Inherited Advantage (L)
United States	Singapore	U.A.E.	Thailand
Canada	Hong Kong SAR, China	Poland	Jordan
Sweden	Denmark	Kuwait	Hungary
Netherlands	Switzerland	Chile	Spain
Australia	Israel	Czech Republic	Philippines
Finland	Belgium	Saudi Arabia	Panama
Germany	Chinese Taipei	Indonesia	Vietnam
Austria	Korea	Malaysia	Dominican Republic
China	France	Mexico	Egypt
United Kingdom	Japan	Oman	Guatemala
New Zealand	Italy	Brazil	Turkey
Iceland		Russia	Morocco
India		Greece	Bangladesh
		Colombia	Cambodia
		Nigeria	Pakistan
		Peru	Croatia
		South Africa	Kyrgyz Republic
		Argentina	Ukraine
		Iran	Kenya
		Venezuela	Sri Lanka
		Libya	

Note: H: high, L: low.

among countries with high created advantages, Group 2, which is weak in inherited advantages, has a higher GDP per capita than Group 1. However, within countries with low created advantages, Group 3 with high inherited advantages displays higher GDP per capita than Group 4. Moreover, through the t-test, we find that the difference in GDP per capita between Groups 1 and 2 is not significant, while that between Groups 3 and 4 is statistically significant (see Table 11-4). The results above show that inherited advantage is a major determinant of wealth at the initial development stage of economic

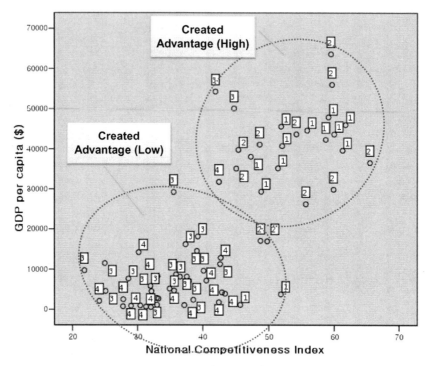

Fig. 11-8   GDP Per Capita and National Competitiveness Index

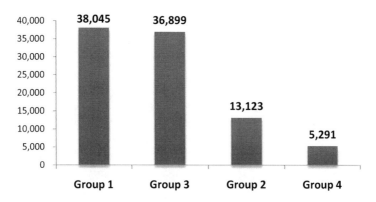

Fig. 11-9   Average GDP Per Capita of Four Groups ($)

Table 11-4   T-test Results

		Levene's Test for Equality of Variances		T-test for Equality of Means	
		F	Sig.	t	Sig. (2-tailed)
Groups 1 & 2	Equal variances assumed	0.002	0.969	−0.276	0.785
	Equal variances not assumed			−0.277	0.784
Groups 3 & 4	Equal variances assumed	3.377	0.074	2.359	0.023
	Equal variances not assumed			2.394	0.023

development. However, when countries step into more advanced stages, they rely more on the creation and upgrade of created advantages, and differences in favorable inheritance become less important.

CONCLUSION

This chapter introduced three types of strategies for enhancing national competitiveness with their empirical analyses and derived important implications as following. First, Korea's competitiveness is comprehensively assessed using the MASI methodology. Measured by double-diamond-based nine-factor model, Korea displays an advanced country-type competitiveness structure: high rankings in Demand Conditions, Entrepreneurs, and Professionals, while low rankings in Factor Conditions. This finding implies that Korea should pursue a differentiation strategy for further enhancement of national competitiveness, rather than a cost strategy like developing countries.

This finding is related to the second finding of this research. In our case study of Korea and China, although the two countries seem to be increasingly competing with each other due to the narrowing gap in their overall competitiveness rankings, their structures of national competitiveness are more complementary than substituting with each other. This implies that they can utilize each other's strengths to offset their weaknesses through cooperation. Both Korea and China can then enhance their overall national competitiveness more effectively.

In addition, this chapter operationalized two concepts of inherited and created advantages, and conducted a series of empirical tests to prove the importance of created advantage for a nation's prosperity. An important finding of this research is that the inherited advantage such as natural resources may be a major determinant of national wealth at the initial stage of economic development, but when countries step up into more advanced stages, they rely more on the creation and upgrade of created advantages.

A comprehensive methodology of this study will assist policymakers in establishing and implementing adequate policies. Analytical frameworks such as the Term-Priority matrix can be very useful for organizing different policies according to different terms and priorities. Highlighting the importance of cooperation rather than just competition with other countries will give broader scope of policy tools. The empirical evidence of the important role of created advantage will assure the policy makers to upgrade the industrial structure rather than just expand the size of the economy. From this study, scholars will also benefit for a better understanding of a variety of policy tools and for a possible extension of these tools. The study of this chapter highlights the case of Korea but a similar methodology can be easily applied to other economies as well.

REFERENCES

Hair, J. F., Anderson, R. E., Tatham, R. L. and Black, W. C. (1998). *Multivariate Data Analysis*, 5th edn., Upper Saddle River, NJ: Prentice Hall.

The Institute for Industrial Policy Studies (IPS). Various Issues. *IPS National Competitiveness Research*, Seoul, Korea: IPS and IPS-NaC.

12

APPLICATION: OTHER AREAS

SUMMARY AND KEY POINTS

With the concepts of economies of scale and reduced transport costs, Paul Krugman, the Nobel Prize winner in Economics, incorporated economic geography into the trade theory. Similarly and actually more systematically, the business economist, Michael Porter, has developed a cluster theory, linking trade (or production) theory to economic geography. This chapter extends Porter's cluster theory, which is domestically oriented, to the international context, i.e., the international cluster of neighboring countries, and applies this new concept to a possible international cluster in Northeast Asia, including Korea, Japan, China, and Russia.

It is often said that Korea is sandwiched or stuck in the middle between Japan and China. However, the economic or business relationship is not a zero sum game. This chapter proves that the relationship in this region is more cooperative than competitive. The relationship among the Northeast Asian countries is not just

Source:
Moon, H. C., and Jung, J. S. (2010). Northeast Asian cluster through business and cultural cooperation. *Journal of Korea Trade*, 14(2): 29–53.

economic, but cultural. For this purpose, we also consider cultural dimensions, in order to enhance the competitiveness of the region, as well as that of the individual countries. The chapter goes over some case studies of selected industries and conducts statistical analysis. The results of this study provide useful implications: from domestic to international clusters; from competition to cooperation; and from trade to cooperative production and business.

So far, we have explained and practiced extended diamond models to various cases at different levels of analysis. This is the last chapter and the study of this chapter demonstrates that this model can be applied to the analysis of cluster and even different topics such as cultural dimensions. Although we have used the double diamond model, the nine-factor model, or the double-diamond-based nine-factor model (IPS model), the origin of these extended models is Porter's diamond model. Without Porter, we could not go "Beyond Porter." Our final comment: we appreciate Professor Porter for his great contribution in the field of competitiveness.

INTRODUCTION

Based on the concepts of economies of scale and reduced transportation costs, Nobel Prize winning economist Paul Krugman explained why an increasingly larger share of the world population lives in cities and why similar economic activities are concentrated in the same geographic locations (*Forbes*, 2008; Fujita *et al.*, 1999; Krugman, 1992). According to Krugman (1992), regions become divided into a high-technology urbanized core and a less developed periphery. The main contribution of Krugman is to relate trade theory with economic geography. However, a more systematic approach on the same topic had been forwarded by the eminent business economist, Michael Porter (1990, 1998a, 1998b, 2000a), who pioneered the cluster theory. Porter's works also link trade (or production) theory to economic geography by introducing the so-called "diamond model" for competitiveness. There are many studies regarding clusters (Anderson, 2006; Russo, 2004; European Commission, 2003; Martin and Sunley, 2003; Reuber and Fisher, 2001; Maskell, 2001). However, Porter's work is the original and incorporates most of the other studies.

Porter's diamond model consists of four endogenous factors (factor conditions, demand conditions, the context for firm strategy, structure and rivalry, related and supporting industries) and two exogenous variables (chance events and government). The interactions in the diamond promote the clustering of a nation's competitive industries or industry segments. Porter's cluster theory is basically as follows. A nation's successful industries are usually linked through vertical (buyer/supplier) or horizontal (common customer, technology, channels, etc.) relationships. One competitive industry then helps create another in a mutually reinforcing process. Such an industry is often the most sophisticated buyer of the products and services.

For example, American leadership in consumer packaged goods and consumer durables contributed to America's preeminence in advertising as well. Japanese strength in consumer electronics meant that Japanese success in semiconductors has been skewed toward memory chips and integrated circuits that are used heavily in these types of products. In other words, once a cluster forms, individual industries in the whole group support each other. Benefits flow forward, backward, and horizontally. Rivalry in one industry spreads to others in the cluster, through spinoffs and related diversification by established firms. Entry from other industries stimulates upgrading and diversity in R&D approaches. Information flows freely and innovations diffuse rapidly through the conduits of suppliers or customers. Furthermore, interconnections within the cluster lead people and ideas to combine in new ways. National competitive advantage resides as much at the level of the cluster as it does in individual industries (Porter, 1990).

A cluster is the manifestation of the diamond at work. Proximity — the collocation of companies, customers, and suppliers — amplifies all the pressures to innovate and upgrade. Economic geography in an era of global competition may pose a paradox. It is often argued that location should no longer be a source of competitive advantage. Open global markets, rapid transportation, and high-speed communications should allow any company to source anything from any place at any time. But in practice, location remains central to competition (Porter, 1998a).

Porter's cluster theory is seminal but is not free from criticism. The most serious problem with Porter's theory is that it was designed mainly with the domestic context in mind and thus lacks an international perspective. Although Porter (1990, 1998a, 1998b, 2000a) attempts to explain international competitiveness of nations or national industries, the sources of competitiveness he emphasizes are only derived from the domestic context. This is to say, Porter's scope of competition is international, but the sources of competitive advantage are limited to the domestic arena. On the other hand, this study considers both domestic and international aspects as the sources of competitive advantage. This perspective is in line with several studies

(Rugman, 1991, 1992a, 1992b; Porter and Armstrong, 1992; Rugman and D'Cruz, 1993; Moon *et al.*, 1998; Dunning, 2003; Cho *et al.*, 2008), which highlight the international source of competitive advantage.

The next section extends Porter's cluster theory to the international context, i.e., the international cluster of neighboring countries. We then apply this extended concept of international cluster to Northeast Asia, including Korea, Japan, China, and Russia. It is often said that Korea is sandwiched by Japan and China. However, the economic or business relationship is not a zero-sum game. We will prove that it is a positive-sum game by applying the concept of international clusters to Northeast Asia. In section three, useful conceptual frameworks of the growth triangle model and cultural model, along with some case studies, will be introduced in order to more systematically analyze the effects of international clusters. Afterwards, a hypothesis will be formulated and empirical analyses will be conducted. It will then prove that the relationship among the four countries in Northeast Asia is more cooperative than competitive. Finally, some useful implications and conclusions will be provided.

EXPANSION OF CLUSTER

According to Porter (1990), geographic concentration of firms in internationally successful industries often occurs because the influence of the individual determinants in the diamond model and their mutual reinforcement are heightened by close geographic proximity within a nation. A concentration of rivals, customers, and suppliers will promote efficiencies and specialization, which eventually lead to improvement and innovation. However, the effective locus of competitive advantage may sometimes encompass regions that cross-national borders.

We are actually now in the midst of a global reallocation of production activities. Driven by the surge of newly industrialized economies, trade liberalization, and decreasing transportation and communication costs, more and more production activities are shifting from high-wage to low-wage countries (Andersen, 2006). On the other hand, many firms from developing countries also enter developed countries for various purposes (UNCTAD, 2006). Other researchers also agree that the ongoing reorganization of production, including off-shoring and internationalization of sourcing, is a sign that new organizational patterns are replacing existing forms (Dicken, 2003). On a similar note, Anderson (2006) suggested the idea of "production relocation dynamics across regional arenas." Moon and Jung (2008) systematically

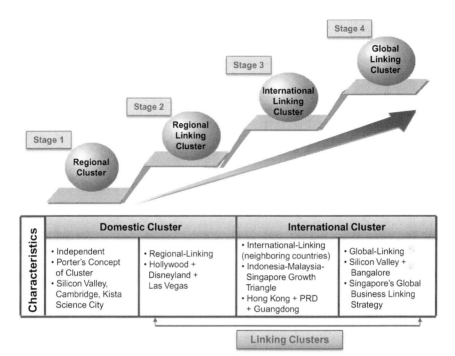

	Domestic Cluster		**International Cluster**	
Characteristics	• Independent • Porter's Concept of Cluster • Silicon Valley, Cambridge, Kista Science City	• Regional-Linking • Hollywood + Disneyland + Las Vegas	• International-Linking (neighboring countries) • Indonesia-Malaysia-Singapore Growth Triangle • Hong Kong + PRD + Guangdong	• Global-Linking • Silicon Valley + Bangalore • Singapore's Global Business Linking Strategy

Linking Clusters

Fig. 12-1   The Cluster Stage Model

Note: PRD means Pearl River Delta.
Source:
Moon and Jung (2008).

modeled the possible expansion of clusters with an introduction of evolutionary stages (see Figure 12-1).

The first stage is the regional cluster which is identical to Porter's original conception where each cluster is independent. Prominent examples of this stage include the early Silicon Valley, Cambridge, and Kista Science City. The second stage is the regional-linking cluster. The combination of related clusters within the national boundaries will generate synergistic effects. The American entertainment cluster, consisting of Hollywood, Disneyland, and Las Vegas, is representative of such regional-linking cluster. All are located in Southwestern part of the U.S. and create synergies between and among each other. The third stage is the international-linking cluster. Through the combination of cross-border neighboring clusters, synergy effects will be further enhanced. An example of this international-linking cluster is the "growth triangle" of Singapore (the core economy) with Malaysia and Indonesia (the peripheral economies). Another example is Hong Kong's linkage with Pearl River Delta (PRD) and Guangdong province. "Front shop, back factory" is the main motivation for this cluster.[1] The final stage is the global-linking cluster. Regardless of the physical distance among them, clusters located in various parts of the world are linked together for maximum synergies. In the field of information technology (IT), for example, the relationship between Silicon Valley (U.S.) and Bangalore (India) can be seen as a form of global-linking cluster. The global network strategy of Singapore is another example of this global-linking cluster.[2]

Of the examples listed above, the evolution of Silicon Valley from regional to global provides an illustrative point. Silicon Valley started as an independent cluster during the 1960s and then rapidly expanded its geographic scope into the neighboring cities, including San Jose and San Francisco. In the process of this evolution, the region's dominant industrial landscape shifted from defense and aerospace to more commercial sectors including computers, multi-media and bio technologies. Silicon Valley then connected with other clusters in Mexico and Canada and eventually Bangalore, located on the other side of the globe, to become a global-linking cluster of high technology. However, it should be noted that this stage model illustrates only generalized paths and a cluster development does not always need to pass through all of these stages. While Silicon Valley is an illustrative example, multiple paths are available towards forming a global-linking cluster.

ANALYTICAL TOOLS AND CASE STUDIES

The Growth Triangle: Korea with China, Japan, and Russia

According to the cluster stage model, explained in the previous section, the Northeast Asian Cluster can be categorized under stage 3. An interesting concept of international cooperation among the neighboring economies is "the growth triangle." The growth triangle is viewed as an exercise in spatial economic organization to "re-territorialize" the contiguous space to achieve economies based on differences in resources, cultural and tech-nological endowments (Sparke *et al.*, 2004; van Grunsven, 1995). Some

---

[1] The role of "front shop" is destined to Hong Kong, while PRD and Guangdong province play the role of "back factory."

[2] Singapore pursues a global strategy, and argues that two-thirds of world business is connected to Singapore.

examples of the growth triangle in the Asian region include the Singapore–Malaysia–Indonesia Growth Triangle, the Southern China Growth Triangle, the Tumen River Area Development Program, Northern ASEAN Growth Triangle, the Eastern ASEAN Growth Triangle, and the Yellow Sea Economic Zone. The growth triangle is not always composed of three countries. For example, the Southern China Growth Triangle consists of Hong Kong, Taipei, China, and the Southern PRC (mainly parts of Guangdong and Fujian provinces). For another example, the Tumen River Area Development Program includes parts of Jilin province in the PRC, Siberia in Russia, the Democratic People's Republic of Korea, Mongolia, the Republic of Korea, and Japan.

The growth triangle emerges as a result of two forces: regional economic cooperation and large flows of foreign direct investment (FDI). Regional cooperation is seen as a means of both enhancing development and providing some measure of insurance against adverse change in the external economic climate (Tang and Thant, 1994). Other scholars also urged the necessity of cooperation among Northeast Asian countries (Moon, 2004; Kim, 2003; Lee and Hong, 1999).

Developing a growth triangle may be a solution for countries which rely on heavily inflows of FDI. By removing barriers to inputs and capital flows, and by cooperating with one another through multiple channels, geographically neighboring countries are able to maintain their industry competitiveness. The most important factors for the success of the growth triangle include economic complementarity, geographical proximity, political commitment, policy coordination, and infrastructure development (Tang and Thant, 1994).

The relationship between the growth triangle and the global value chain is very important (Toh, 2006). The value chain describes the full range of activities that are required to bring a product from its conception to its end use and beyond, including design, production, marketing, distribution, and support to the final consumers. When developing a growth triangle, policy makers and business leaders have to consider the optimal combination of activities they wish to undertake at the growth triangle, based on prudent analysis of the global value chain of the product or industry.

There are some other considerations for developing growth triangles. De Long and Summers (1991) showed that countries tend to trade with their neighbors if transportation and communication costs can be minimized. Moreover, similarities in language and cultural background, which often

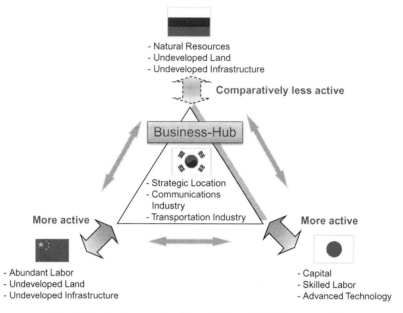

Fig. 12-2 A Prospective Growth Triangle in Northeast Asia

prevail between geographically proximate areas, are conducive to better understanding and closer business relationships (Tang and Thant, 1994). The country similarity theory of Linder (1961) can also be applied to the concept of the growth triangle among neighboring countries.

In accordance with the above discussion, Korea, China, Japan, and Russia can enhance their economic competitiveness by developing an international-linking cluster or a growth triangle through cooperation among the four nations. Figure 12-2 shows a prospective model for a growth triangle in this region, based on their differences in factor endowments and other national characteristics.

Next, Korea's potential as a Northeast Asian Hub will be discussed. A hub can be described as a place of an activity when it is a very important center for that activity or the central part of a circular object. Korea has hub potential for the following reasons. First, the Korean peninsula is strategically located at the center of all the nations. Korea's locational advantage is evidenced by the fact that there are more than 50 cities, exceeding one million in population, within one and half hours flight time from Korea. Second, from the perspective of economic development stages, Korea's position is between the more developed country (Japan) and less developed countries (China and

Russia). Therefore, an effective collaboration can be made, through the hub position of Korea, by combining the natural resources of Russia, the labor force of China and the technologies of Japan, together with Korea's semi-skilled labor and some advanced sectors in communication (e.g., information technology) and transportation (e.g., shipbuilding and automobiles). Through the formation of this international-linking cluster, the market in this region will also expand and become more sophisticated. Third, contrary to popular sentiment, Korea and its neighboring countries share more cooperative than competitive aspects in terms of their competitiveness variables. This is one of the main points of this chapter and will be proven in the next sections through case studies and empirical analysis.

Cooperative Cases between Korea and other Countries

A number of cooperative ventures between Korea and its neighboring countries are already taking place. A more systematic integration of these business activities will enhance the competitiveness of the region as well as that of the individual country. Here are some illustrative examples of cooperation among the four countries.

Cooperation between Korea and China

China is an important trading and investment partner to Korea. In many fields, cooperation between Korea and China has progressed. Examples include the resource development plan; electric power development project; Chinese west province development project; and collaboration in the distribution industry.[3] In these projects, China's abundant labor is well matched with Korea's capital and technology. However, the relationship between Korea and China is not simply a one-way transfer of capital and technology from Korea to China. Recently, China also made substantial investments in Korea, including the acquisitions of Hynix LDD parts (Korea) by BOE (China) and SsangYong Motors (Korea) by Shanghai Automotive Industry Corporation (China). These investments are unconventional from the view point of orthodox FDI theory (Dunning, 2003) and represent good examples of collaboration mechanism between the two countries in terms of acquiring new technologies and sharing other business activities.

---

[3] www.mke.go.kr (21st century common prosperity through the expansion of Korea–China economic cooperation, (In Korean), 5 December, 2012.

Cooperation between Korea and Japan

There is a great potential for mutual benefits through cooperation between Korea and Japan. Firms from these two countries often form joint ventures or alliances in order to enhance their competitiveness. For example, Hitachi-LG Data Storage (HLDS) Inc. and Toshiba Samsung Storage Technology (TSST) Corporation have established themselves as leaders in the global market for optical disk drives through joint ventures, which can create synergies by combining the technological capability of Japanese partner and the manufacturing expertise of Korean counterpart.[4] Another example is a close connection for technological interchange between the Korean Gumi Cluster, which is famous for its world-class electronic display sector, and the Japanese TAMA (Technology Advanced Metropolitan Area) Cluster. This linkage of clusters has made substantial progress in joint investments, component trade, technological alliances, and cooperative research and development (R&D), thus leading to mutual benefits for both countries.[5]

Cooperation between Korea and Russia

Much discussion has progressed, applying the concept of comparative advantage and complementarity to Korea-Russia cooperation for the development of resources and the improvement of infrastructure in the area of Primorskiy Krai. Specifically, energy resources and international transportation networks are of particular interest to these two countries. Recently, Korea's advancement into the fishing grounds of the Russian Far East has raised an issue, related to the long-term development plan of the Far East Zabaikal region and the possibility of a cooperative scheme between the two countries (Kim and Choi, 2005). In September 2008, the presidents of Korea and Russia made an agreement that the relationship between the two countries will be strengthened to the level of strategic partnership. Further cooperation will then include the development and transmission of natural gas; the cooperative petroleum development; space development; harbor construction; and fishery quotas.[6]

---

[4]Invest Korea Journal (Sn. 58, NO. 3, May-June 2008) (http://www.investkorea.org/).
[5]Available at: http://www.ohmynews.com/NWS_Web/view/at_pg.aspx?CNTN_CD=A0000 268230. Accessed 9 November 2008.
[6]Available at: http://todaykorea.tistory.com/505. Accessed 9 November 2008.

EMPIRICAL ANALYSIS

Hypothesis

The four countries in Northeast Asia can be first categorized into two groups: resource-rich, less developed countries (China and Russia) and resource-poor, more developed countries (Japan and Korea). Further differences exist between the countries, although they are classified under the same subgroups. In terms of the main source of competitiveness, China's strength lies in its labor force while Russia's major strength is in the field of natural resources. Differences can also be found between Japan and Korea. Although the overall level of Japanese technology and skill is higher than that of Korea, Korea has world-class strengths in some manufacturing segments and in some industrial sectors such as information technology, electronics, shipbuilding and other machinery.

As competitiveness is an organization's relative position compared to its rivals (Moon and Peery, 1995), competitiveness indexes differ according to the country. If the levels of competitiveness in some factors among these four countries are different, cooperative potential through complement is larger than competitive potential. In case of cooperative potential, it is likely to enhance the competitiveness of these countries through cooperation.

For example, in terms of the overall level of science and technology, Japan is ranked higher than Korea. Therefore, if Japan is classified as a different group from Korea, it can be said that the overall science and technology between Korea and Japan has a more cooperative rather than competitive potential. Based on such reasoning, we can conclude that technology and skill can be regarded as a cooperative factor between Japan and Korea. On the other hand, if Korea and Japan are classified in the same group in the energy resource sector, then the relationship between Korea and Japan in energy resource has competitive potential. Thus, energy resource is considered a competitive factor between the two nations.

This logic is consistent with that of the traditional trade theory, which assumes a cooperative potential between labor-abundant and capital-abundant countries. This chapter extends this two-factor model to a multiple-factor model and assumes the same cooperative potential between two countries if they are not in the same group. Similarly, we assume countries to have competitive potential if they are in the same group for a certain competitiveness factor. In other words, even if the two countries have different factor or competitiveness conditions, they do not necessarily have to cooperate with each other but we can assume the existence of a potential for cooperation between the two countries.[7] Therefore, we can formulate the following hypothesis.

There is more cooperative than competitive potential in competitiveness factors between Korea and the other Northeast Asian three countries (China, Japan, and Russia).

Analysis

Analytical model

Criticizing traditional trade theories, Porter (1990) introduced the diamond model, which systematically incorporates not only the production factor conditions that most traditional theorists have employed but also other important variables into a single model. Since then, Porter's diamond model has been extended in two directions, i.e., scopes and sources of national competitiveness. First, the scope of the original model has been extended from purely domestic to the international context. The double diamond model additionally incorporates multinational activities into Porter's framework in order to illustrate the influences of non-domestic activities on overall national competitiveness (Rugman, 1991; Rugman and D'Cruz, 1993; Moon *et al.*, 1995, 1998; Dunning 2003). Second, the original model has been extended to the nine-factor model (Cho, 1994; Cho and Moon, 2000).[8] This model divides the sources of competitiveness into physical and human variables in order to portray the more granular aspects of national competitiveness. The two upgraded versions of Porter's single diamond model have been designed specifically to explain the sources of national competitiveness of developing countries where human factors and international strategies are very important for enhancing national competitiveness. Porter's original diamond model was sufficient to explain the sources of national competitiveness of large developed countries such as the U.S. but left some loopholes in terms of providing a viable explanation for the competitiveness of developing countries.

Figure 12-3 visualizes the two changes made to Porter's original diamond model. In model 2, a new diamond of human factors is introduced as an

---

[7] For a related study, see Moon (2004) and Moon and Kim (2006a, 2006b).

[8] The nine-factor model consists of three parts, which are physical factors, human factors, and chance events.

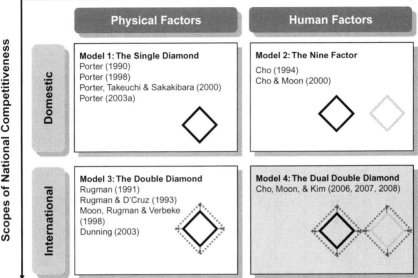

Fig. 12-3 Extension of Porter's Diamond Model

extension to the original sources of national competitiveness. In model 3, the original diamond is doubled in order to expand the scope of national competitiveness from a purely domestic context to the international context. Therefore, the integration of these two extensions into a single framework results in a dual double diamond (DDD) model, which provides an all-encompassing model that mitigates many of the flaws inherent in Porter's original model (Cho *et al.*, 2008). The DDD model considers both physical and human factors in both domestic and international contexts, and, consequently, provides a more comprehensive explanation for national competitiveness than other existing models. This study will employ the DDD model for the following empirical tests.

Data and Methodology[9]

Data for the empirical analysis were selected from IPS National Competitiveness Research (IPS, 2007), published by the Institute for Industrial Policy

---

[9]Methodologies of Moon (2004) and Moon and Kim (2006a, 2006b) are used for this part. However, data are updated; Russia is added; and some parts of methodologies are upgraded.

Table 12-1 Criteria for the Calculation of the National Competitiveness Index

Main Factors		Sub-Factors	Number of Criteria
Physical Factors	Factor Conditions	Energy Resources	6
		Other Resources	9
		Strategy & Structure	5
	Business Context	Global Mindset	5
		Business Culture	7
		Foreign Investment	11
	Related & Supporting Industries	Transportation	9
		Communication	10
		Finance	23
		Education	9
		Science & Technology	7
		Cluster Development	3
		Overall Living Environment	15
	Demand Conditions	Demand Size	11
		Demand Quality	8
Human Factors	Workers	Quantity of Labor Force	6
		Quality of Labor Force	1
	Politicians & Bureaucrats	Politicians	11
		Bureaucrats	32
	Entrepreneurs	Personal Competence	6
		Social Context	5
	Professionals	Personal Competence	7
		Social Context	6
TOTAL			212

Note: 212 criteria (among total 275 criteria) are used for this study.

Studies. The report includes competitiveness variables for 66 countries based on categories of the DDD model. Table 12-1 lists the specific criteria of this study.[10]

Eight factors of the DDD model are utilized and the chance event variable is excluded in the analysis. The economic competitiveness index is measured

---

[10]The report uses the most up-to-date 137 hard data collected through various statistical sources published by international or government organizations, and 138 soft data collected by the foreign offices of the Korea Trade-Investment Promotion Agency (KOTRA).

as an average of the eight factors. Each of the eight factors is calculated as an average of sub-factors under each factor, and each of the 23 sub-factors is also calculated as an average of the criteria under each sub-factor. Finally, 212 criteria are selected to calculate the national competitiveness index.

Although productivity is the internal competence of an organization, competitiveness is an organization's relative competitive position compared to its rivals (Moon and Peery, 1995). Therefore, this study utilizes a cluster analysis approach in order to find the relative position of each nation. Cluster analysis is a statistical technique that classifies objects into clusters according to the characteristics of the objects. Objects in the same cluster share significant homogeneity, while significant heterogeneity exists among objects in different clusters (Hair *et al.*, 1998).

A cluster analysis was conducted with the following steps. First, the relevant variables and their proxies based on the DDD model were selected. Second, four countries in each variable were classified into three clusters (High = A, Middle = B, and Low = C) according to their respective competitiveness.[11] For each competitiveness factor, we define the relationship between any two countries as competitive if the cluster analysis results indicate that these two countries can be classified under the same cluster. If not, they are considered to have a cooperative relationship. The cooperation can be both downward from a more developed country to a less developed country (Dunning, 1981, 1988) and upward from a less developed country to a more developed country (Moon and Roehl, 2001). Third, a K-means methodology was conducted to classify the entire sample of 66 countries into three groups. This methodology was used by the original IPS study. In this study, however, there is also an interest in the relationship between Korea and other neighboring countries; therefore, for the specific purpose of this study the sample was reclassified using the hierarchical clustering analysis.

Results and Discussions

Table 12-2 shows the results of the K-means cluster analysis and hierarchical cluster analysis of main factors in both physical and human factors of the DDD model, with the cooperative and competitive positions of Korea, China, Japan, and Russia. Each country is classified into three competitive groups of A, B, and C, according to the results of the cluster analyses of 66 countries. Cluster A includes the group of countries with high competitiveness; Cluster B with

---

[11] Some outliers are excluded and marked in the related table.

Table 12-2 Results of Cluster Analysis in Main Factors

Main Factors		K-Means Cluster Analysis			Hierarchical Cluster Analysis Competitive Group[#]				Rankings				Relationship with Korea[##]	
		Cluster Mean Square	Error Mean Square	F-Value	Korea	China	Japan	Russia	Korea	China	Japan	Russia	Cooperation	Competiton
Physical Factors	FC	2997.946	8.391	357.281***	C	A	C	A	59	5	54	3	C, R	J
	BC[a]	5339.880	32.724	163.179***	B	B	B	C	32	42	21	58	R	C, J
	RS	5108.184	21.704	235.355***	B	B	A	C	24	28	11	43	J, R	C
	DC	3015.040	15.130	199.276***	A	B	A	B	11	23	2	21	C, R	J
Human Factors	W[b]	1612.004	18.548	86.911***	B	A	B	B	53	3	35	44	C	J, R
	P&B	8036.935	49.363	162.813***	C	B	B	C	42	26	24	59	C, J	R
	E	5797.076	43.446	133.433***	A	B	B	B	15	50	30	61	C, J, R	
	P	6398.132	34.025	188.044***	A	B	A	B	16	52	23	47	C, R	J

Note: *** p<0.001

[#] A is the most competitive group, and C is the least comptitive group.

[##] K, C, J, and R represents Korea, China, Japan, and Russia, respectively.

[a,b] Two outliers — Libya and Nethetlands for Business Context, India and Mexico for Wokers — are excluded in hierarchical cluster analysis.

middle competitiveness; and Cluster C with low competitiveness. For example, in the case of factor conditions, Korea has potential to forge cooperative relationship with China and Russia while engaging in competitive relationship with Japan. In cases of business context (i.e., firm's strategy, structure, and rivalry) and workers, all three countries demonstrate a competitive relationship with Korea. On the other hand, in the case of entrepreneurs, Korea has a potential for cooperative relationship with all three countries. In this area, Korea can be a cooperative partner with all three countries because the level of Korean entrepreneurs is higher than that of the other three countries. In other areas, cooperative and competitive relationships are mixed among countries.

To analyze the relationship among the four countries in more detail, the same methodology is applied to the 23 sub-factors and the results are summarized in Table 12-3. The results show that the number of cooperative cases is 44 and the number of competitive cases is 25 between Korea and the other three countries. In the areas of foreign investment, China, Japan, and Russia all show a competitive relationship with Korea, while in the areas of science and technology, cluster development, overall living environment, and entrepreneurs' personal competence all three countries display a cooperative relationship with Korea. As the number of cooperative cases exceeds that of competitive cases, it can be concluded that the hypothesis presented in the chapter has been proven. Another notable finding is the higher cooperative ratio in the cluster analysis of sub-factors ($44/69 = 0.638$) (see Table 12-3) than that of the main factors ($15/24 = 0.625$) (see Table 12-2). Such finding indicates that further sub-categorization would yield more results towards cooperative relationship.

Table 12-4 illustrates specific avenues for cooperation and competition by each of the three countries *vis-à-vis* Korea. For example, China shows a competitive relationship with Korea in Global Mindset, Business Culture, Foreign Investment, Finance, Bureaucrats, Entrepreneurs' Social Context and Professionals' Social Context while cooperative relationship can be observed in other areas. To sum up, since each country is equipped with different competitive advantages and disadvantages, sharing the diversities of these countries will create additional synergies and enhance competitiveness of the Northeast Asian region as well as that of the individual countries.

While the main hypothesis of this study has been proven through empirical work, other considerations can be given to realize the cooperative

Table 12-3   Results of Cluster Analysis in Sub-Factors

Main Factors		Sub-Factors	K-Means Cluster Analysis F-Value	Hierarchical Cluster Analysis Competitive Group#				Relationship with Korea##	
				Korea	China	Japan	Russia	Cooperation	Competiton
Physical Factors	FC	Energy Resources	312.639***	C	B	C	A	C, R	J
		Other Resources[a]	213.003***	C	A	C	B	C, R	J
	BC	Strategy & Structure	114.380***	A	B	A	B	C, R	J
		Global Mindset	156.694***	B	B	B	C	R	C, J
		Business Culture	157.187***	C	C	B	C	J	C, R
		Foreign Investment	190.728***	C	C	C	C	C, J, R	C, J, R
	RS	Transportation[b]	123.104***	B	A	A	B	C, J	R
		Communication	271.202***	A	B	A	C	C, R	J
		Finance	281.483***	B	B	A	C	J, R	C
	RS	Education	188.076***	B	C	C	B	C, J	R
		Science & Technology	203.041***	B	C	A	C	C, J, R	
		Cluster Development	143.173***	B	A	A	C	C, J, R	
		Overall Living Environment	210.010***	B	C	A	C	C, J, R	
	DC	Demand Size[c]	87.297***	B	A	A	B	C, J	R
		Demand Quality	150.204***	B	C	A	B	C, J	R

(Continued)

Table 12-3 (*Continued*)

Main Factors		Sub-Factors	K-Means Cluster Analysis F-Value	Hierarchical Cluster Analysis Competitive Group[#]				Relationship with Korea[##]	
				Korea	China	Japan	Russia	Cooperation	Competiton
Human Factors	W	Quantity of Labor Force[d]	136.170***	C	A	C	B	C, R	J
		Quality of Labor Force	152.152***	B	A	A	B	C, J	R
	P&B	Politicians	176.038***	C	B	B	C	C, J	R
		Bureaucrats	133.379***	C	C	B	C	J	C, R
	E	Personal Competence[e]	133.843***	A	C	B	B	C, J, R	C, R
		Social Context	127.652***	B	B	B	C	R	C, J
	P	Personal Competence	148.331***	A	B	A	B	C, R	J
		Social Context	199.015***	B	B	A	C	J, R	C

Note: ***p<0.001

[#]A is the most competitive group, and C is the least competitive group.

[##]K, C, J, and R represents Korea, China, Japan, and Russia, respectively.

a,b,dOne outlier — Canada in a, USA in b, India in d — is excluded in hierarchical cluster analysis.

cThree outliers — USA, Hong Kong, and Singapore — are excluded in hierarchical cluster analysis.

eTwo outliers — Libya and The Netherlands — are excluded in hierarchical cluster analysis.

Table 12-4   Cooperative and Competitive Relationship with Korea

Main Factors		Sub-Factors	Relationship with Korea		
			China	Japan	Russia
Physical Factors	Factor Conditions	Energy Resources	O	X	O
		Other Resources	O	X	O
	Business Context	Strategy & Structure	O	X	O
		Global Mindset	X	X	O
		Business Culture	X	O	X
		Foreign Investment	X	X	X
	Related & Supporting Industries	Transportation	O	O	X
		Communication	O	X	O
		Finance	X	O	O
		Education	O	O	X
		Science & Technology	O	O	O
		Cluster Development	O	O	O
		Overall Living Environment	O	O	O
	Demand Conditions	Demand Size	O	O	X
		Demand Quality	O	O	X
Human Factors	Workers	Quantity of Labor Force	O	X	O
		Quality of Labor Force	O	O	X
	Politicians & Bureaucrats	Politicians	O	O	X
		Bureaucrats	X	O	X
	Entrepreneurs	Personal Competence	O	O	O
		Social Context	X	X	O
	Professionals	Personal Competence	O	X	O
		Social Context	X	O	O

Note: O is cooperative relationship with Korea, while X is competitive relationship.

or competitive relationship among the Northeast Asian countries. First, the weights of the competitiveness variables may differ depending on the specific country context. Second, historical and political situations, including the process of the Six Party Talks on the Korean peninsula, need to be considered. Third, cultural dimensions must also be examined and will be discussed in the following section.

A FURTHER CONSIDERATION: CULTURAL DIFFERENCES

An Analytical Model

The competitiveness of the four countries in the Northeast Asian region can be further enhanced through sharing cultural as well as economic diversity. Cultural differences may become barriers to business when the discrepancy is large and lead to culture clashes between countries. However, cultures can also be sources of unique competitive advantages and thus enhance national competitiveness. The four countries in the Northeast Asian regions have distinct cultural identities but the differences are at a level where the potential for mutual understanding and learning can be cultivated toward enhancing the region's overall competitiveness.

Of all the models for cultural analysis, Hofstede (1983) model is the most widely used and covers most of the cultural variables in other models such as Hall and Hall (1990), Trompenaars and Hampden-Turner (1998). However, Hofstede has been criticized by other scholars (McSweeney, 2002; Hampden-Turner and Trompenaars, 1997) and, in particular, Moon and Choi (2001) points out that the Hofstede model misses Perlmuter's (1969) EPG Profile — ethnocentrism (home-country orientation), polycentrism (host-country orientation), and geocentrism (host-country orientation). The EPG Profile is particularly important in explaining the changing competitiveness of developing countries as it represents the degree of *internationalization* or *openness*. Furthermore, some of the variables utilized in the Hofstede model either overlap or incorporate inappropriate factors. Thus, Moon and Choi (2001) suggested a new cultural model dubbed the OUI model, which consists of three variables that removed the overlaps and unnecessary variables found in the Hofstede model and added a new variable. Later, Moon (2004) and Moon and Jung (2007) demonstrated the validity of this model through empirical analyses.

The OUI model explains cultural differences utilizing *Openness, Uncertainty Avoidance*, and *Individualism*. *Openness* consists of *Attractiveness* and *Aggressiveness*. *Attractiveness* is the willingness to accept foreign values and cultures through import, immigration, and inward FDI, and so on. *Aggressiveness* is the tendency to push home country values abroad through export, emigration, and outward FDI, and so on. *Uncertainty Avoidance* includes *Disciplinism* and *Frontierism*. *Disciplinism* refers to rules, laws, and standards and *Frontierism* incorporates challenge, originality, and innovation.

Individualism is made up of *Responsibility* and *Reward*, and is measured by how much reward is awarded for responsible behavior.

Data and Methodology[12]

For an empirical analysis, data were selected from IPS National Competitiveness Research (IPS, 2007). The cultural variables and their indices of the four countries are presented in Table 12-5. For example, in *Individualism*, the proxies for *Responsibility* are job description and individual roles, corporate governance and labor-management relations. Whether or not the job description and individual roles are clear is an important criterion in defining each person's responsibility. Furthermore, if a country's corporate governance reflects well-defined responsibility, each employee and employer can be faithful to his or her own duty by maintaining a cooperative relationship between labor and management. The proxies for *Reward* are measured by reward on performance, firm's decision process, and compensation to professionals. A country's culture can be economically more productive if: reward is based on performance rather than seniority; professionals are appropriately compensated; the firm's decision process is transparent. A similar logic can be established for other variables, as shown in Table 12-5.

Results and Discussions

Tables 12-5 and 12-6 and Figures 12-4, 12-5, and 12-6 show the results regarding the cultural differences among the four countries. For *Individualism*, Japan has a high score in both *Responsibility* and *Reward*. Korea also has a high score in *Reward* but is relatively lower than Japan in *Responsibility*. China is in the middle position for both *Responsibility* and *Reward*. On the other hand, Russia's *Reward* position is extremely low, while its *Responsibility* is in the middle.

In *Uncertainty Avoidance*, both Japan and Korea have high scores, but Japan is relatively more disciplined and Korea is relatively more frontieristic. China's *Disciplinism* is in the middle, but its *Frontierism* is relatively low. Russia's *Disciplinism* is very low, while its *Frontierism* is in the middle but higher than that of China. In *Openness*, Korea and Japan, have similar scores on both *Aggressiveness* and *Attractiveness*, while China is a little below these two countries for *Aggressiveness*. In contrast, Russia has a very low score in

---

[12]Methodologies of Moon (2004) and Moon and Kim (2006a, 2006b) are used for this part. However, data are updated; Russia is added; and some methodologies are changed.

Table 12-5   Cultural Variables and Their Indices of Korea, China, Japan, and Russia

Measured Items	Korea	China	Japan	Russia
Individualism				
Responsibility				
Job description and individual roles	44.38	36.83	69.58	21.34
Corporate governance	47.24	45.27	61.73	55.64
Relationship between labor and management	34.99	42.72	63.61	27.06
Average	42.20	41.61	64.97	34.68
Reward				
Reward on perfomance	52.10	36.48	43.72	3.90
Transparency of the firm's decision process	34.40	12.14	29.72	0.72
Compensation to professionals	55.81	54.79	56.02	7.74
Average	47.44	34.47	43.15	4.12
Uncertainty Avoidance				
Disciplinism				
Keeping public order	61.89	41.85	78.60	18.91
Bureaucracy	36.43	45.95	54.52	16.26
Bribery and corruption	37.00	24.92	43.87	2.84
Average	45.11	37.57	59.00	12.67
Frontierism				
Mindset for innovativeness and creativity	58.61	41.52	56.22	22.72
Dfferentiated competence of entrepreneurs	95.39	25.35	57.64	64.34
Ability to take opportunities	73.58	37.08	64.61	60.74
Average	75.86	34.65	59.49	49.27
Openness				
Aggressiveness				
[Outward FDI, stock index ($) + Outward FDI, stock index (% of GDP)]/2	1.75	1.50	11.03	5.90
Adaptation of firms to international changes	56.34	32.91	50.56	27.74
Willingness to accept new ideas	64.13	63.07	50.96	37.96
Average	40.74	32.49	37.52	23.87
Attractiveness				
[Inward FDI, stock index ($) + Inward FDI, stock index (% of GDP)]/2	3.12	11.99	3.31	6.81
Equal treatment of domestic and foreign firms	51.77	63.52	41.05	22.10
Openness of professional jobs to foreigners	29.68	17.94	43.68	54.75
Average	40.73	40.73	42.37	27.89

Table 12-6 Results of Measured Cultural Variables based on OUI Model

Cultural Variables		Japan	Korea	China	Russia
Individualism	Responsibility	64.97	42.20	41.61	34.68
	Reward	43.15	47.44	34.47	4.12
	Ratio	1.51	0.89	1.21	8.42
Uncertainty	Disciplinism	59.00	45.11	37.57	12.67
Avoidance	Frontierism	59.49	75.86	34.65	49.27
	Ratio	0.99	0.59	1.08	0.26
Openness	Aggressiveness	37.52	40.74	32.49	23.87
	Attractiveness	42.37	40.73	40.73	27.89
	Ratio	0.89	1.00	0.80	0.86
The Sum of Individualism		108.13	89.64	76.08	38.80
The Sum of Uncertainty Avoidance		118.49	120.97	72.22	61.94
The Sum of Openness		79.88	81.47	73.22	51.75
The Sum of All Cultural Variables		306.49	292.07	221.52	152.49

Source:
IPS National Competitiveness Research 2007.

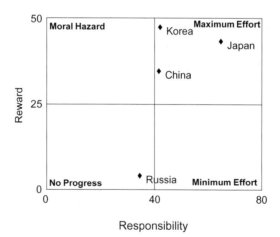

Fig. 12-4 Individualism of the Four Countries

Attractiveness. The low level of Russia's *Openness*, particularly in *Attractiveness*, is well contrasted by that of China, which scores substantially higher than Russia. An important implication is then that the recent success of the Chinese economy is mainly due to its active internationalization or openness (especially

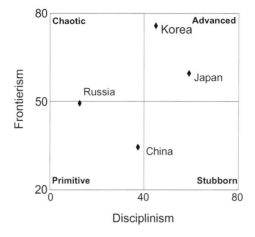

Fig. 12-5 Uncertainty Avoidance of the Four Countries

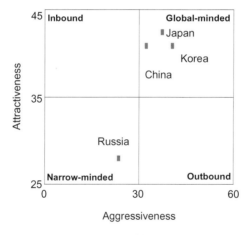

Fig. 12-6 Openness of the Four Countries

compared to Russia), and this will be an important piece of policy advice for Russia. As we have seen from the economic differences discussed in the previous section, sharing cultural differences among the four countries will enhance their competitiveness.

The view that cultural differences can become a source of competitive advantage rather than a barrier to business is consistent with the ideas forwarded in Porter (2000b). Such findings provide policy makers with an important insight. For example, a distinctly Korean cultural trait, commonly referred to as *pali pali* (or quick quick), may be a disadvantage in and of itself. However, when combined with Japan's *disciplinism* or other cultural characteristics of China, a negative cultural trait such as *pali pali* can become a source of new competitive advantage of frontierism and entrepreneurship.

CONCLUSION

This chapter has extended Porter's domestically independent cluster to an internationally linking cluster and applied this concept to four countries in the Northeast Asian region. The four countries in the region have significantly different sources of competitive advantages from each other, so an appropriate combination of these advantages will create enormous benefits to these countries. These benefits can be maximized and the process can be optimized if the four countries possess their own world-class clusters and combine them across the four countries. Although there are some cooperative ventures among the countries in the region, a more systematic and cluster-based cooperation is yet to be developed.

Free trade agreements (FTAs) have been discussed in the region, but obtaining concrete results seem like a distant possibility. If the Northeast Asian countries link internationally through clusters, however, there will be little need for formal contracts such as FTAs. Compared to FTAs, which simply promotes free flow of the goods produced mostly in one country, international-linking cluster can combine the best activities in the international value chain and generate powerful positive influences on the region's competitiveness. Furthermore, an international-linking cluster can be formed without much political tension or resistance.

This chapter has provided some different but useful implications: from domestic to international clusters; from competition to cooperation; and from trade to all business activities in the international value chain. In addition, this chapter has suggested that sharing cultural diversity is as important as sharing economic diversity in terms of enhancing national competitiveness. The cultural aspect of clustering is an important area of additional research that deserves further attention from business scholars and policy makers. Other avenues for extension include applying the analytical frameworks of this chapter to other levels of analysis such as industrial and firm levels. Moreover, interactive terms between clusters and cultures for different business activities can also be further investigated.

REFERENCES

Anderson, P. H. (2006). Regional clusters in a global World: Production reloca-tion, innovation, and industrial decline. *California Management Review*, **49**(1): 101–121.

Cho, D. S. (1994). A dynamic approach to international competitiveness: The case of Korea. *Journal of Far Eastern Business*, **1**(1): 17–36.

Cho, D. S. and Moon, H. C. (2000). *From Adam Smith to Michael Porter*, Singapore: World Scientific.

Cho, D. S., Moon, H. C. and Kim, M. Y. (2006). Competitive strategy to enhance national competitiveness. *Proceedings of the Academy of International Business 2006 Annual Meeting*, Beijing, China, 23–26 June.

Cho, D. S., Moon, H. C. and Kim, M. Y. (2007). Beyond Porter's single diamond: A dual double diamond model approach to national competitiveness. *Proceedings of the Academy of International Business 2007 Annual Meeting*, Indianapolis, Indiana, 25–28 June.

Cho, D. S., Moon, H. C. and Kim, M. Y. (2008). Does one size fit all? A dual double diamond approach to country-specific advantages. *Asian Business & Management*, **8**(1): 83–102.

De Long, J. B. and Summers, L. H. (1991). Equipment investment and economic growth. *The Quarterly Journal of Economics*, **106**: 445–502.

Dicken, P. (2003). *Global Shift: Reshaping the Global Economic Map in the 21st Century*, New York: Guilford Publications.

Dunning, J. H. (1981). *International Production and the Multinational Enterprise*. London: George Allen & Unwin.

Dunning, J. H. (1988). The eclectic paradigm of international production: A restate-ment and some possible extensions. *Journal of International Business Studies*, **19**(1): 1–32.

Dunning, J. H. (2003). The role of foreign direct investment in upgrading China's competitiveness. *Journal of International Business and Economy*, **4**(1): 1–13.

European Commission (2003). Final Report of the Expert Group on Enter-prise Clusters and Networks, Brussels: European Commission. Available at: http://ec.europa.eu/enterprise/entrepreneurship/support_measures/cluster/final_report_clusters_en.pdf. Accessed August 2008.

Forbes (2008). Paul Krugman, Nobel, 13 October. Available at: http://www.forbes.com/2008/10/13/krugman-nobel-economics-oped-cx_ap_1013panagariya.html.

Fujita, M., Krugman P. and Venables, A. J. (1999). *The Spatial Economy: Cities, Regions, and International Trade*, MA: The MIT Press.

Hair, J. F., Anderson, R. E., Tatham, R. L and Black, W. C. (1998). *Multivariate Data Analysis*, 5th Edn, Upper Saddle River, N.J.: Prentice Hall.

Hall, E. and Hall, M. R. (1990). *Understanding Cultural Differences*, Yartmouth, Maine: Intercultural Press.

Hampden-Turner, C. and Trompenaars, F. (1997). Response to Geert Hofstede. *International Journal of Intercultural Relations*, 21(1): 149–159.

Hofstede, G. (1983). The cultural relativity of organizational practices and theories. *Journal of International Business Studies*, 14(2): 75–89.

Institute for Industrial Policy Studies (IPS) (2007). IPS National Competitiveness Research 2007 Report, Seoul: IPS and IPS-NaC.

Kim, C. S. and Choi, D. O. (2005). A scheme for the trade increase between Korea and Russia through the enhancement of fisheries cooperation. *Journal of Korea Trade*, 9(2): 47–70.

Kim, W. B. (2003). *A Research on Strategies of Cooperative Regional Development toward Integrated National Territory*, Seoul: Korea Research Institute for Human Settlements.

Krugman, P. (1992). *Geography and Trade*, MA: The MIT Press.

Lee, C. J. and Hong, I. P. (1999). A new approach to enhance Northeast Asian economic cooperation. *Journal of International Economic Studies*, 3(3): 100–137.

Linder, S. B. (1961). *An Essay on Trade and Transformation*, New York: John Wiley.

Martin, R. and Sunley, P. (2003). Deconstructing clusters: Chaotic concept or policy panacea? *Journal of Economic Geography*, 3(3): 5–35.

Maskell, P. (2001). Towards a knowledge-based theory of the geographical cluster. *Industrial and Corporate Change*, 10(4): 921–943.

McSweeney, B. (2002). Hofstede's model of national cultural differences and their consequences: A triumph of faith — A failure of analysis. *Human Relations*, 55(11): 89–118.

Moon, H. C. (2004). Cooperation among Japan, Korea, and China through sharing business and cultural advantages. *The Review of Business History*, 19(3): 33–51.

Moon, H. C. and Choi, E. K. (2001). Cultural impact on national competitiveness. *Journal of International and Area Studies*, 8(2): 21–36.

Moon, H. C. and Jung, J. S. (2007). A strategic approach to culture and economic performance for different stages of economic development: The OUI model and its empirical analysis (In Korean). *International Business Journal*, 18(1): 111–136.

Moon, H. C. and Jung, J. S. (2008). A stage approach to the cluster evolution and the development of a new global-linking cluster (In Korean). *The Review of Business History*, 23(1): 77–104.

Moon, H. C. and Kim, M. Y. (2006a). Cooperation and competition between Korea and BRICs (In Korean). *Journal of International Trade and Industry Studies*, 11(2): 69–94.

Moon, H. C. and Kim, M. Y. (2006b). Enhancing cooperation between Korea and Japan: An interdisciplinary approach of business competitiveness and culture. *Hitotsubashi Journal of Commerce and Management*, 40: 19–33.

Moon, H. C. and Peery, N. S. (1995). Competitiveness of product, firm, industry, and nation in a global business. *Competitiveness Review*, 5(1): 37–43.

Moon, H. C. and Roehl, T. (2001). Unconventional foreign direct investment and the imbalance theory. *International Business Review*, 10(2): 197–215.

Moon, H. C., Rugman, A. M. and Verbeke, A. (1995). The generalized double diamond approach to international competitiveness, in Rugman, A. M., den Broeck, J. V. and Verbeke, A. (eds.), *Research in Global Strategic Management, Vol. 5: Beyond the Diamond*, Greenwich, CT: JAI Press, pp. 97–114.

Moon, H. C., Rugman, A. M. and Verbeke, A. (1998). A generalized double diamond approach to the global competitiveness of Korea and Singapore. *International Business Review*, 7: 135–150.

Perlmutter, H. V. (1969). The tortuous evolution of the multinational corporation. *Columbia Journal of World Business*, 4: 9–18.

Porter, M. E. (1990). *The Competitive Advantage of Nations*, New York: Free Press.

Porter, M. E. (1998a). Clusters and the new economics of competition. *Harvard Business Review*, 76(6): 77–90.

Porter, M. E. (1998b). *On Competition*, Boston: Harvard Business School Press.

Porter, M. E. (2000a). Location, competition, and economic development: Local clusters in a global economy. *Economic Development Quarterly*, 14(1): 15–34.

Porter, M. E. (2000b). Attitudes, values, beliefs, and the microeconomics of prosperity, in Harrison, L. E. and Huntington, S. P. (eds.), *Culture Matters*, New York: Basic Books, pp. 14–28.

Porter, M. E. (2003). *Malaysia's Competitiveness: Moving to the Next Stage*, Kuala Lumpur, Malaysia (Presentation slides).

Porter, M. E. and Armstrong, J. (1992). Canada at the crossroads: Dialogue (Response by Porter). *Business Quarterly*, 56(4): 6–10.

Porter, M. E., Takeuchi, H. and Sakakibara, M. (2000). *Can Japan Compete?* Cambridge, MA: Perseus Publishing.

Reuber, R. and Fisher, E. (2001). *Industrial Clusters and SME Promotion in Developing Countries*, Commonwealth Secretariat.

Rugman, A. M. (1991). Diamond in the rough. *Business Quarterly*, 55(3): 61–64.

Rugman, A. M. (1992a). Porter takes the wrong turn. *Business Quarterly*, 56(3): 59–64.

Rugman, A. M. (1992b). Canada at the crossroads: Dialogue (Counter-response by Rugman). *Business Quarterly*, 57(1): 7–10.

Rugman, A. M. and D'Cruz, J. R. (1993). The double diamond model of international competitiveness: The Canadian experience. *Management International Review*, 33(2): 17–39.

Russo, M. (2004). The ceramic industrial district facing the challenge from China-innovation processes and relations among different types of firms inside and outside the Sassuolo district. Paper presented at *Clusters, Industrial Districts and*

Firms: The Challenge of Globalization, conference in Honor of Professor Sebastino Brusco, Modena, Italy.

Sparke, M., Sidaway, J. D., Bunnell, T. and Grundy-Warr, C. (2004). Triangulating the borderless world: Geographies of power in the Indonesia-Malaysia-Singapore Growth Triangle. *Transactions of the Institute of British Geographers*, **29**: 495–498.

Tang, M. and Thant, M. (1994). Growth triangles: conceptual issues and operational problems. *Staff Paper No. 54*, Manila: Asian Development Bank.

Toh, M. H. (2006). Development in the Indonesia-Malaysia-Singapore Growth Triangle. Department of Economics SCAPE Working Paper, *Series Paper No. 2006/06-31*, March 2006, National University of Singapore.

Trompenaars, F. and Hampden-Turner, C. (1998). *Riding the Waves of Culture: Understanding Cultural Diversity in Global Business*, New York: McGraw-Hill.

UNCTAD (2006). *World Investment Report: FDI from Developing and Transition Economies: Implications for Development*, New York and Geneva: United Nations.

van Grunsven, L. (1995). Industrial regionalization and urban-regional transformation in Southeast Asia: The SIJORI growth triangle considered. *Malaysian Journal of Tropical Geography*, **26**(1): 47–65.

REFERENCES

Anderson, P. H. (2006). Regional clusters in a global world: Production reloca-tion, innovation, and industrial decline. *California Management Review*, **49**(1): 101–121.

Baker, M. J. and Hart , S. J. (1989). *Marketing and Competitive Success*, New York: Philip Allan, pp. 5–8.

Baldwin, R. (ed.) (1988). *Trade Policy Issues and Empirical Analysis*, Chicago: University of Chicago Press.

Bark, T. and Moon, H. C. (2002). Globalization of technologies: The role of foreign direct investment. *Tech Monitor*, **19**(1): 20–25.

Bonacich, E. and Appelbaum, P. P. (2000). *Behind the Label: Inequality in the Los Angeles Apparel Industry*, Berkeley, CA: University of California Press.

Brander, J. and Spencer, S. (1985). Export subsidies and international market share rivalry. *Journal of International Economics*, **February**: 83–100.

Brown, C. and Sheriff, T. D. (1978). De-industrialization: A background paper, in Blackaby, F. (ed.), *De-industrialization*, London: Heinemann.

Buckley, P. J. and Casson, M. C. (1976). *The Future of the Multinational Enterprise*, London: MacMillan, pp. 33–65.

Buckley, P. J. and Casson, M. C. (1991). Multinational enterprises in less developed countries: Cultural and economic interactions, in Buckley, P. J. and Clegg, J. (eds.), *Multinational Enterprises in Less Developed Countries*, Chap. 2, London: MacMillan, pp. 27–55.

BusinessWeek (2003). The Samsung way, 16 June.

Cartwright, W. R. (1993). Multiple linked diamonds: New Zealand's experience. *Management International Review*, **33**(2): 55–70.

Cho, D. S. (1994). A dynamic approach to international competitiveness: The case of Korea. *Journal of Far Eastern Business*, **1**(1): 17–36.

Cho, D. S. and Moon, H. C. (2000). *From Adam Smith to Michael Porter*, Singapore: World Scientific.

Cho, D. S. and Moon, H. C. (2006). *The National Competitiveness: Theory and Practice* (In Korean). Seoul, Korea: The Korea Economic Daily.

Cho, D. S., Moon, H. C. and Kim, M. Y. (2006). Competitive strategy to enhance national competitiveness. *Proceedings of the Academy of International Business 2006 Annual Meeting*, Beijing, China, 23–26 June.

Cho, D. S., Moon, H. C. and Kim, M. Y. (2007). Beyond Porter's single diamond: A dual double diamond model approach to national competitiveness. *Proceedings of the Academy of International Business 2007 Annual Meeting*, Indianapolis, Indiana, 25–28 June.

Cho, D. S., Moon, H. C. and Kim, M. Y. (2008a). Characterizing international competitiveness in international business research: A MASI approach to national competitiveness. *Research in International Business and Finance*, **22**(2): 175–192.

Cho, D. S., Moon, H. C. and Kim, M. Y. (2008b). Does one size fit all? A dual double diamond approach to country-specific advantages. *Asian Business & Management*, **8**(1): 83–102.

Cho, D. S., Choi, J. and Yi, Y. (1994). International advertising strategies by NIC multinationals: The case of a Korean firm. *International Journal of Advertising*, **13**: 77–92.

Christerson, B. and Appelbaum, R. P. (1995). Global and local subcontracting: Space, ethnicity, and the organization of apparel production. *World Development*, **23**(8): 1363–1374.

Chung, H. K., Yi, H. C., Jung, K. H. and Lee, H. C. (1997). *Korean Management: Global Strategy and Cultural Transformation*, New York: Walter de Gruyter, Inc.

Chungang Daily Newspaper (1995). Wages of Korea and other major countries, February.

Crocombe, F. T., Enright, M. J. and Porter, M. E. (1991). *Upgrading New Zealand's Competitive Advantage*, Auckland: Oxford University Press.

De Long, J. B. and Summers, L. H. (1991). Equipment investment and economic growth. *The Quarterly Journal of Economics*, **106**: 445–502.

Dialogue (1992). Canada at the crossroads. *Business Quarterly* (Winter, Spring, and Summer).

Dicken, P. (2003). *Global Shift: Reshaping the Global Economic Map in the 21st Century*. New York: Guilford Publications.

Dickerson, K. (1999). *Textiles and Apparel in the Global Economy*, 3rd Edn, New York: Prentice-Hall.

Dietrich, W. S. (1991). *In the Shadow of the Rising Sun: The Political Roots of American Economic Decline*, University Park: Pennsylvania State University Press.

Dunning, J. H. (1981). *International Production and the Multinational Enterprise*, London: George Allen & Unwin.

Dunning, J. H. (1988). The eclectic paradigm of international production: A restatement and some possible extensions. *Journal of International Business Studies*, **19**(1): 1–32.

Dunning, J. H. (1992). The competitive advantage of countries and the activities of transnational corporations. *Transnational Corporations*, **1**(1): 135–168.

Dunning, J. H. (1993). Internationalizing Porter's diamond. *Management International Review*, **33**(2): 7–15.

Dunning, J. H. (2003). The role of foreign direct investment in upgrading China's competitiveness. *Journal of International Business and Economy*, **4**(1): 1–13.

Europa Publications Limited (1995). *The Europa World Year Book 1995*, London, England: Europa Publications Limited.

European Commission (2003). *Final Report of the Expert Group on Enterprise Clusters and Networks*, Brussels: European Commission. Available at: http://ec.europa.eu/enterprise/entrepreneurship/support_measures/cluster/final_report_clusters_en.pdf. Accepted August 2008.

Fallows, J. (1993). How the world works. *The Atlantic Monthly*, **December**: 60–87.

Fashion View (2001). Big changes in apparel market. *Fashion View*, **1**(6): 1–6 (In Korean).

Feenstra, R. (ed.) (1988). *Empirical Methods for International Trade*, Chicago: University of Chicago Press.

Financial News (2001). Apparel industry expanding to Chinese market, 27 November (In Korean). Available at: http://www.fnnews.com/html/fnview/2001/1127/091850249115111100.html. Accessed 6 February 2002.

Forbes (2001). Look out Sony, 16 April.

Forbes (2008). Paul Krugman, Nobel, 13 October. Available at: http://www.forbes.com/2008/10/13/krugman-nobel-economics-oped-cx_ap_1013panagariya.html.

Fortune (2002). Samsung's golden touch, 17 March.

Foster, M. J. and Wang, Z. (2007). Nanjing's performance as China's FDI inflows grow. *International Journal of Management and Decision Making*, **8**(2): 426–439.

Francis, A. and Tharakan, P. K. M. (eds.) (1989). *The Competitiveness of European Industry*, London and NY: Routledge, pp. 5–20.

Frear, C. R., Metcalf, L. E. and Alguire, M. S. (1992). Offshore sourcing: Its nature and scope. *International Journal of Purchasing and Materials Management*, **28**(3): 2–11.

Fujita, M., Krugman, P. and Venables, A. J. (1999). *The Spatial Economy: Cities, Regions and International Trade*, MA: The MIT Press.

Garten, J. E. (1992). *A Cold Peace: America, Japan, Germany, and the Struggle for Supremacy*, New York: Times Books.

Gereffi, G. (1994). The organization of buyer-driven global commodity chains: How US retailers shape global production networks, in Gereffi, G. and Korzeniewicz, M. (eds.), *Commodity Chains and Global Capitalism*, Westport, CT: Greenwood Press, pp. 95–122.

Gereffi, G. (1999). International trade and industrial upgrading in the apparel commodity chain. *Journal of International Economics*, **48**: 37–70.

George, A. (1998). Li & Fung: Beyond 'filling in the mosaic', 1995–1998. *Manuscript no. 9-398-092*, Boston MA: Harvard Business School Press.

Glass, G. V. and Hopkins, K. D. (1996). *Statistical Methods in Education and Psychology*, 3rd Edn, Needham Heights, MA: Allyn and Bacon.

Goldsmith, W. and Clutterbuck, D. (1984). *The Winning Streak: Britain's Top Companies Reveal Their Formulas for Success*, Weidenfeld & Nicolson.

Grant, R. M. (1991). Porter's competitive advantage of nations: An assessment. *Strategic Management Journal*, **12**(7): 535–548.

Grossman, G. M. (ed.) (1992). *Imperfect Competition and International Trade*, Cambridge: MIT Press.

Gwynne, P. (1993). Directing technology in Asia's dragons. *Research Technology Management*, **32**(2): 12–15.

Hair, J. F., Anderson, R. E., Tatham, R. L. and Black, W. C. (1998). *Multivariate Data Analysis*, 5th Edn, Upper Saddle River, N. J: Prentice Hall.

Hall, E. and Hall, M. R. (1990). *Understanding Cultural Differences*, Yartmouth, Maine: Intercultural Press.

Hampden-Turner, C. and Trompenaars, F. (1997). Response to Geert Hofstede. *International Journal of Intercultural Relations*, **21**(1): 149–159.

Han, D. H. *et al.* (2003). Competitiveness of Samsung electronics versus SONY, in Moon, H. C. (ed.), *Managing Competitiveness*, Seoul: The Institute for Industrial Policy Studies (IPS).

Han, S. (2003). The Korea textile news, 6 March (In Korean). Available at: www.ktnews.com. Accessed 19 May 2003.

Heckscher, E. F. (1949) (1919). The effect of foreign trade on the distribution of income, in Howard, S. E. and Metzler, L. A. (eds.), *Readings in the Theory of International Trade*, Homewood: Irwin.

HMSO (1985). *Report from the Select Committee of the House of Lords on Overseas Trade*, The Aldington Report.

Hodgetts, R. M. (1993). Porter's diamond framework in a Mexican context. *Management International Review*, **33**(2): 41–54.

Hofstede, G. (1983). The cultural relativity of organizational practices and theories. *Journal of International Business Studies*, **14**(2): 75–89.

Hofstede, G. (1997). *Cultures and Organizations: Software of the Mind*, New York: McGraw-Hill.

Hymer, S. H. (1976) (1960). *The International Operations of National Firms: A Study of Direct Foreign Investment*, Cambridge, M.A.: MIT Press.

IMD (1992). *The World Competitiveness Report*, Lausanne, Switzerland.

IPS (2005). *IPS National Competitiveness Research 2005 Report*, Seoul: IPS and IPS-NaC.

IPS (2006). *IPS National Competitiveness Research 2006 Report*, Seoul: IPS and IPS-NaC.

IPS (2007). *IPS National Competitiveness Research 2007 Report*, Seoul: IPS and IPS-NaC.

IPS (2012). *IPS National Competitiveness Research 2012 Report*, Seoul: IPS and IPS-NaC.

Ipsos Reid (2002). Internet use continues to climb in most markets, 10 December. Available at www.ipsos-reid.com. Accessed 22 March 2003.

International Monetary Fund (1996). *International Financial Statistics*, February.

Jin, B. and Koh, A. (1999). Differences between South Korean male and female consumer in the clothing brand loyalty formation process: Model testing. *Clothing and Textiles Research Journal*, **17**(3): 117–127.

Jin, B. and Moon, H. C. (2006). The diamond approach to the competitiveness of Korea's apparel industry: Michael Porter and beyond. *Journal of Fashion Marketing and Management*, **10**(2): 195–208.

Kim, C. S. and Choi, D. O. (2005). A scheme for the trade increase between Korea and Russia through the enhancement of fisheries cooperation. *Journal of Korea Trade*, **9**(2): 47–70.

Keegan, W. J. (1989). *Global Marketing Management*, 4th Edn, Englewood Cliffs, NJ: Prentice-Hall.

KIET (1987). Future picture of automobile industries. *Series of Future Industries*.

Kim, M. Y. (2006). Inequality in globalization: An extension of the Gini index from the perspective of national competitiveness. *Journal of International Business and Economy*, **7**(1): 119–140.

Kim, W. B. (2003). *A Research on Strategies of Cooperative Regional Development toward Integrated National Territory*, Seoul: Korea Research Institute for Human Settlements.

Kindleberger, C. P. (1969). *American Business Abroad*, New Haven: Yale University Press.

Kogut, B. (1985). Designing global strategies: Comparative and competitive value-added chains. *Sloan Management Review*, **Summer**: 15–28.

Korea Electronic Industries Promotion Institute (1989). Prospect for Long-term Development of Electronic Industries.

Korea Federation of Textile Industries (2002). Available at: www.kofoti.org/textile/introduction/introduction_main.htm (In Korean). Accessed 19 May 2002.

Korea Federation of Textile Industries (2005). Available at: www.kofoti.or.kr/info/index03.php (In Korean). Accessed 25 July 2005.

Krugman, P. R. (1979). Increasing returns, monopolistic competition and international trade. *Journal of International Economics*, **9**: 469–479.

Krugman, P. (1992). *Geography and Trade*, MA: MIT Press.

Krugman, P. R. (1994). Competitiveness: A dangerous obsession. *Foreign Affairs*, **73**(2 and 4): 28–44.

Krugman, P. (2011). The competition myth. *New York Times*, 23 January.

Kreinin, M. (1965). Comparative labor effectiveness and the Leontief scarce factor paradox. *American Economic Review*, **64**: 143–155.

Krugman, P. (ed.) (1986). *Strategic Trade Policy and the New International Economics*, Cambridge: MIT Press.

Krugman, P. and Smith, A. (eds.) (1994). *Empirical Studies of Strategic Trade Policy*, Chicago: University of Chicago Press.

Lancaster, K. J. (1979). *Variety, Equity and Efficiency*, New York: Columbia University Press.

Lee, C. J. and Hong, I. P. (1999). A new approach to enhance Northeast Asian economic cooperation. *Journal of International Economic Studies*, 3(3): 100–137.

Leontief, W. (1953). Domestic production and foreign trade: The American capital position re-examined. *Proceedings of the American Philosophical Society*, 97: 331–349. Reprinted in Caves, R. and Johnson, H. (eds.) (1968), *Readings in International Economics*, Homewood, Illinois: Richard D. Irwin, Inc.

Leontief, W. (1956). Factor proportions and structure of American trade: Further theoretical and empirical analysis. *Review of Economics and Statistics*, 38(4): 386–407.

Linder, S. B. (1961). *An Essay on Trade and Transformation*, New York: John Wiley.

Lui, T. L. and Chiu, S. W. K. (2001). Flexibility under unorganized industrialism? The experience of industrial restructuring in Hong Kong, in Deyo, F. C., Doner, R. F. and Hershberg, E. (eds.), *Economic Governance and the Challenge of Flexibility in East Asia*, New York: Rowan and Littlefield, pp. 55–77.

Luttwak, E. N. (1993). *The Endangered American Dream: How to Stop the United States from Becoming a Third World Country and How to Win the Geo-economic Struggle for Industrial Supremacy*, New York: Simon and Schuster.

Magaziner, I. C. and Patinkin, M. (1990). *The Silent War: Inside the Global Business Battles Shaping Americas Future*, New York: Vintage Books.

Magaziner, I. C. and Reich, R. B. (1983). *Minding America's Business. The Decline and Rise of the American Economy*, New York: Vintage Books.

Magretta, J. (2000). Fast, global and entrepreneurial: Supply chain management, Hong Kong style: An interview with Victor Fung, in Clark, K. B., Magretta, J., Dyer, J. H., Fisher, M., Fites, D. V. and Baldwin, C. Y. (eds.), *Harvard Business Review on Managing the Value Chain*, Boston, MA: Harvard Business School Press.

Makino, S., Isobe, T. and Chan, C. M. (2004). Does country matter? *Strategic Management Journal*, 25(10): 1027–1043.

Management Today (1989). Guru on the riverbank, August, pp. 52–56.

Martin, R. and Sunley, P. (2003). Deconstructing clusters: Chaotic concept or policy panacea? *Journal of Economic Geography*, 3(3): 5–35.

Maskell, P. (2001). Towards a knowledge-based theory of the geographical cluster. *Industrial and Corporate Change*, 10(4): 921–943.

McGuire, S. (2001). Fast fashion: How a secretive Spanish tycoon has defied the post war tide of globalization, bringing factory jobs from Latin American and Asia back to Continental Europe. *Newsweek International*, 17 September, p. 36.

McSweeney, B. (2002). Hofstede's model of national cultural differences and their consequences: A triumph of faith–A failure of analysis. *Human Relations*, 55(11): 89–118.

Ministry of Knowledge Economy (2003). 21st Century Common Prosperity through the Expansion of Korea–China Economic Cooperation. Available at: http://www.mke.go.kr/news/coverage/bodoView.isp?seg=5531&srchType=1&srchWord=1T&pCtx=1&pageNo=22 (In Korean). Accessed 5 December 2012.

Moon, H. C. (1992). New challenges for Korean conglomerates, in Chen, T., Choi, Y. B. and Lee, S. (eds.), *Economic and Political Reforms in Asia*, New York: St. John's University Press.

Moon, H. C. (1994). A revised framework of global strategy: Extending the coordination-configuration framework. *The International Executive*, 36(5): 557–574.

Moon, H. C. (2004). Cooperation among Japan, Korea, and China through sharing business and cultural advantages. *The Review of Business History*, 19(3): 33–51.

Moon, H. C. and Choi, E. K. (2001). Cultural impact on national competitiveness. *Journal of International and Area Studies*, 8(2): 21–36.

Moon, H. C. and Jung, J. S. (2007). A strategic approach to culture and economic performance for different stages of economic development: The OUI model and its empirical analysis (In Korean). *International Business Journal*, 18(1): 111–136.

Moon, H. C. and Jung, J. S. (2008). A stage approach to the cluster evolution and the development of a new global-linking cluster (In Korean). *The Review of Business History*, 23(1): 77–104.

Moon, H. C. and Jung, J. S. (2010). Northeast Asian cluster through business and cultural cooperation. *Journal of Korea Trade*, 14(2): 29–53.

Moon, H. C. and Kim, M. Y. (2006a). Cooperation and competition between Korea and BRICs (In Korean). *Journal of International Trade and Industry Studies*, 11(2): 69–94.

Moon, H. C. and Kim, M. Y. (2006b). Enhancing cooperation between Korea and Japan: An interdisciplinary approach of business competitiveness and culture. *Hitotsubashi Journal of Commerce and Management*, 40: 19–33.

Moon, H. C. and Lee, D. H. (2004). The competitiveness of multinational firms: A case study of Samsung Electronics and Sony. *Journal of International and Area Studies*, 11(1): 1–21.

Moon, H. C. and Lee, K. C. (1995). Testing the diamond model: Competitiveness of U. S. software firms. *Journal of International Management*, 1(4): 373–387.

Moon, H. C. and Peery, N. S. (1995). Competitiveness of product, firm, industry and nation in a global business. *Competitiveness Review*, 5(1): 37–43.

Moon, H. C. and Roehl, T. W. (1993). An imbalance theory of foreign direct investment. *Multinational Business Review*, 1(1): 56–65.

Moon, H. C. and Roehl, T. (2001). Unconventional foreign direct investment and the imbalance theory. *International Business Review*, 10(2): 197–215.

Moon, H. C., Rugman, A. M. and Verbeke, A. (1995). The generalized double diamond approach to international competitiveness, in Rugman, A. M., den Broeck, J. V. and Verbeke, A. (eds.), *Research in Global Strategic Management, Vol. 5: Beyond the Diamond*, Greenwich, CT: JAI Press, pp. 97–114.

Moon, H. C., Rugman, A. M. and Verbeke, A. (1997). The new global competitiveness of Korea and the generalized double diamond approach. *The Korean Economic and Business Review*, **Fall**: 48–57.

Moon, H. C., Rugman, A. M. and Verbeke, A. (1998). A generalized double diamond approach to the global competitiveness of Korea and Singapore. *International Business Review*, 7: 135–150.

Moon, H. C. and Kim, J. Y. (2010). Comparing the competitiveness of Korea and Singapore after ten years of Asian economic crisis. *The Review of Business History*, 25(1): 75–91.

Newsweek (2002). Samsung in the bloom, 15 July, pp. 32–33.

New York Times (1992). Economic analyst says U.S. needs long-term investments, 7 September.

OECD (2002). Broadband access in OECD countries per 100 inhabitants, OECD, September. Available at: www.oecd.org/EN/document/0,EN-document-29-no directorate-no-1-39262-29,00.html. Accessed 24 March 2003.

Perlmutter, H. V. (1969). The tortuous evolution of the multinational corporation. *Columbia Journal of World Business*, 4: 9–18.

Phillips, K. P. (1984). *Staying on Top: The Business Case for a National Industrial Strategy*, New York: Random House.

Porter, M. E. (1980). *Competitive Strategy: Techniques for Analyzing Industries and Companies*, New York: Free Press.

Porter, M. E. (1986). Competition in global industries: A conceptual framework, in Porter, M. E. (ed.), *Competition in Global Industries*, Boston: Harvard Business School Press, pp. 15–60.

Porter, M. E. (1990a). The competitive advantage of nations. *Harvard Business Review*, March–April: 73–93.

Porter, M. E. (1990b). *The Competitive Advantage of Nations*, New York: Free Press.

Porter, M. E. (1994). Competitiveness of the Korean economy. *Mae-il-kyung-jai* (*Daily Economic Review*).

Porter, M. E. (1996). What is strategy? *Harvard Business Review*, 74(6): 61–78.

Porter, M. E. (1998a). Clusters and the new economics of competition. *Harvard Business Review*, 76(6): 77–90.

Porter, M. E. (1998b). *On Competition*, Boston, M.A.: Harvard Business School Press.

Porter, M. E. (2000a). Location, competition, and economic development: Local clusters in a global economy. *Economic Development Quarterly*, **14**(1): 15–34.

Porter, M. E. (2000b). Attitudes, values, beliefs, and the microeconomics of prosperity, in Harrison, L. E. and Huntington, S. P. (eds.), *Culture Matters*, New York: Basic Books, pp. 14–28.

Porter, M. E. (2003a). *Malaysia's Competitiveness: Moving to the Next Stage*, Kuala Lumpur, Malaysia (Presentation slides).

Porter, M. E. (2003b). Building the microeconomic foundations of prosperity: Findings from the business competitiveness index, in World Economic Forum, *The Global Competitiveness Report*, Oxford and New York: Oxford University Press, pp. 29–56.

Porter, M. E. and Armstrong, J. (1992). Canada at the crossroads: Dialogue (Response by Porter). *Business Quarterly*, **56**(4): 6–10.

Porter, M. E., Takeuchi, H. and Sakakibara, M. (2000). *Can Japan Compete?* Cambridge, MA: Perseus Publishing.

Porter, M. E. and The Monitor Company (1991). *Canada at the Crossroads: The Reality of a New Competitive Environment*, Ottawa: Business Council on National Issues and Minister of Supply and Services of the Government of Canada.

President's Commission on Industrial Competitiveness (1985). *Global Competition: The New Reality*, Washington, D. C.: U. S. Government Printing Office.

Prestowitz, Jr., C. V. (1988). *Trading Places: How We Allowed Japan to Take the Lead*, New York: Basic Books.

Reich, R. B. (1990). Who is us? *Harvard Business Review*, **68**(1): 53–64.

Reuber, R. and Fisher, E. (2001). *Industrial Clusters and SME Promotion in Developing Countries*, Commonwealth Secretariat.

Ricardo, D. (1971) (orig. pub. 1817). *The Principles of Political Economy and Taxation*, Baltimore: Penguin.

Rugman, A. M. (1981). *Inside the Multinationals*, New York: Columbia University Press.

Rugman, A. M. (1990). *Multinationals and Canada-United States Free Trade*, Columbia: University of South Carolina Press.

Rugman, A. M. (1991). Diamond in the rough. *Business Quarterly*, **55**(3): 61–64.

Rugman, A. M. (1992a). Porter takes the wrong turn. *Business Quarterly*, **56**(3): 59–64.

Rugman, A. M. (1992b). Canada at the crossroads: Dialogue (Counter-response by Rugman). *Business Quarterly*, **57**(1): 7–10.

Rugman, A. M. and D'Cruz, J. R. (1991). *Fast Forward: Improving Canada's International Competitiveness*, Toronto: Kodak Canada Inc.

Rugman, A. M. and D'Cruz, J. R. (1993). The double diamond model of international competitiveness: The Canadian experience. *Management International Review*, **33**(2): 17–39.

Rugman, A. M. and Verbeke, A. (1990). *Global Corporate Strategy and Trade Policy*. London, New York: Croom Helm, Routledge.

Rugman, A. M. and Verbeke, A. (1992). A note on the transnational solution and the transaction cost theory of multinational strategic management. *Journal of International Business Studies*, **23**(4): 761–771.

Russo, M. (2004). The ceramic industrial district facing the challenge from China-innovation processes and relations among different types of firms Inside and outside the Sassuolo district. Paper presented at *Clusters, Industrial Districts and Firms: The Challenge of Globalization*, conference in Honor of Professor Sebastino Brusco, Modena, Italy.

Ryan, R. (1990). A grand disunity. *National Review*, **42**(13): 46–47.

Saaty, T. L. (1980). *The Analytic Hierarchy Process*, New York: McGraw-Hill.

Samsung Electronics (2003). Annual Report 2002.

Samuelson, P. (1948). International trade and the equalization of factor prices. *Economic Journal*, **58**: 165–184.

Sandholtz, W., Borrus, M., Zysman, J., Conca, K., Stowsky, J., Vogel, S. and Weber, S. (1992). *The Highest Stakes: The Economic Foundations of the Next Security System*, Berkeley Roundtable on the International Economy (BRIE), New York: Oxford University Press.

Shan, W. and Hamilton, W. (1991). Country-specific advantage and international cooperation. *Strategic Management Journal*, **12**(6): 419–432.

Shin, U. S. (1988). *Resource Economics*, (In Korean) Seoul: Park-Young Sa.

Smallwood, J. E. (1984). The product life cycle: A key to strategic marketing planning, in Weitz, B. A. and Wensley, R. (eds.), *Strategic Marketing: Planning Implementation and Control*, Boston, MA: Kent Publishing Company, pp. 184–192.

Smith, A. (1937) (orig. pub. 1776). An inquiry into the nature and causes of the wealth of nations, in Eliot, C. W. (ed.), *The Harvard Classics*, New York: P. F. Collier & Son Corporation.

Sony (2003). Annual Report 2002.

Sparke, M., Sidaway, J. D., Bunnell, T. and Grundy-Warr, C. (2004). Triangulating the borderless world: Geographies of power in the Indonesia-Malaysia-Singapore growth triangle. *Transaction of the Institute of British Geographers*, **29**: 495–498.

Speer, J. K. (2001). Mexico: Mapping out a course of action. *Bobbin*, **January**: 16–22.

Stolper, W. and Samuelson, P. (1941). Protection and real wages. *Review of Economic Studies*, **9**: 58–73.

Suh, S. M., Hong, B. S. and Jin, B. (2002). *Fashion Business* (In Korean), Seoul: Hyung-Sul Publication Co.

Sureshchandar, G. S. and Leisten, R. (2006). A framework for evaluating the criticality of software metrics: An analytic hierarchy process (AHP) approach. *Measuring Business Excellence*, **10**(4): 22–33.

Tang, M. and Thant, M. (1994). Growth triangles: conceptual issues and operational problems, *Staff Paper No. 54*, Manila: Asian Development Bank.

Techexchange (2005). An introduction to the DAMA project. Available at: www.dama.tc2.com. Accessed 23 July 2005.

Thain, D. H. (1990). The war without bullets. *Business Quarterly*, 55(1): 13–19.

The Economist (1994). Professor Porter Ph.D., 8 October: 75.

(The) US Commercial Service (2001). Overview of the apparel market, 14 April. Available at: www.usatrade.gov/website/mrd.nsf/MRDurl/ISA_KOREA_APP_OVERVIEW-OF-THE-APPA_001A8052. Accessed 26 September 2003.

Thurow, L. C. (1992). *Head to Head: The Coming Economic Battle among Japan, Europe, and America*, New York: Morrow.

Time (2002). Samsung moves upmarket, April, pp. 31–33.

Toh, M. H. (2006). Development in the Indonesia-Malaysia-Singapore Growth Triangle. Department of Economics SCAPE Working Paper, *Series Paper No. 2006/06-31*, March, National University of Singapore.

Trompenaars, F. and Hampden-Turner, C. (1998). *Riding the Waves of Culture: Understanding Cultural Diversity in Global Business*, New York: McGraw-Hill.

The Economist Intelligence Unit (1992). *South Korea 1992–93: Annual Survey of Political and Economic Background*, EIU Country Profile.

Tyson, L. D. (1992). *Who's Bashing Whom: Trade Conflict in High-Technology Industries*, Washington: Institute for International Economics.

UNCTAD (2006). *World Investment Report: FDI from Developing and Transition Economies: Implications for Development*, New York and Geneva: United Nations.

United Nations Development Programme (1994). *Human Development Report 1994*, New York: Oxford University Press.

United States Department of Commerce (1995). *Statistical Abstract of The United States 1995*.

van Grunsven, L. (1995). Industrial regionalization and urban-regional transformation in Southeast Asia: The SIJORI growth triangle considered. *Malaysian Journal of Tropical Geography*, 26: 47–65.

Vanek, J. (1963). *The Natural Resource Content of United States Foreign Trade, 1870–1955*, Cambridge: MIT Press.

Vernon, R. (1966). International investments and international trade in the product cycle. *Quarterly Journal of Economics*, 80: 190–207.

Vernon, R. (1979). The product cycle hypothesis in a new international environment. *Oxford Bulletin of Economics and Statistics*, 41(4): 255–267. Reprinted in Wortzel, H and Wortzel, L. (eds.) (1985), *Strategic Management of Multinational Corporations: The Essentials*, New York: John Wiley & Sons.

Vitzthum, C. (2001). Just-in-time fashion: Spanish retailer Zara makes low-cost lines in weeks by running its own show. *Wall Street Journal* (Eastern Edition), 18 May, p. B1.

Wanniski, J. (1978). *The Way the World Works*, New York: Basic Books.

Winters, W. (2003). 6th annual rising star awards. Available at: www.fgi.org. Accessed 19 May 2003.

World Bank (1995). *World Development Report: Workers in An Integrating World*, Oxford: Oxford University Press.

World Economic Forum (1996–1999). *The Global Competitiveness Report*, Geneva, Switzerland.

Yamazawa, I. (1970). Intensity analysis of world trade flow. *Hitotsubashi Journal of Economics*, **10**(2): 61–90.

INDEX